Civilization in Crisis

Civilization in Crisis

Human prospects in a changing world

Joseph A. Camilleri

Lecturer in Politics,
La Trobe University

Cambridge University Press
Cambridge
London   New York   Melbourne

Published by the Syndics of the Cambridge University Press
The Pitt Building, Trumpington Street, Cambridge CB2 1RP
Bentley House, 200 Euston Road, London NW1 2DB
32 East 57th Street, New York, NY 10022, USA
296 Beaconsfield Parade, Middle Park, Melbourne 3206, Australia

Photoset and Printed in Malta by Interprint (Malta) Ltd

Library of Congress Cataloguing in Publication Data

Camilleri, Joseph A. 1944–

Civilization in Crisis.

Includes bibliographical references and index.

1. Civilization, Modern—1950– I. Title.

CB428.C325 909.82 76–4240

ISBN 0–521–21248–0

ISBN 0–521–29078–3 pbk.

Contents

To Rita, Kristian
and all who are struggling to build a better world

Preface

Until very recently, when confronted with the grim reality of scarcity and disorder, western man has tended to place his hopes in technological progress as the sure path to consumer affluence, legal order and political stability. However, the increasing strains and stresses which now afflict the human condition have gradually compelled a drastic reassessment of the time-honoured faith in man's 'tool-making, utensil-shaping, machine-fabricating' genius. For, along with the benefits of technological engineering, usually measured in terms of economic productivity, have come the costs of environmental damage, economic inequality, social conformism, a deeply ingrained sense of political impotence, and the suicidal march of military technology.

Throughout the twentieth century, there has developed, both nationally and internationally, a clearly discernible trend towards the bureaucratization of authority, the concentration of wealth and power, and the increasing recourse to social and physical coercion. In this sense, the widespread psychological disorder which we are witnessing in most advanced industrial societies reflects much more than the dissolution of an established morality. It indicates man's inability to adjust to a social milieu in which he is frequently reduced to an object, a mere pawn in the impersonal and inhuman game of economic, political and military competition.

In focussing attention on the decadence of industrial culture, the fragility and inequity of economic and political institutions, the dangers of ecological collapse and military destruction, the aim of this book is to identify those forces which threaten not only man's capacity for self-expression and communal living but the very survival of the species. Any attempt to illuminate the reality of the crisis which confronts modern man must, therefore, rest on normative criteria. It is only on the basis of clearly stated ethical options that one can hope to

evaluate the current global state of social pathology and formulate alternative goals for the future. It is precisely the
function of the utopian vision to challenge the existing order
by establishing a sharp contrast between two models of social
organization, one actual and the other potential. The ensuing
tension between these two images may be said to provide the
necessary impetus for action.

However, the formulation of ultimate values and long-term
goals is only the first step in any concrete programme of social
transformation, and has to be complemented by a realistic
strategy for change, in which the means are adapted to the
current reality as well as to the desired end. In other words,
the strategy must provide an effective bridge between the actual
and the potential, between what is and what should be. It is
the intention of this study to contribute to this bridging enterprise by examining the manner in which both dominant and
emergent forces are tending to modify the existing pattern of
wealth, power and authority. Needless to say, the questions
raised by such an undertaking are extremely complex and
varied. What follows does not pretend to give complete or
definitive answers. It is at best a personal and provisional
view of present trends and future options, but to the extent
that this small book helps to shed some light on the critical
choices now confronting man, it will have amply served its
purpose.

November 1975   J. A. Camilleri

Note: $ sign denotes American dollars throughout.

1. The world crisis: an overview

From the earliest years of the paleolithic age the human species has had to struggle to adapt to a complex and often hostile environment. Before the development of agriculture, man had to sustain the process of living by depending on what he could catch or collect from wild nature, assisted only by the use of the most primitive tools. To achieve his dominance as a hunter, he had to confront the powerful and unknown forces of climate and terrain, vanquish animals larger, faster and stronger than himself, and devise new forms of social cooperation. In the ensuing millenia, the uneven but accelerating rate of technological progress appeared to bring complete mastery over the natural environment within the realm of human possibility. The dramatic breakthrough of agriculture some ten thousand years ago was followed five thousand years later by the invention of the wheel. However, it is only in the relatively short historical space of the last hundred years that we have witnessed the radical impact of the mathematical and physical sciences upon technology, and the opening up of such new realms as nuclear energy, supersonic transportation, cybernetics, and satellite communication systems. Paradoxically, this revolutionary shift from man's primeval state to the new 'megatechnics' has left him more vulnerable than ever, for the immense gains in valuable knowledge and productivity have been offset by even greater increases in waste, destruction and violence.

The contemporary human crisis is so profound and pervasive that the very attempt to analyse it – let alone resolve it – seems to defy the power of human reason and imagination. The battle for survival is currently being waged by millions of men whose precarious existence is one of poverty, squalor and even hunger. Man's predicament impinges on the future of entire nations that are threatened by external attack or internal disintegration. It dominates the vast network of international relations so delicately poised on the dangerous and ultimately

1

unstable 'balance of terror'. It pervades the whole ecological system whose growing disequilibrium could undermine centuries of economic and political development.

Though understandable and largely unavoidable, the marked tendency in the social sciences to interpret the flow of history through the actions and objectives of large human collectivities must not be allowed to obscure through excessive abstraction or generalization, the real quality, intensity and diversity of human suffering. It is one thing to know that a large fraction of the world's population suffers from hunger and malnutrition, and quite another to identify with the victims of material necessity. Recent estimates indicate that some 40,000 people die every day from starvation alone; but chronic undernourishment saps the mental and physical health of hundreds of millions more, stifles the desire or opportunity for self-improvement and with it any sense of dignity or personal freedom.

Nowhere is the dehumanizing experience of underdevelopment more evident than in the field of education. Although literacy programmes have been initiated in all underdeveloped countries, the fact remains that there are each year at least five million more adult illiterates in the world. During the Development Decade their number actually increased from 700 to 800 million. At the end of a ten-year major project to improve education in Latin America, it was found that, in spite of compulsory primary education, less than two out of every four children were completing the first six years of primary school. For the vast majority of drop-outs, who relapse into a state of virtual illiteracy, schooling would merely have served to inculcate a deep sense of incompetence, of inferiority in relation to the deserving minority, and a fatalistic acceptance of the status quo.

However, the phenomenon of social and economic underdevelopment is not confined to Third World countries. Though less conspicuous or widespread, it is also in evidence in the technologically advanced societies of North America, Western Europe and Japan, where, segregated from the rest of the community, exploited at all levels, deprived minorities eke out a sub-human existence in ghettos and shanty-towns which cannot provide even the barest necessities of life.

Accompanying the experience of acute scarcity are the many prevalent forms of human enslavement and political tyranny.

Of particular significance is the institutionalized practice of racial discrimination, most stridently manifested in South Africa but also evident in many other countries, including the United States and Australia. South Africa's official policy of apartheid, committed to the indefinite preservation of white supremacy, has necessitated the removal of more than one million Africans from the 'white' areas; the prosecution of another million Africans every year for statutory offences under the pass laws, influx control and related laws; the secret detention of an undisclosed number of persons for indefinite periods in jails and police cells; the imposition of numerous restrictions over African workers and their employment, denying them access to most jobs, the right to engage in collective bargaining and the right to strike.

In the United States, structural racism has left enduring scars on much of urban life. The Negro drift to the cities has thrust families into a thread-bare existence which effectively destroys in the Negro male any semblance of self-respect and drives him to drink, drugs, gambling, debauchery and violence. Similarly, for the majority of Australian Aborigines, contact with the urban environment inevitably produces a deep sense of frustration for having broken their cultural roots while acquiring few or none of the benefits of so-called civilized living. Ultimately, racial conflict, whether in Southern Africa, in the United States or in Australia, is symbolic of the much larger confrontation between those who are prepared to use violence in the defence of power and privilege and those who see no alternative but violence in the struggle for liberation.

In spite of the many solemn declarations by the United Nations, the violation of basic human rights has become accepted practice in many parts of the world. The atrocities of the Spanish Civil War, the terror of the Stalinist purges, and the mass extermination of the Jews in Nazi Germany have been succeeded in the last three decades by a grotesque record of unbridled genocide, mass torture, widespread suppression of civil liberties and indiscriminate recourse to the political weapons of detention, imprisonment and forced labour. One need only bring to mind the massive repression carried out by innumerable Latin American military elites and police authorities anxious to stem the growing revolutionary ferment within their respective countries; the policy of arbitrary arrest, jailing and assassination resulting in the bloody Greek Civil War; the savagery with which Russian tanks and artillery crushed the resistance of the Hungarian people; or the ruthlessness, bordering on genocide, with which colonial and neo-colonial powers have sought to subdue the revolt of their subject peoples. The atrocities perpetrated in Vietnam for nearly two decades (e.g. indiscriminate use of napalm, phosphorus, defoliating and herbicidal products; killing of the wounded on the battlefield; summary executions; torture by electricity, water, burns, and blows; devastation of fields; destruction of stock; forcible displacement of entire villages to so-called 'secure' zones) represent perhaps the most dramatic, though certainly not unique, example of this phenomenon.

The extremely fragmentary profile of human misery that we have sketched should nonetheless be sufficient to convey the extent and intensity of the present pathological state of the human condition. The affluent western world may, at first sight, appear to be a major exception to this general picture of unrelieved violence. On closer scrutiny, however, we find that it is at best a partial exception. Advanced industrial society may not engage in the same type of wholesale physical repression, or create the same obstacles to sheer survival, nevertheless it has seriously degraded the quality and the meaning of life.

Man experiences the crushing force of the technological society most dramatically and most immediately in his 'work' situation. Wage labour may be less tiring and of shorter duration than it has been for many generations. Yet, the toll that it takes of the human personality may be greater than ever before. In the name of productivity and abundance, the rational utilization of the machine has led to the systematic division of labour and the efficient assembly line whose inevitable by-products are boredom, mental sluggishness and psychological constraint. The demand for ever-growing levels of production, which in turn necessitates a constantly expanding rate of consumption, has become, with the aid of a highly sophisticated and elaborate advertising industry, the ultimate goal around which all human toil is organized. For many, work is no longer a means of personal development or cultural enrichment but a subordinate factor in a technical order that operates with little regard for human purpose or moral justification.

Traditional conceptions of time space and movement have been overthrown by the technological revolution and the shift to an exploitative, power-centred culture. The ensuing social and psychological discontinuity and moral vacuum have produced a severe crisis of conscience and a large-scale flight from reality. The student who turns to LSD and other hallucenogenic drugs, the family man who withdraws for hours on end to the fantasy world of television, the hippie drop-out who leaves the corrupt urban jungle in search of the elusive paradise of unspoilt nature, the teenager who suddenly goes on the rampage smashing windows and wrecking cars, the tramp who seeks refuge in alcoholic stupour, the over-strained executive or alienated housewife who seeks salvation on the psychiatrist's couch – all these are the victims of the pervasive climate of anxiety, insecurity and neurosis. Theirs is a raging anger that turns to impotence and retreat in the face of a future they do not comprehend and cannot control.

In reviewing the arduous struggle against scarcity, the physical and psychological enslavement wrought by various forms of institutionalized inequality and the brutalizing impact of a machine technology, attention so far has been focussed on the strictly human dimension of the world crisis. But each of these social phenomena impinges also on the fabric and development of national communities. When entire populations suffer from chronic illiteracy, unemployment, disease and hunger, it is the very body politic which is diseased and not merely its constituent members. The ensuing climate of despair and resignation stifles the very incentive, consciousness and skills required to envisage and construct an alternative society. The striking inequalities between the various strata of society express and reinforce the self-perpetuating pattern of social conflict, economic underdevelopment and political fragmentation.

In many underdeveloped countries, the emergence of an indigenous elite in the wake of independence has often served to increase the incentives and opportunities for corruption by multiplying the power positions which can be used to make gain for self, family or kin group. In spite of ambitious industrial programmes and an ever-expanding bureaucratic machinery, many of the urban or metropolitan centres which continue to absorb the mass migration from rural areas, have become parasites rather than promoters of development. Cities with limited industrial capacity are little more than export–import centres established and maintained by the upper and middle classes in order to take advantage of the labour and produce of the countryside. Accentuating the already explosive character of economic inequality is the demographic factor. The increase in life expectancy brought about by medical innovation and the consequent fall in the mortality rate have added to the problems of over-population. The failure to create favourable conditions for responsible family planning, accompanied by the gradual but steady replacement of labour by capital-intensive industries, has seriously compounded the persistent problem of massive unemployment and underemployment.

In conditions of economic exploitation, human dislocation and material wastage, it is only to be expected that the social and political institutions of these countries should become vulnerable to deep-seated discontent, conflict and instability. Physical violence, however, must be seen as the symptom rather than the cause of insufficient capital accumulation, deficient political institutionalization and weak social mobilization. The political and military upheavals which followed the independence struggles of the newly emerging nations have demonstrated that expectations of rapid economic development are likely to unleash a revolutionary dynamic not easily contained by conservative regimes even with the assistance of outside military intervention. The resulting sense of crisis and frustration has called into question the whole process of nation-building initiated in the early stages of the post-independence period.

Though the recent history of the Third World may indicate a high vulnerability to dismemberment and internal dissolution, it is well to remember that national crises have not been altogether absent from the contemporary experience of either the First or the Second World. One need only refer to the recurring convulsions in the French political system, the growing manifestations of dissent in the United States and the intermittent signs of decay in the Soviet Union's Eastern European empire. Moreover, the gigantic war machines which the United States and the Soviet Union have constructed since 1945, far from producing the desired strategic advantage, have merely resulted in a spiralling arms race which demands ever-increasing military expenditures and steadily accentuates the psychological crisis of national insecurity.

But the crisis of violence which has marked advanced industrialized societies has not been confined to deterrence or the mere preparation for war. Quite frequently it has found expression in the actual use of force, as reflected in the various interventionist wars undertaken by the great powers and especially the United States, France, Britain and the Soviet Union. Almost invariably such violence has rebounded on the political and social fabric of the metropolitan country. The profound political upheavals caused by the Algerian, African and Vietnam wars in France, Portugal and United States respectively were highlighted not only by sharp internal divisions but by a collective crisis of conscience. A point was eventually reached when a large proportion of the society was no longer willing to accept the official ideology of the state or its interpretation of the 'national interest'.

The moral and psychological trauma which the Vietnam War helped to create within the consciousness and institutions of American society has provided perhaps the most explicit revelation of the bureaucratic growth and political polarization characteristic of all advanced capitalist and even socialist societies. The very magnitude of industrial production dictates the use of ever more complex machinery, sophisticated techniques and elaborate decision-making structures. The ensuing pyramid of power reduces most people to spectators of a profound social disorder which they perceive but cannot correct. As for the small elite situated at the top of the pyramid, it is hardly in a position to take remedial action, for the basis of its power lies precisely in the process of continuing over-production, rising arms expenditures, luxurious consumption, planned obsolescence and elitist education. In this sense, the economic and political organization of the nation-state in both developed and underdeveloped societies is in a state of decay. Its demise may not be imminent and its destructive power in time of peace and war may yet increase, but its capacity to meet real human needs and aspirations is now in rapid decline.

Not unexpectedly, the various upheavals which have marked the recent history of both the old and the new states have rebounded on to the international plane, which is not to say that

the disorder in interstate relations is a mere reflection of the
current crisis of the nation-state. The distinctive character of
the international crisis derives from the very nature of the
system of sovereign states. The self-defeating search for security
in a fragmented system of states predates the emergence of the
city-state in Hellenic civilization. But a new factor has rapidly
transformed the age-old problem of war into a major crisis of
survival. That factor is technology.

One need only consider the development of nuclear warheads and their means of delivery. In 1945 the atomic bomb,
which was dropped on Hiroshima, killing 78,000 people and
injuring 45,000 more, had an explosive power of 20,000 tons of
TNT or 20 kilotons. The weapons developed by the United
States and the Soviet Union since 1945 are measured in megatons or thousands of kilotons. One B-52 bomber carrying the
equivalent of 25 megatons of explosive power could unleash
more than twelve times the devastation caused by all the bombs
dropped during World War II. In the 1960s, the bomber,
although still in active use in Vietnam, was superseded by the
inter-continental ballistic missile (ICBM) which can travel at
18,000 mph and reach any point on the globe. Recently, an
even more accurate and deadly missile system, consisting of
multiple independently-targeted re-entry vehicles (MIRVs) has
resulted in a qualitative jump in the spiralling arms race, further
destabilizing the already precarious nuclear balance.

The suicidal march of military technology is also reflected in
the astronomical sums devoted to defence expenditure. Current
military budgets throughout the world are estimated to be in
excess of $250,000 million, averaging approximately 7 per cent
of the world's gross product, an amount greater than the total
gross domestic product of the one thousand million people
living in Africa, South and Southeast Asia. Moreover, the war
machines which the great powers have built with such pains-
taking care since World War II have not in fact been idle. While
the atomic weapon has not been used since 1945, it is calculated
that in the last 30 years there have been more than 100 wars
resulting in more deaths than for the whole of World War II.

The dominance of actual and threatened force in international relations points not only to the absence of a world
community but to the gradual dissolution of the existing order.

International violence and the gradations of military power are only the tip of the iceberg, the apex of a global system of inequality in wealth, power and prestige, which is reflected in diplomatic arrangements, in legal institutions and above all in the structure of the world economy. The power of veto enjoyed by the five permanent members of the UN Security Council symbolizes rather pointedly the hierarchical structure of international relations. The most advanced industrial nations of the world have tended to dominate trade flow patterns in underdeveloped countries, to monopolize their manufacturing outlets, to channel the great bulk of both public and private investment and, until recently, to determine the prices of their main exports.

In spite of the powerful military component underpinning the pyramidal structure of the world economy, it has not been possible thus far – and undoubtedly it will become increasingly difficult in the future – for existing economic disparities to be maintained without violent resistance. The widespread recourse to urban fighting, the increasing incidence of aerial piracy and armed attack against civilians are but the most visible signs of anger and frustration in the face of poverty and exploitation. However, the forces of the existing order, far from acceding to the increasingly militant demands of distributive justice, appear more determined than ever to defend present institutions and power structures, and, where necessary, to do so by force. The international system thus appears set on a collision course which will inexorably lead to more violence.

The crisis which confronts twentieth-century man is truly global, not simply by virtue of the fact that it threatens directly the lives of countless men and women, but in the more far-reaching sense that it permeates and vitiates the whole fabric of human relations and human institutions, and is now distorting man's entire relationship with the natural order. After a period of economic, political and cultural stability lasting some fifteen hundred years, the ideological revolution of the Reformation and the Renaissance in the fifteenth and sixteenth centuries, and the commercial, scientific and industrial revolutions of the seventeenth and eighteenth centuries produced a process of radical acceleration and discontinuity in human history. The ensuing rapid growth in population, the large-scale migration from the countryside to the cities, the increasing use of energy, food supplies and minerals were but the first hesitant steps towards the overwhelming demographic and technological explosion of the twentieth century.

On the basis of existing demographic trends, the 1968 medium United Nations forecast projected a world population of slightly under 6,500 million in the year 2000; that is, an increase of 2,500 million within the next 25 years, the greater part of which will occur in those underdeveloped regions which even now are unable to support a very large section of their population. Demographic calculations must of course take account of such potentially limiting factors as space, heat, available energy, non-renewable resources, water and food. The limitations of space are already apparent in the intolerable conditions of the many crowded cities in Asia and Latin America. But aside from the physical limitation of space, serious doubts have arisen as to whether technological progress can act as a substitute for the earth's finite natural resources. It is by no means certain that the utilization of new sources or greater quantities of existing sources of energy can be indefinitely multiplied without exhausting known reserves of non-renewable resources or causing irreparable damage to the natural environment.

In any case, it is not industrial production but agriculture which will continue to provide for the foreseeable future the best index of man's capacity to feed himself. Since World War II, the rich countries have shown a steady upward trend in the amount of food produced per person. In the developing nations, however, the picture has been ambiguous and, generally, much less encouraging. In 1968 the average country in Africa and Latin America grew less food per capita than it had done in 1956. Most underdeveloped countries had been unable to develop the economic and administrative infrastructure needed to take advantage of improved farming techniques, fertilizer technology or more extensive irrigation systems. Moreover, the short-term economic benefits of these technological innovations are often offset by the long-term destabilizing effects of human interference with the natural processes of the ecological system.

Clearly, man is not a totally autonomous agent able to superimpose on nature his own schemes and designs without regard to the laws and rhythms of nature on which he remains vitally dependent. The current trends toward environmental breakdown are of especial significance because they both confirm and illuminate the universal character of the world crisis. No human community, no individual, no corner of the globe, however remote or isolated, however powerful or well endowed, can now escape from the disorder which afflicts the entire planet. The earth constitutes a highly integrated ecosystem where variation in any one of its components is likely to have far-reaching political, economic and cultural ramifications. Thus, for example, changes in the economic organization of any one society will have repercussions on the whole international economy. Similarly, any shift in a nation's economic priorities are likely to be reflected in its cultural, legal or political system. This undeniable web of interdependence is particularly evident in the various monetary crises, trade imbalances and cycles of spiralling inflation which now confront the international economy. These phenomena are so closely interrelated that they may be regarded as manifestations of the same crisis, as different sides of the same coin. Perhaps, we can best describe the global crisis in terms of a fundamental disequilibrium which severely limits, and may ultimately destroy, man's capacity for biological and cultural adaptation to his environment. It is an uncomfortable but nonetheless real possibility that inadequate human organization may prevent man from continuing to transmit the secret of life to future generations and thus put an end to his leading role in the process of evolution. Contemporary man may well be facing a crisis of survival.

2. Underlying causes of disorder

The growing signs of conflict and disorder in the world have led observers to paint a gloomy picture of man's fate as he gropes for purpose and direction on his erratic journey to the twenty-first century. Some have even argued that the human machine is set for an uncontrollable explosion or at least a gradual breakdown. Such future projections are no doubt alarmist, but they do raise the central question regarding the adaptive or maladaptive functioning of the human species in relation to its natural and increasingly man-made environment. As our discussion in the previous chapter has shown, considerable and mounting evidence now points to the emergence of a global disequilibrium which, for purposes of analysis, we may regard as the expression and summation of several separate yet closely interconnected and mutually reinforcing imbalances. In the next few chapters we shall attempt to make more explicit the nature of these imbalances, the significance of their interaction, and the conceptual fallacies and social myths on which they rest.

The psycho-social imbalance

We have already observed how in the present context of rapid and accelerating technological and social change, man finds himself increasingly disoriented. The rate of change appears to be far greater than his capacity to absorb it. There exists, in actual fact, a dangerous gap between the resources at the command of the individual and the power at the disposal of the state and other large bureaucratic and economic organizations. It is these institutions which invariably wield a virtual monopoly of the wealth, the means of violence and the knowledge resources of society. This is not to say that the imbalance between the individual and the institution stems chiefly from a trend towards more authoritarian government and bureaucratic control. Such a trend is clearly discernible but it is the symptom rather than the cause of the imbalance. The explanation lies rather in the ever rising potential of the institution (as opposed to the individual) to define social goals and devise economic and political strategies with little or no regard for human need or volition. There has arisen a growing distance between man and the structures, the tools and the techniques which he has created. Far from controlling them, he is often brought under their control. Far from making history, it is he who is made by it. The profound disharmony between man and his creation, which enslaves him and transforms him into an object, may be termed the *psycho-social imbalance*. The so-called 'mass society' and its distinguishing characteristics of political apathy, social anomie and mental or emotional disorder are the product of the dual process of domination and alienation to which the technological society subjects the human psyche.

Lewis Mumford has attempted to explain the growing enslavement of the individual in terms of the 'megamachine',[1] which he considers as the central phenomenon of modern industrial culture, in which the desire for rational organization and centralized coordination inevitably results in a constant increase in order, power, predictability and constraint. In such a society, every major area of human activity – political, economic, cultural – is brought under the jurisdiction of the expert. Indeed, as Theodore Roszak has pointed out, there is no limit to this process, for the authority and prestige of technical skill assert themselves not only over the conduct of major public policy but also over the most personal aspects of human conduct whether it be sexual relations, child rearing, mental health or recreation.[2] The rationale and dynamic of the process of bureaucratization in which 'everything aspires to become purely technical, the subject of professional attention', have received their most lucid exposition in Jacques Ellul's masterful study of technique. Extreme though his thesis may appear at first sight, a careful scrutiny of the bureaucratic industrial system soon reveals the irreconcilable conflict between human autonomy and the application of technique whose net effect is to obliterate any trace of 'personal determination' from 'the perfect design of the organization'.[3]

But what are the requirements of technique? According to

Erich Fromm,[4] they are essentially twofold: the actualization of everything that is technically possible irrespective of social consequences (e.g. development of nuclear, chemical and biological weapons) and the maximization of efficiency and output, on the basis of bureaucratic organization and quantifiable economic growth.[5] It is precisely at this point that several theorists[6] have sought to identify the internal logic of technique with the very rationale of capitalist development. It is in this context that Herbert Marcuse takes issue with Max Weber's pure definition of technical rationality, and his emphasis on the neutrality of technical reason. For Marcuse, the very concept of technical reason is perhaps ideological. The principle of domination is inherent in the notion of technology and not simply in its application. The possibility of control afforded by scientific and rational calculation is not external to but enters 'the very construction of the technical apparatus'.[7] According to this view, the rationality of science and technology is the reflection of a substantive, historically derived, economic process. In *One Dimensional Man*, where he has considerably refined this analysis, Marcuse argues that the principles of modern science have been so structured as to become the 'conceptual instruments for a universe of self-propelling, productive control', thereby ensuring the coincidence of theoretical and practical operationalism.[8]

But awareness of the totalitarian implications of modern science has not been confined to contemporary Marxist analysis, as Aldous Huxley's indictment of twentieth-century capitalism clearly indicates. For him the trend towards increased centralization and government intervention in the immediate future as in the immediate past is in direct response to economic and social confusion which is itself a consequence of mass production and rapid technological change.[9] Huxley's interpretation may lack the conceptual rigour or depth of insight that we find in Marcuse's analysis, but it does serve to highlight the fact that the totalitarianism of technique, whatever its historical origins, is not the direct expression of any particular ideology or political system but of the mass-producing, energy-intensive economy.

It is true that throughout the advanced capitalist world, we are witnessing the emergence of a 'bureaucratic society of manipulated consumption'.[10] But the effort to integrate and subordinate man into large-scale enterprise is not restricted to capitalism. As Roszak rightly argues, technocracy is not the exclusive product of the capitalist mode of production, but rather the consequence of mature and accelerating industrialism regardless of the role ascribed to the profit motive.[11] The socialist societies of the Soviet Union and Eastern Europe operating in the name of Marxism, but severely limited by considerations of party discipline, industrial growth and capital accumulation, have reaffirmed rather than undermined the empire of technological necessity. Comparing them with the 'suave technocracies' of the western capitalist world, Roszak describes these collectivist societies as 'vulgar, grim-faced, heavy-handed technocracies', even more strongly committed than their western counterparts to scientific and technical orthodoxy.[12] In Russia's case, the Tsarist tradition of secrecy and autocratic control and the Soviet conception of power and ideological infallibility, which provides no focal points of organization outside the Party itself, have compounded the totalitarian tendencies of the technocratic state.[13] In other words, the revolutionary seizure of state power in these societies may have transformed the bourgeois mode of production, but it has not restructured those deeply embedded elements of domination and the authoritarian model of socialization which the psyche experiences within the cultural superstructure. The central fact of contemporary life is not the agent but the nature of social control, which derives from the very division of labour and the technical apparatus 'that spans and maintains the whole society'.[14]

In our discussion so far of the psycho-social imbalance we have stressed the almost complete domination which the rule of technique exercises over the individual. Such domination, however, implies much more than mere submission to external or even internalized authority, rules and regulations; it entails a far-reaching process of psychological alienation. The concept of alienation has of course a long history probably dating back to the earliest period of civilization. It is certainly one of the major recurring themes of the Judeo-Christian tradition, to which both Marxism and existentialism[15] are deeply indebted. It was Marx, however, who first developed a general theory of alienation in the context of the rise of the modern state.[16] For

Marx, alienation was a form of self-estrangement, that is, a condition whereby man is alienated from nature, from himself (from his own activity), from his 'species-being' (from his membership of the human species), from other men. All these four aspects of alienation have gained dramatically in magnitude and intensity over the last hundred years, although not always in keeping with Marx's own descriptions or predictions.

It has become increasingly apparent that the crisis of existential emptiness and despair, as portrayed in Kafka's novels and in Sartre's plays, is not merely a function of the relationship between men of different classes but of a deep-rooted sickness within all men. Erich Fromm has compared the alienation of the worker, experienced as frustration of his inner creativeness, curiosity and independence of thought leading to a flight from being, to apathy, destructiveness and psychic regression, with the alienation of the manager, experienced as impersonal and repressive intercourse with the competing interest groups which dominate the corporate economy as well as with the anonymous consumer who has to be manipulated into choosing what is produced today and rejecting what was produced yesterday.[17]

In a complex society governed by the forces of the marketplace, the individual's personality is submerged by his exchange value as if he were no more than a commodity, as if he had no sense of self, no unique identity, no personal dignity. Similarly, in the enforced collectivist economy, the individual has no value except in so far as he contributes materially to the fulfilment of unintelligible economic plans and industrial targets. In each case, the individual's labour, the physical and mental energy which he expends, is determined by an apparatus over which he has no control. Such labour may result in higher standards of material consumption, but the net effect is an act of self-consumption and a state of pseudo-satisfaction, for the commodities that are consumed correspond to the dictates of advertising technique or ideological propaganda which specializes in pseudo-experience and fictitious image-making.

The psychological condition of alienation inevitably leads to the abstraction of the individual who becomes a mere number in the computerized calculations, predictions and decisions of the investor, the strategist, the administrator, the politician. The person is objectified into a vast abstract process of manipulation. Similarly, events concerning large numbers of human beings, whether a company take-over, the launching of a new industry, a military battle or a natural disaster, are invariably assessed in terms of some large abstract quantitative element rather than in terms of the concrete aspects of human experience and human suffering. Thus political discourse and economic decision-making come to rest on mathematical rationality rather than on the awareness of the basic problems of human existence. Zbigniew Brzezinski's 'technetronic society',[18] Herman Kahn's 'doomsday machine',[19] Alvin Toffler's 'modular man'[20] are the necessary products of this new cult of the abstract.

Nor is it coincidence that ours should have been the age of abstract art, for the artist's impressions of the world no longer reflect manageable human dimensions.[21] All that he can portray that is distinctive of the modern period is one-dimensional culture, which manifests itself in the contempt of form, the destruction of privacy, the vulgar display of violence and brutality, and the monotonous succession of new fads and fashions. Thus the generalized pattern of spectacular advertising and mass consumption succeeds in stunting the public imagination and debasing moral, aesthetic and intellectual values, in dissolving real experience into soporific make-believe, in substituting for real communication 'the one way dissemination of directives and symbols.[22] Domination and alienation are mirrored in the technocratic culture, in its philosophy, in its attitude to the future. The resulting psycho-social imbalance is such that the distinctions between progress and decay, illusion and reality, reason and unreason, normality and abnormality almost imperceptibly fade away as man struggles to retain his balance in a world seemingly devoid of all psychological stability.

The structural imbalance

The contemporary disorientation of the human personality and its societal and political implications will be the subject of a more detailed analysis in the next chapter. Enough will have been said, however, to suggest the character of the other major imbalances which derive from this psycho-social disorder and which threaten, even more directly, or at least more obviously, the survival of the species. It is now generally accepted that in spite of their virtual monopoly of the economic, political and intellectual resources of society, the technocracy and its accompanying institutions are finding increasing difficulty in fulfilling their promise of material abundance and psychic gratification for all. We are thus confronted with a second major anomaly in human organization which we may call the *structural imbalance* since it involves the main political and economic structures in the ordering of society. This imbalance refers primarily to the widening gap between the promise of the corporate state and its actual performance, between its destructive and creative power, between the power of the few and the impotence of the many.

Whatever its precise historical origins, the development of an industrial system committed to the production of goods and services in vast and increasing volume has now assumed global proportions. The growth of science, the wedding of science and technology to the means of production, and the increasing integration of the means of production with the political apparatus of society are the dominant characteristics of our age. The ensuing social structure has been variously described as the 'socio-industrial order',[23] the 'new industrial state',[24] the 'contract state',[25] or even the 'military–industrial complex'.[26] Whichever term is used to describe the phenomenon, the inescapable fact of modern history is the continuing acceleration of industrialization in all regions of the world irrespective of ideological system or particular stage of economic development. The twin processes of technological growth and capital accumulation are increasingly brought under the unifying power of state planning which coordinates, adjusts and equilibrates social forces. The gradual abandonment of laissez-faire economics in the United States as a result of the increasing complexity of production and economic organization,[27] the continued reliance of communist systems on central planning in spite of some greater acceptance of market mechanisms and material incentives, the constant elaboration of national and regional development plans in the Third World, all testify to the expanding role of the state in the functioning of the economy[28] and the emergence of a corporate technostructure.

As already indicated, the underlying rationale and overriding objective of the industrial system is economic growth.

Undeniably, this growth has produced in the twentieth century a significant rise in living standards in both capitalist and communist societies. But the statistical measurement of growth, usually in terms of gross national product, does not necessarily give a true indication of the degree of economic well-being.[29] The gross national product is at best an index of the productive performance of society; it does not indicate the quality of health, literacy, education, culture, housing, employment or recreation. In fact, the post-war prosperity of developed industrial countries in both East and West has been achieved at significant social cost whether in terms of air and water pollution, soil contamination, traffic congestion, slums, crime, alcoholism, or drug addiction. The very development of the industrial system, especially under capitalism where it has reached its most advanced stage, appears to have produced both nationally and internationally a social order based on inequality, stratification and exclusiveness. As Schneider has observed, the economic and social disparities characteristic of the industrial system are created and maintained by the very nature of 'the rat race' which both losers and winners are conditioned to accept.[30]

In spite of the unprecedented expansion of the productive capacity of advanced capitalist nations, the sharp inequalities in income, wealth, education and employment opportunities have not disappeared.[31] Despite higher income taxes the richest 20 per cent of Americans have not had their share of income appreciably reduced since 1944. In 1962, the richest 20 per cent earned 45.5 per cent of the national income, while the poorest 20 per cent earned only 4.6 per cent.[32] Significantly, the education system, which claims to act as the great equalizer in society, is often instrumental in transmitting inequality,[33] and has even been described as an 'institutional prop for privilege'.[34] The close correlation between low education qualifications and unemployment is well established. In the United States, a non-white is almost three times as likely as a white man to be in a low paying job as a labourer or service worker. A low income region is inevitably reflected in slums and extremely inadequate housing, a situation reinforced and perpetuated by patchwork planning and the unpredictable play of market forces.

The industrial system, far from producing growth for everyone, has a large number of victims, whom Baran and Sweezy have correctly identified as those who, because of their class, ethnic background or age, are unemployed or unemployable and thereby deprived of the purchasing power to avail themselves of 'the gratifications of consumption'.[35] Understood in this sense, institutional racism, sexual discrimination and even political repression[36] are not passing aberrations but the logical consequence of the technocratic drive to rationalize and expand production. Admittedly, all advanced industrialized societies, whether communist or capitalist, provide in varying degrees and in different forms, a certain minimum level of welfare, but such public expenditures merely strengthen the stability of the technostructure by limiting political opposition and by maintaining a disciplined and productive labour force.

Thus far, we have confined our attention to those costs of economic growth normally incurred by deprived minorities, but perhaps even more significant are those costs which affect the entire society, that is, both the losers and the winners of the technocratic rat race. The most obvious cost in this regard concerns the marked deterioration in the natural environment resulting from the toxic substances dispersed by industrial plants into the atmosphere, and the wastes deposited into streams, lakes and subsoil. The aesthetic perspective, the ideal of freedom and creativity, the conservation ethic have all fallen victim to the mystique of exploitation and power, to vulgar highways and machines for land despoliation, to squalid slums, septic streams and razed deserts.[37] Once again, these external diseconomies are not rare anomalies but an inherent part of the process of corporate production. It is not mere coincidence that, along with the highest measured growth rate Japan should have achieved also the most polluted atmosphere in the world. The industrial state, especially in the capitalist world, has tended to neglect the collective needs of society by encouraging, in Galbraith's words, a sharp divide between 'private opulence and public squalor'.[38] The predominance of the private car at the expense of public transport is but the most striking example of this widespread bias which promotes urban decay, unbalanced regional development and a general decline in the quality of life.[39] The overpowering interests of mass production and mass consumption are by their very nature conducive to the impoverishment of the cultural environment and the neglect of those moral and intellectual faculties in man which enable him to make life a meaningful and creative experience.[40]

The industrial technocracy appears, in fact, to have evolved into a quasi-totalitarian system of manipulation able to regulate the needs, perceptions and values of society. Its dominant institutions, the state and the corporation, have achieved not only a monopoly of economic power but a general organizational ascendancy that is reflected in almost every aspect of social behaviour. Paradoxically, however, such institutional supremacy, precisely because it rests on control rather than participation, on competition rather than cooperation, destroys the associative character of society and the moral autonomy of man. Organic unity is replaced by the distant state, whose institutions are too complex, impersonal and bureaucratized to meet the psychological needs of the community.

In the economic realm, Galbraith has devised the term 'revised sequence' to describe the demise of consumer sovereignty and the emergence of the corporate technostructure, whose continued expansion depends on the control of the market and hence on the ability to shape the behaviour and social attitudes of the customer.[41] For Ivan Illich, it is the concept of 'radical monopoly' which best expresses the ascendance exercised by the production process over public needs and the restriction of the market to one type of commodity or expertise. The ability of the car to shape the entire traffic system in its image, the unchallenged dominance of the school in discharging the education function, and the supremacy of medical prescription in the caring of the sick are so many instances of 'radical monopoly' where 'a major tool rules out natural competence'.[42] The net effect of this process is a form of social polarization which deprives the majority of the power to control the goods and services which are supposedly produced for their benefit, and concentrates this power in the hands of a relatively small professional elite.

It is this growing distance between the objectives of the productive machine and the needs of the individual which explains the widening gulf between the internal rationality of technocratic organization and the irrationality of its consequences upon the larger functions and purposes of society. There may be a high level of rationality in advertising techniques and strategic calculations, but there is an even greater irrationality in the massive allocation of resources which they entail for ends that are wasteful or positively destructive. It is not surprising, then, that such a manipulative and irrational system should have generated scattered but far-reaching dissenting responses from various sections of society. Among these one would include not only student protest and industrial unrest, but also the demonstrative rejection of technocratic values by the beat and the hippie, as well as the increasingly common neurotic response to environmental pressures and frustrations. In this sense, the politics of withdrawal and the politics of protest are but two sides of the same coin. They both reflect the profound, though as yet dimly perceived, dissatisfaction with the structural imbalance in social organization and with the irreparable damage it is causing to nature, society and the human psyche.

The systemic imbalance

At this point, it is important to note that the structural gap between promise and performance, which we have observed in highly developed industrial systems, is even more apparent in economically backward societies. In these countries, domestic institutions often constitute in-built impediments to social change. For example, the educational system, instead of providing effective literacy and vocational skills for both children and adults, often creates an immense pool of illiterate drop-outs and a small highly educated minority that provides the membership and the social base of the ruling oligarchy.[43] Mirroring the pattern of educational elitism is the administrative infrastructure which permits and often encourages corruption and exploitation.[44] In such circumstances, it is not surprising that a great divide should separate the interests of the rural masses from the aspirations of economic, political and military elites. In most cases the peasantry has yet to be convinced of the need to identify with the interests and objectives of the state. More often than not, the actions of government meet with indifference and at times even rebellion and revolt against the whole process of modernization and national integration.[45]

But the vicious circle of contemporary underdevelopment is not simply the product of domestic institutions. It is to a large extent set and kept in motion by the overwhelming dependence of these underdeveloped economies on foreign industrial and financial interests.[46] It is estimated that in Latin America, where the process of external domination is in its most advanced stage, 70 to 90 per cent of raw materials are under the control of United States corporations. The net effect of the economic satellization of Third World countries is to frustrate the possibilities of radical change in the structure of their economies, since it is in the interests of the major centres of industrial development to retain the existing hierarchy of wealth and power. The far-reaching impact of the psychological and structural imbalances on the international system thus becomes readily apparent. The ensuing stratified world order points, however, to yet another imbalance. For the economic, national, racial and ideological divisions are not merely a function of institutional decay, they are the expression of a *systemic imbalance*.

It need hardly be said that the institutions which have been created to deal with the inequalities between the rich and poor nations of the world have been singularly unsuccessful. Indeed the international organizations dominated by the capitalist system and the vested interests which it incorporates have ensured the diminishing share of the underdeveloped countries in the world economy.[47] The dependent nations of Asia, Africa and Latin America have been obliged to pursue a form of development conditioned by the structure and function of the world market and by the international division of labour over which they have had no control and little influence. The determination of the great powers to retain and expand their economic and political spheres of influence has been amply demonstrated by the continued operation of restrictive trading policies and capital transactions whose benefits have accrued largely to the developed economies.

To complement and reinforce these economic techniques of statecraft the major industrial powers have often resorted to subversive 'intelligence' activites and to various forms of military intervention. The anti-colonial wars which so exhausted and demoralized the French nation, first in Indochina, and then in North Africa, the counter-insurgency operations conducted by Britain in Greece, Malaya and East Africa, the joint Anglo-French expedition that led to the 1956 Suez War, the Soviet invasion of Hungary in 1956 and of Czechoslovakia in 1968, America's large-scale military involvement in Korea, Vietnam, Laos, Cambodia, the Dominican Republic, have all conformed to the same interventionist strategy.[48] An equally critical, though more subtle, form of involvement has occurred through the policy of arms transfers.[49] Rather than despatch troops to the theatre of conflict, great powers have often preferred to wield military influence through such institutional mechanisms as military bases, joint military manoeuvres, 'contingency' planning, standardization of weapons, and metropolitan training programmes for the senior military officers of Third World states. This form of involvement has been clearly demonstrated by both Soviet and American policy in the Middle East Wars, by the British and French involvement in the Nigeria–Biafra civil war, as well as by the Soviet, American and British roles in the recurring hostilities between India and Pakistan.[50]

Although extremely cursory, our discussion of the role of economic inequality and international violence has already indicated two salient characteristics of the systemic imbalance, which we may designate as stratification[51] and fragmentation.[52] By its very nature, a system of sovereign states functions without the international authority which alone can give expression to the interests of the world community as a whole. The consequent state of anarchy may not approximate the war of all against all, but it does represent a condition of unrelenting competition. Every major actor on the international stage– not only the state, but also the regional organization and above all the multinational corporation – operates in accordance with narrow vested interests, limited perceptions and divisive ideologies. For the state, the ever-present problem is that of security. By acting on the perennial anticipation of external threats, a state tends to confirm the similar expectations of other states. Thus expectations of violence become self-fulfilling prophecies.

With the development of nuclear weapons, the self-defeating search for security in a fragmented system of states has been taken to its most logical and perilous conclusion. Nuclear deterrence, far from providing effective national defence, risks unleashing a total war which would destroy the very substance of national life, the very existence of the state. Essentially, the rationale of nuclear deterrence is that each nuclear power can help prevent war by threatening its opponent with such massive or graduated retaliation that he will not dare attack. Given the risk of unacceptable damage, it is argued, the would-be aggressor will desist from attack because the cost involved is greater than any possible gain. The problem with this argument is that it depends on the rationality of the decision-maker, for which history provides no guarantee. In any case, the deterrence strategy is itself irrational, for the destructiveness of total war is seen as a condition of peace, and the power of annihilation as the prerequisite of survival.[53]

The hierarchy of military power thus reflects and reinforces the stratification of the international economy. The resulting violent conflicts and economic antagonisms are producing strains and stresses which an increasingly crowded, shrinking and interdependent planet may no longer be able to sustain. The adversary relationship between the United States and the Soviet Union, which dominated the cold war era and which persists to this day though in somewhat more subdued form, is now complicated by the ideological and security confrontation between the two communist giants and by the fierce economic competition which operates among the major capitalist states, and which in the last decade has given rise to a series of recurring international monetary upheavals. The continuing and widening gap between rich and poor nations and the expanding proliferation of nuclear weapons provide the other important dimension to the systemic imbalance in the authoritative allocation of values and resources. The net effect of this imbalance is to deprive international society of the regulatory mechanisms able to balance or overcome the disruption caused by a hierarchical, fragmented and conflict-ridden system.[54] The widespread incidence of international violence and the threat of nuclear extinction are the ultimate expression of this systemic imbalance.

The failure to create a viable international community reflects not only the systemic imbalance in international relations, but also the increasing tyranny of the nation-state and the growing disorientation of the human personality. In other words, it is closely interrelated with the structural and psycho-social imbalances. The all-pervasive nature of international violence and the mounting sense of insecurity are contributing greatly to the erosion of national loyalties and the consequent crisis of legitimacy. The instinctive reaction of ruling elites, which is to strengthen the coercive powers of the state in the hope of arresting the rapid decline of its authority, merely serves to reinforce the tendency towards social malintegration, ideological discontinuity, contradictory economic expectations and political sclerosis.

The ecological imbalance

In referring to the imbalances which affect the role and distribution of wealth, power and authority within the international system and its various political and economic subsystems, we have highlighted those aspects of human disorder which derive more or less directly from various forms of maladaptive social organization. But apart from the sharp conflicts which divide men and the human oppression to which millions are subjected, the technocratic mode of industrial development, which has been gradually encompassing the entire world, has seriously disturbed the natural balance between man and his biological and physical environment. The resulting *ecological imbalance* impinges on the three other imbalances and thereby expresses most dramatically the current condition of global disequilibrium.

With the benefit of hindsight, it is possible to see how technical reason and the spirit of industrial conquest which have activated man's relationship with the natural universe, far from ensuring his ascendancy, now threaten his destruction. It is becoming painfully clear to all those who are willing to examine the available evidence that the exponential growth in human technology and the resulting impact of man's technical intervention in the natural order have seriously disturbed the delicate equilibrium which the evolutionary process has established between the biosphere and the world of inanimate matter. The unrestrained technological optimism, which has dominated for more than half a century the priorities of institutionalized science, is now increasingly under attack.[55]

Man may have reached the apex of the tree of life, but he still remains an integral branch of that tree and of its life-sustaining environment. He cannot divorce himself from this organic structure without risking his own survival. Nor can he arbitrarily decide to alter various elements of the existing biological, physical or chemical framework of life without seriously endangering the indispensable symbiotic relationship which exists between man and various forms of animal and plant life.[56] The indiscriminate cultivation of land, the destruction of forests, the extermination of active species have had precisely this effect. The introduction of pollutants into the earth's ecosystem, whether it be through the use of pesticides and herbicides, industrial wastes or automotive emissions, represents a major and perhaps lasting hazard to life. For these toxic substances are likely to be spread by wind, water movement and animal migration over large areas of the earth's surface, and to be reconcentrated to unpredictable and perhaps dangerous levels by virtue of the food webs through which energy passes from plants to herbivores to carnivores.[57]

But the uncontrolled growth of technology and the consequent disturbance of those natural regulating mechanisms helping to preserve the ecological balance have been compounded by two other interacting and limiting processes. In 1960, the world's population, estimated at 2,700 million, was doubling every fifty years.[58] Within a decade the population had increased to 3,700 million while the doubling time had been reduced to forty years. This uncontrolled increase in the human population was occurring on a planet with a finite capacity to provide for man's needs and absorb his waste products, and in the context of an exploitative attitude to the environment leading to the irretrievable diminution of vital resources. According to one recent estimate, known reserves of aluminium at the present rate of consumption will last only 31 years. The comparable period for copper is given as 21 years, lead 21 years, and mercury 13 years.[59] Even if these calculations are regarded as making insufficient allowance for new discoveries and new technologies and, therefore, unduly alarmist, the fact remains that, even if world population growth were suddenly to stop, copper production would have to increase almost sixfold, oil production sevenfold, lead production eightfold, and similarly with all other non-renewable resources, if global per capita consumption were to reach the present level of the United States.

This leads us to a subtler and more profound sense in which man has become the victim of an ecological imbalance. For both the costs of and the responsibility for the environmental crisis have not been equally distributed.[60] The detrimental impact of human intervention in the ecosphere stems largely from the technocratic mentality which has governed the behaviour of western man since the close of the Middle Ages, and has found its highest expression in the capitalist mode of production. In such a profit-motivated economic system, it is the privileged strata of society which are least affected by the costs of depletion and pollution and best equipped to secure the benefits of growth. As for that large fraction of humanity situated at the 'world's political and economic periphery', overcrowding, lack of hygiene and scarcity are the inescapable conditions of everyday existence.

The degradation of the physical environment must therefore be seen as the manifestation of structural inequality within the existing world order as well as of the enormous gulf between man's boundless thirst for dominance and his limited understanding of the natural order. The doctrine which has exalted and sacralized the concept of technical supremacy, and the various forms of domination to which it has given rise can now be said to have stemmed from ignorance rather than knowledge. True human development can take place only through the cultivation of symbiotic rather than predatory or parasitic relationships both among men and with other forms of life.[61] It is precisely man's lack of planetary perspective, the misconception of his own role and purpose in the evolving cosmos, which form the essence of the ecological imbalance.

The psycho-social, structural, systemic and ecological imbalances which we have just outlined constitute one method of describing and interpreting the more obvious threats to human survival and the quality of life. It is now commonly understood that any of these critical trends, if allowed to persist, could unleash a major local or even global crisis. What is much less appreciated is that each of these trends feeds into the other, each imbalance accentuates the other. The major risk to human life on this planet does not stem from any one of these crises or imbalances taken in isolation but from their constant inter-action. It is this basic but far-reaching insight which will need to guide and inform our analysis of present trends and future possibilities.

3. The decadence of industrial culture

Having sketched in broad outline the most critical imbalances underlying the contemporary organization of human society, we are now in a position to consider their manifestation in the political realm, understood as the realm of freedom, in which man raises himself above the realm of pure necessity.[1] Central to our analysis will be the impact of the growth of technical civilization and the dominance of bureaucratic rationality on the political culture of advanced industrial societies.

There is, of course, no rigidly uniform political culture encompassing all human societies, as the many differences between political and ideological systems readily demonstrate. Nevertheless, one can discern an unmistakable universal tendency towards the centralization of power and the specialization of technique. Significantly, even in the Third World, the drive towards modernization has almost invariably promoted 'the bureaucratic interest in centralized governmental institutions'[2] and the accompanying belief that it is a progressive force of higher value than traditional commitments and loyalties. We may, therefore, justifiably speak of the psycho-social and structural imbalances as worldwide political phenomena. As we shall see, the separation of individual experience from social reality and the gap between autonomous activity and the monopoly of organized power are conducive to an order-maintaining system and a rarified life-style singularly ill-adapted to meet the challenges of the present age. We shall attempt to characterize the decadence of industrial culture[3] in relation to four clearly discernible trends: conformism, privatism, psychic repression and moral decay.

Conformism

It is now widely recognized that the elaborate bureaucratic technological society depends for its efficient organization on a system of anonymous or impersonal control. The mechanism through which such control is exercised is the principle of conformity, whereby adjustment to prevailing norms preempts any question of right or wrong.[4] Human beings become efficiently administered units to the extent that they find their identity in the corporate society rather than in their individuality. As Ronald Laing has observed, by inducing people to experience the same desires and emotions, entertain the same expectations, perceive the same threats, their social behaviour not only becomes predictable but 'is already captive'.[5] The net result of this process is the 'mass man' hardly capable of choice or spontaneous action, a creature conditioned by commercial or ideological salesmanship to conform to the objectives of modern business or to the policies of totalitarian government.[6] It should be readily apparent that in a society of 'mass men', or in a 'mass society',[7] political discourse and public opinion are shaped by a one-way vertical flow in communication emanating from the controlling authorities and spreading downwards to an undifferentiated mass of individuals.

Compliance with the requirements of mass behaviour is assured, in part, through the natural workings of ambition and elitist selection. Though bureaucratic structures may vary from one society to another, advancement is invariably subject to acceptance of existing norms, regulations and organizational practice.[8] For Karl Mannheim, the conformist implications of the bureaucratic process are evident in its selection of 'methodical workers' able to respond to every situation in terms of existing rules and regulations, and in its rejection of individuals with 'free-ranging interests and propensities for improvisation'.[9] The modern corporation with its emphasis on technological and managerial innovation may appear to favour initiative at the lower levels of the administrative apparatus, but such initiative is still contained within the strict parameters set by established norms and centralized decision-making.

The tendency towards conformity does not stem merely from bureaucratic ambition, which is, in any case, a product of economic and political competition. The competitive character of technocratic society pervades every aspect of human relations – even the most intimate sexual relationships – and thereby creates the widespread climate of anxiety and neurosis.[10] Placed in this context, conformity may be seen as a defence mechanism against the general feeling of insecurity produced by impersonal technical forces and accelerating social and technological change. Increasingly, the individual is faced with the prospect of psychological breakdown and even material insecurity, or the option of complying with the dictates of the social machine. It is hardly surprising that the majority in any society should choose, often unconsciously, the latter alternative. However, once the individual has made this choice, then the corporate society is able to mount a large-scale invasion into his life, and achieve a position of unassailable dominance, for, as Adorno has rightly observed, this process of regimentation does not confront the mind from without, but immigrates 'into its immanent consistency'.[11]

In a sense, the mass man is the product of the mass institution, whether it be the state, the corporation, the political party or the voluntary association. In each case, the bureaucratic structure, by virtue of its size, complexity and impersonality, integrates and systematizes the life of the individual, but fails to meet his need for 'recognition, fellowship, security and membership'.[12] Whyte has described how even the romantic concept of marriage has been bureaucratized by the company which evaluates the employee's wife as part of his assets and liabilities. C. Wright Mills has shown that the voluntary association, presumably designed to promote the specific interests of its members, once it is mass in scale, becomes immune to the influence of the individual. Nearly half a century earlier, Robert Michels had demonstrated the bureaucratic trend in the organization of mass parties and the consequent decline of democracy and loss of original enthusiasm and spontaneity.[13] For Marcuse, the psychological result of this societal process, demanded by the very efficiency of the system, is the disappearance of the 'inner dimension of the mind', the loss of the 'critical power of reason', 'submission to the facts of life'.[14]

The organization man is thus transformed into a passive and substantially inert creature that merely responds as if by conditioned reflex to the pressures of society. His actions and decisions consistently follow the line of least resistance; they are predicated on the search for immediate gratification and the indefinite postponement of painful choices. This ideal-type construct is of course little more than a caricature of the contemporary man who remains a much more complex and varied personality. Nevertheless, this oversimplified portrait does reveal certain significant sociological characteristics which Thorstein Veblen was able to discern with penetrating accuracy much earlier than most of his contemporaries. The 'hedonistic man', whatever buffeting he may receive from social forces that propel him in one direction or another, is always content to return to a state of equilibrium, the same 'self-contained globule of desire as before'.[15] It should not surprise us then that the progress of the hedonistic society, under the guise of the welfare state, should have been equated with the end of chiliastic hopes, of utopian thinking, of ideology.[16] The growth of affluence in the most advanced capitalist economies, and more recently in the industrialized socialist world, has provided the managers of society with a ready-made instrument for distracting public opinion from the central issue of the structure of power, and focussing attention on the pleasures of the consumptive life.[17] The redefinition of the pleasure principle in terms of the demand for consumption ultimately leads to intolerance of all unpleasurable experience, to 'entropy of feeling', to political and cultural inertia.[18]

Apart from the material rewards of the 'post-scarcity' society, another important factor contributing to cultural conformism is the mass media which not only provide information about the world, but set the standards and the criteria by which that information is interpreted and evaluated. They become such powerful mediators between the individual's everyday experience and the wider social reality that he is reduced to a passive recepient of their inputs. The progressive centralization of the media in the hands of government or of a few private interests has markedly accentuated the quasi-totalitarian control over the perceptual apparatus of the consumer. To the extent that there is still some residual element of diversity or competition in either the content or the analysis of the information that is presented, it tends to be concerned primarily with trivial or marginal events. The net effect of mass media communication is very much one of falsification and trivialization.

The major socializing institutions are thus able to impose their general monopoly not so much by force as by 'pruning the social imagination'. The many forms of communication and the endless succession of messages, which constantly bombard the individual, seek to govern every aspect and every moment of his existence. No need, real or imaginary, is overlooked. Inevitably, people lose the sense of their own competence, of their capacity to make decisions. For Illich, the industrial institutionalization of values and the substitution of 'the standard package for the personal response' have created a new source of 'scarcity', 'privilege' and 'dependence'.[19] Even learning is transformed into a commodity. Education, traditionally considered a means of developing a critical awareness of self and the surrounding milieu, is now primarily a means of ensuring access to the rewards of consumption, and of adjusting the individual to the vast complex of man-made tools.

No doubt the consumer retains a degree of choice between competing car models and cigarette brands and even between alternate doctors and schools, but this element of autonomy does little to lessen his dependence on professional service or general compliance with established consumption patterns. It is precisely the same advertising technique – so successful in the marketing of goods and services – which is used to sell political images and social and economic policies. The choice between competing political parties and personalities thus acquires the same cosmetic quality as that between rival soap powders and tooth-pastes. In so far as political choice still exists, it resides between competing bureaucracies rather than between conflicting ideologies. In countries, where parties compete for votes, the public may be able to bring about a change of government, but seldom one of policy. In more authoritarian political systems, there may not even be the option for a change in personnel. The widespread deleterious effects of such enforced political conformism are reflected not only in the corruption of the mass which has exchanged moral autonomy for instant gratification, but in the corruption of the elite for the precondition of its rule is the creation of an inferior culture. Michael Harrington has aptly described the resulting dialectic as 'the decadence of an entire society'.[20]

Privatism

The inadequacy of the individual's response to the technocratic society is not purely a function of his impotence in relation to the institution. It stems to a large extent from the very magnitude of the issues and events which confront him. How can the ordinary citizen effectively respond to the complex and technical questions posed by the strategy of nuclear deterrence, the international monetary crisis, atmospheric and fluvial pollution, the use of supersonic transport, the implications of future energy requirements, the ambivalent consequences of the 'green revolution'? All these issues are so large and so remote from his everyday experience that he lacks any normative or cognitive standards by which to make judgements or reach conclusions, and so, in self-defence, retreats to his private world where he hopes to find meaning and reward.

This withdrawal into a privatized universe abstracted from the larger social totality reflects the deep sense of alienation characteristic of mass production society and the gradual decline of individual initiative and responsibility. Even in the large metropolis with its diverse life-styles and cultural patterns, the life of most individuals unfolds within the confines of a narrow and largely routinized environment. They perceive the world, not through the stimulating variety of opposing worldviews, but through the same shared stereotyped preconceptions of their social milieu. Higher levels of formal education are powerless to undermine this parochialism for more often than not they merely succeed in producing the 'illiterate specialist', the man who has acquired an 'education' in order to operate some minute component of the productive machine and thus earn the right to taste of the fruits of consumption. Such an education will almost certainly not have created a deeper consciousness of self or of society.

In the *Lonely Crowd*, David Riesman, has greatly overstated the liberating impact of leisure and the popular culture. The man who has satisfied 'society's requirements on the productive front' may be able to do 'as he pleases on the pleasure front',[21] but can he suppress the essential emptiness, the dreaded loneliness that haunts the life of the acquisitive consumer, and drives him with obsessive compulsion to fill in every available moment of free time? In T. S. Eliot's dramatized form we can capture something of the inner solitude which afflicts modern man and finds such penetrating expression in his heroine, Cilia:

> No, I mean that what has happened has made me aware
> That I've always been alone. That one always is alone
> Not simply the ending of one relationship,
> Not even simply finding that it never existed –
> But a revelation about my relationship
> With *everybody* . . .
>
> No . . . it isn't that I *want* to be alone,
> But that everyone's alone – or so it seems to me
> They make noises, and think they are talking to each other,
> They make faces, and think they understand each other
> And I am sure that they don't. Is that a delusion?[22]

Certainly not a delusion but a profound insight into the contemporary condition of 'ontological insecurity' in which the individual can no longer take the reality, aliveness, autonomy and identity of himself and others for granted.[23]

A more empirical observation of another facet of this same phenomenon is to be found in Jeffrey Hadden's analysis of the *Private Generation*,[24] a phenomenon which he describes with great accuracy but is at a loss to explain. Following a comprehensive student survey, the author reports that the present generation 'rejects meaning or authority outside of the self',[25] and even argues that 'the new style of privatism' aspires to escape from the control of established institutions, and even 'rejects their legitimacy'.[26] The ideology of privatism would seem to have an altruistic quality in so far as it favours the extension of 'the privileges of private existence' to all men. How then is this altruism to be reconciled with the practice of privatism and its emphasis on self-indulgence, non-involvement and acceptance of the status quo?

As Hadden correctly points out, the student rejection of existing institutions is actually far less drastic than we are often led to believe. Indeed, they see many of these institutions, especially government and business, as essential to their future advancement. They have, moreover, an extremely vague and unrealistic conception of the requirements of social and political action. They are committed to idealistic concerns only so long as these do not come into conflict with the demands of privatism. This assessment, valid though it may be, nevertheless overlooks the central fact that ambivalent idealism and committed privatism are not necessarily antagonistic but two sides of the same coin; they both express the same withdrawal from the real world, the same sense of helplessness to affect the course of events or change the existing structure of society. Indeed, they both reveal the same fragmented and stereotyped view of social reality. What is true of the younger student generation is bound to apply still more forcefully to the other private worlds of the mass society where even lip-service to idealism may be in short supply.

What Hadden has not grasped in relation to the nature and function of privatism, Jürgen Habermas has clearly understood. The industrial system justifies itself not by reference to some ultimate political principle but in terms of the 'technocratic consciousness' and the 'allocations of money and leisure time'.[27] In other words, the legitimacy of the system is maintained by the very promise of rewards for 'privatized needs', whether they be expressed in terms of power, success, status or wealth. By dangling these carrots before the eyes of the mass, thereby giving rise to a 'possessive individualism' which measures achievement in terms of the private acquisition of goods and services,[28] passive compliance with the dictates of bureaucratic rationality is upheld.

By devaluing communicative interaction among men and between man and nature, the object orientation of industrial culture justifies and depoliticizes the established order. The consequent separation of society from the state, so clearly perceived by Marx, inexorably leads to an 'essential schism' within the individual because as 'citizen of the state' he must renounce his membership of civil society. His citizenship of the state adds nothing to his 'pure bare individuality' while 'his existence in civil society is complete without the state'.[29] In this sense, the growth of privatism and the decline of meaningful political discourse may be seen both as the expression and the consequence of the psycho-social and structural imbalances which dominate technocratic society. They reflect both man's inner alienation and the almost unbridgeable gap which now separates him from the technical apparatus of the state.

Psychic manipulation

Very closely related to the mechanism of conformism and privatism and underlying the whole process of bureaucratic organization is that very subtle form of manipulation which influences the inner recesses of the human mind and gradually undermines its capacity to oppose the existing order. Everyone is aware of the crude forms of political propaganda – by no means limited to totalitarian systems – which seek to mould opinion by repeated assertions, deceptive slogans and the irrational association of ideas. Ellul has outlined at some length the far-reaching effects of propagandistic manipulation in terms of the 'hypnotic' conditioning of mental processes, 'the suppression of the critical faculty' by 'the creation of collective passions', the formation of an acceptable 'social conscience', the creation of a sphere of the sacred, and the falsification of reality.[30]

But the already large repertoire of propaganda techniques is being constantly expanded by the development of other more exotic methods of behavioral and personality change. Indicative of this trend is Herman Kahn's exercise in futurology which envisages more pervasive techniques of surveillance of individuals and organizations; stimulation of the brain; new counter-insurgency measures; new drugs for the control of fatigue, mood, perception and fantasies; and various forms of genetic control.[31] Somewhat euphemistically, Alvin Toffler has termed this type of human engineering 'psychic gratification'. He foresees a great 'psych-corps' which will sell experiences so organized as to provide 'colour, harmony or contrast to lives that lack these qualities'.[32] Though these forecasts may not be realized in the foreseeable future, the fact remains that several manipulative psychological techniques are already in operation. Much of industrial psychology and psychoanalytic therapy is being used even now to adapt individuals to the demands of an oppressive society. Treating the patient means persuading him or her to accept a repressed condition as the normal state of affairs.

Less direct, more subtle and, in the long-term more efficacious is the form of manipulation which derives from the very process of socialization, in which the reality of compulsion is made to coexist with the illusion of freedom. Henri Lefebvre's analysis of the 'over-repressive society' is most illuminating for it highlights the efforts of that society to banish from public view any gesture or attitude which may give the appearance of conflict.[33] In a society, where 'self-repression' is an integral part of organized everyday life, the inner man has scarcely any chance to exist. From his earliest years the child is taught to struggle against his spontaneous urges and feelings which are inevitably portrayed as evil, immoral and uncivilized. Ronald Laing, who has developed at some length the Freudian theme of childhood repression, has laid special stress on the repressive function of the family, its strong tendency 'to promote respect, conformity, obedience'.[34] The inner world of the human personality is thus transformed into a demon which the individual feels obliged to repress by every psychological mechanism at his disposal, whether it be by reaction, rationalization, splitting, projection or introjection. The end-result of the various forms of destructive action on experience is a shrivelled, dessicated fragment of the human personality, radically estranged from the structure of being and from the human processes caused by the very condition of alienation.

It would be a mistaken view, however, which considers the family as the sole agent of repressive socialization. Marcuse may have exaggerated the degree to which the classical psychoanalytic model has been invalidated by the declining role of the father figure and other family ties and traditions, but he is surely right in stressing the manipulative function of the school, the media and the various recreational institutions. No one can deny that continually escalating mass production and consumption and the increasing concentration of power in the hand of an all-embracing technocratic administration have markedly reduced the inner space available for the development of mental processes.

In the age of scarcity, economic conditions created within the individual an inner compulsion to focus psychic energies on the achievement of mastery over nature. The Protestant work ethic was an indispensable element in the process of capital accumulation, capable of generating those forms of compulsive activity most adapted to the competitive market economy. Why then has the successful termination of the first stage of industrialization and the replacement of scarcity by affluence not put an end to the system of socio-economic domination and psychological repression? The question is too far-reaching and complex to be adequately treated at this point. Suffice it to say that industrialization has given rise historically to an industrial performance principle based on technical innovation and bureaucratic rationalization. Marcuse denotes the additional controls arising from these social phenomena as the 'surplus repression' characteristic of the contemporary period. He differentiates 'surplus repression' from 'basic repression' by which he understands 'the modifications of the instincts' necessary for the survival of human civilization.[35] It is here that Freud and Marcuse are in substantial disagreement.

For Freud, the reality principle, which is inseparable from scarcity and restrains the full and painless gratification of individual needs, makes domination an unavoidable aspect of civilization.[36] Marcuse, on the other hand, argues that surplus repression is not a social or biological necessity but merely the product of the repressive character of technocratic consciousness which depends on repression for its continued existence.[37] Though one may not wish to accept the Marcusean thesis in its totality, it is nonetheless clear that the manipulative administration of society is a direct expression of the prevailing mode of social and economic organization and hence of the dominant ideology. In the case of the contemporary technocracy, it is the 'technical' organization of society and the ideology of 'bureaucratic rationality' which give rise to a machine-centred technology and to the underlying process of psychic manipulation. The machine has come to dominate the human environment by entering the deepest recesses of the human personality and modifying its very essence. There is no more dramatic illustration of this fact than technological man's almost complete dependence on the clock which transforms his experience in time into a rigid and mechanical abstraction.[38]

It is worth noting at this point that the tyranny of technique is by no means confined to the capitalist mode of production. For as the Russian Revolution has demonstrated, the Bolshevik minority which seized power in October 1917 has singularly failed to promote the communist transformation of society. That failure is attributable not only to the bureaucratic apparatus which was inherited almost intact from the Tsarist state, but more fundamentally to the authoritarian mode of socialization from which neither the masses nor the new leadership were able to emancipate themselves.[39] Indeed, the revolutionary movement, far from liberating the individual psyche, initiated a forced programme of large-scale industrialization, which was to instil 'a grotesque fear of initiative and responsibility'[40] at every level of administration and to subordinate all intellectual and cultural activity to bureaucratic and political control.

The orgy of the Stalinist purges in the 1930s was but the most visible and extreme manifestation of the coercive force which was to form the foundation of the Soviet technocracy. In time, the brutalizing use of terror would become less conspicuous but more insidious. The more mature and sophisticated authoritarianism, gradually emerging in the communist systems but especially evident in its most refined form in advanced capitalist societies, has developed a high degree of 'absorbent power'; that is, a capacity to generate material satisfaction on the one hand while disarming protest on the other. In fact, as Roszak convincingly argues, the sexually permissive society serves to consolidate the technocratic status quo, for its 'casual, frolicsome and vastly promiscuous' character, by discouraging 'binding loyalties' and 'personal attachments', reinforces the commitment to 'career and social position, and to the system generally'.[41] This form of repressive tolerance or safety valve is not, however, within the reach of everyone nor is it fully effective as the increasing evidence of psychological stress clearly indicates.

It has been estimated that in Britain the average child stands a ten times greater chance of being admitted to a mental hospital than to a university. In the United States some $25,000 million are spent annually on alcoholic beverages and tobacco, while in the female population aged between 30 and 60 one in four makes regular use of psychoactive prescription drugs.[42] If, in addition, one takes into account the large and growing reliance on illicit drugs, especially among the younger generation, one gains some impression of the present pathological state of society. The resulting nervous tension and psychic pressure, which threaten to paralyse the social machine, have thus made necessary the psychic manipulation of stress and the redefinition of normality. The drug and the mental hospital have become the indispensable lubricating oil and reservicing factory needed to prevent the complete breakdown of the human engine. The eventual outcome, however, is far from certain for in the process man is extended to the limit of his endurance 'like a steel cable which may break at any moment'.[43]

Moral decay

Conformism, privatism, psychic manipulation, these are the three main features which dominate the physiognomy of modern culture. The net effect of all three phenomena is to reduce the individual into a helpless automaton whose only function is to serve the gigantic organizational network that surrounds him. The monolithic and routinized pattern of his day-to-day experience strongly militates against the development of the non-conformist conscience and, therefore, against the formation of ethical concerns. The conforming, isolated, psychically manipulated individual is powerless to construct group standards and norms in opposition to those prescribed by the industrial technocracy. He cannot defy the bureaucratic ethic, for conflicting normative principles are antithetical to the rule of the bureaucracy, whose mentality Marx has succinctly expressed as 'the deification of its authority'.[44] The rule of technique is in fact governed by an ethic whose precise function is to exclude all other ethics, to obstruct all moral considerations likely to conflict with or threaten its continued operation.

As Habermas has observed, the suppression of the normative sphere is reflected not so much in the authoritarian personality as in 'the destructuring of the superego'.[45] The apparent freedom exercised by the voter, the consumer or the man of leisure masks a more fundamental subordination to an ideology which eliminates the distinction between the practical and the technical, distorts the process of human communication and depoliticizes the mass of society. The consequent collapse of the normative order is most dramatically reflected in the progressive abandonment of the Judeo-Christian impulse towards transcendance. The spiritual–ethical imperative to renounce the self, to give up wealth and worldly comfort, to endure any sacrifice for the cause of justice,[46] is now considered by the secular, super-industrial system as an 'embarrassing', 'anachronistic', 'irrational' assertion of the ideal.

What we are witnessing in the most advanced industrial societies is the gradual impoverishment, if not complete elimination, of the transcendental element of culture, of its capacity to offer a critical perspective on social reality. Marcuse has described this flattening out of the antagonism between the actual and the possible in terms of the 'liquidation of two-dimensional culture' and the integration of cultural values into the established order.[47] The massive reproduction and consumption of culture in the modern period, the so-called democratization of art, have led to a qualitative as well as quantitative change which robs the work of art of its 'power of negation', of its critical function in society. In two-dimensional culture, the great work of art stands in 'terrifying or elevating contrast' to the mediocrity of everyday life.[48] Whereas today, the artistic creation is incorporated into the technological society and serves the same function as an advertisement, which is to 'sell, comfort or excite'.[49] Marcuse may have overstated the changing role of culture and the one-dimensional character of present-day civilization, but he has accurately perceived the general trend which separates today from yesterday. The breakdown of narrative time in Joyce, the despairing evocation of memory in Proust, the experimentation with atonality and dissonance in Stravinsky's and Schoenberg's music, the geometrical design of abstract art, and the use of deliberate distortion and stylization to depict the grotesque and the fantastic as in Picasso, Matisse and Epstein, are the symptoms of nervous shock, the reflection of the violence and disintegration of modern civilization.

The stifling impact of one-dimensional culture, the suffocating rationale of the bureaucratic ethic, the oppressive thrust of the ever-accelerating machine have undoubtedly contributed to the pathological explosions characteristic of the present epoch. The disappearance and liquidation of peoples in Stalinist Russia and Nazi Germany and the genocidal reflexes triggered both in the Second World War and in subsequent wars, though carried out with the aid of technology, may well represent man's instinctive revolt against the machine. Steiner has detected in this destructive impulse 'a lashing out of the choked psyche', an attempt to escape from the oppressive confinement of 'an intolerably thronged condition'.[50] The twentieth-century experience of wholesale human and material devastation is indicative not only of the irrationality of the social machine, but also of man's desperate need for free space, for escape from the totalitarian rule of technique. The aggressiveness of technological man is, at least in part, a form of psychological release, a controlled reaction to an escalating and ultimately intolerable level of frustration.

In this sense, the cold war ideology developed by the superpowers may be regarded as the institutionalized efforts of both elites to mobilize the aggressive energies of their respective populations, energies which could not be channelled into the life of their domestic societies. The construction of two permanent military–industrial complexes fulfilled this purpose while highlighting the wasteful and destructive energy that inevitably accompanies the growth of technical power.[51] Their very awesomeness, remoteness and permanence have drastically lowered the human threshold of apprehension. The paralyzing effect of destructive technology has made possible the increasing acceptance and tolerance of the most callous bestiality, the most grotesque violence. While nearly all Americans were provided in their very living rooms with the most detailed information about the atrocities committed by their troops in the Vietnam War, only a relatively small number appeared able to grasp the intensity or the enormity of the crime. Morally, psychologically, killing and torture have been neutralized by a 'realistic' ordering of the facts, by the rationalization of precisely that which is least acceptable in reality.

The euphemistic references to rationality and realism in fact serve to conceal a condition of almost total political cynicism. The revelations of the Pentagon Papers are significant not merely because they expose the real nature of American interventionist policy or deflate the 'rational' argument advanced in favour of indiscriminate warfare, but primarily because they highlight the 'use of the total lie by the total state'. They illuminate the function of advertising technique in the manipulation of public opinion and political dogma. In this sense, the end of ideology simply points to the decline of public morality, a decline which 'pragmatists' and 'realists' apparently interpret as an index of progress and material well-being. In reality, ideology has become an integral part of the social system which it justifies and represents as the best of all possible worlds. In this regard, we need only cite the intellectual absurdities that provide strategic thinking with its façade of toughmindedness and pseudoscience and the flagrant distortion of the facts by which governments seek to contrast the purity of their own motives with the diabolical intentions of the enemy. What we are witnessing, then, is not the end of ideology but the suppression or trivialization of those beliefs which can act as levers for the transformation of society. The end result is the 'ideology of non-ideology' designed to justify a system of repression and to produce the required degree of conformity.

The fiction of the purely technical, pragmatic, non-ideological character of 'post-industrial society' has been considerably encouraged by the welfare state technician and social scientist who is not concerned with questioning values or threatening privilege but with technical adjustments of the existing order which 'improve its efficiency and blur its inequities'.[52] Were the technician or scientist to go beyond marginal social engineering and engage in radical inquiry, he might well jeopardise his newly found position of prestige, security and affluence. Not surprisingly, much that has passed for science and objective investigation turns out to be 'scientism' and dubious philosophy. It is only recently that there has emerged overt opposition to the interpretation of the social sciences as 'a set of bureaucratic techniques' whose 'methodological pretensions' and 'obscurantist conceptions' merely serve to obfuscate or trivialize the most burning issues in the present phase of man's cultural and moral evolution.[53] The so-called objective, value-free, scientific observer can perceive only the behavioural façade of the observed subject. To simply observe and record the behaviour of the voter, the political leader or the schizophrenic and to establish the general pattern to which he conforms is to impose enormous limitations on the uniqueness, the reality and psychic coherence of what is perceived. To refuse to enter into the life of the human subject, to sympathize and identify with his moral or psychological dilemma, is to reduce him into an incomprehensible and alienated object whose only meaning is that which has been attributed to it by the observer.[54]

The simplistic, instrumental, even quantitative conception of social science can operate only by minimizing the importance of conscious, purposeful, creative activity, by abstracting man from his physical and bio-social environment, and by assigning to him a passive function in the existing social order, which is thereby reduced to an aggregate of impersonal, disparate, antagonistic forces.

Such a mechanistic model of society merely justifies, rationalizes and reinforces the integration of the individual into a scientific and technical order over which he can exert little or no influence. Politics then becomes the mere regulatory mechanism for the maintenance of this 'natural' order rather than the means whereby man can transcend and transform it.[55] The 'scientific' and intellectual resources as well as the political and cultural conditions created by the technocratic society would thus appear to have set in motion a self-perpetuating social order. However, such a conclusion may be somewhat premature for until now we have restricted ourselves to an examination of the dominant trends operating within industrial culture, and while not disputing the powerful momentum which they have unleashed, it is clear that account must also be taken of emerging political and cultural developments pointing in quite different directions. However, before exploring the possible implications of these more positive trends, we need to complete our investigation of the various imbalances in contemporary human relations and their economic, ecological and military ramifications.

4. World economy in disarray

Our discussion of industrial culture has only hinted at the structural imbalance which is progressively undermining the institutional framework of both national and international society. To gain a clearer appreciation of the nature of institutional breakdown, we need to consider the contemporary evolution of economic organization, which underlies the widening gap between promise and performance, power and impotence, disturbance and regulation. These gaps are most dramatically evident in the widespread phenomenon of underdevelopment, but increasingly also in the crisis which threatens the future growth of the major capitalist economies, and which may be considered as the opening stage of a struggle for a new world order. Having made the crisis of 'neo-capitalism'[1] the starting point of our analysis, we shall then be in a better position to examine the structural sources of underdevelopment, the systemic implications of multinational enterprise and the ecological dimension of the 'energy crisis'.

Inflationary growth

Since the Great Depression of the late 1920s and early 1930s and the subsequent Keynesian revolution, economic theorists and practitioners alike have been preoccupied with the prospects and the problems of growth. In the case of the United States, World War II acted as a great catalyst for growth. By 1944, American war production had exceeded the entire value of the gross national product in 1933, while unemployment had been reduced to a mere 670,000 compared to eight million in 1939. Within little more than a decade GNP (at current prices) had doubled in value and by 1960 had reached the figure of $500,000 million only to double again in 1971. Much of this increase was simply the monetary expression of inflationary trends, but there was nonetheless a significant and

47

prolonged expansion in the production of goods and services. As for the West European and Japanese economies, although they had been gravely damaged by war, their knowledge resources had remained more or less intact and were effectively complemented by a programme of massive re-capitalization, greatly facilitated by the bipolar division of the world and the economic and political institutions of the cold war. Recovery gradually gave way to an 'economic miracle', for by the end of the 1950s the levels of Japanese, French and German industrial production had more than doubled those of 1938. Dramatic though it was, however, the fact remains that growth was achieved at a price, often unrecorded but nonetheless substantial. Several analysts have attempted to take account of the considerable human and environmental costs of growth by introducing notions such as the gross national disproduct[2] and the diseconomics of growth.[3] Kenneth Boulding has, in fact, suggested that the net value of growth may have been zero or even negative.[4]

But quite aside from the material costs associated with pollution, the depletion of resources, wasteful military production, the mediation of conflicts, bureaucratic coordination, and the less tangible, though perhaps more lasting, damage suffered by the human personality, growth in the capitalist economies has given rise to a set of interconnected structural imbalances which have already produced a series of recessions and may eventually culminate in a general depression. Without engaging in needlessly alarmist speculation, it is important to note that, in spite of the general upward trend in the growth curve, the United States economy has performed sluggishly on several occasions, and particularly during the late 1940s, late 1950s and early 1970s, when a marked contraction of economic activity was reflected in high and rising levels of unemployment and much idle productive capacity. On the other hand, periods of sustained growth have tended to generate higher price levels as demonstrated by the thirty-five per cent rise in the overall price level in the 1960s. Generally speaking, governments have been willing to tolerate a measure of inflation in order to retain the benefits of growth and honour their commitment to full employment. Both macro-economic theory[5] and government fiscal policy, mindful of the dangers posed by depression, have come to accept rising prices as the lesser of two evils.

While it is true that in 1973–5 prices rose on a scale unprecedented since World War II (according to data released by the Organization for Economic Co-operation and Development (OECD), consumer prices for 1973 in 24 major western economies had increased at four times the average annual rate of the 1960s[6]) inflationary trends have been in evidence throughout the post-war period. The average annual decline in the value of money in the 1960s was 2.2 per cent for the United States, 2.4 per cent for Canada and Australia, 3.4 per cent for Britain, 3.7 per cent for Sweden and France, and 5 per cent for Japan. By 1969, the lowest rate of price increases for a major country was for West Germany at 3.8 per cent. The inflationary phenomenon was no mere accident but the result of a conscious policy of 'controlled' inflation, which considered a gradual rise in prices as the economic stimulant most likely to encourage capital investment and the sale of consumer durable goods, to provide opportunities for credit expansion, and generally accelerate the process of economic growth. Government, business and trade unionism alike became fervent exponents of the philosophy of growth through inflationary expansion.

Growth was now seen as one of the overriding responsibilities of all western governments. In accordance with Keynesian theory, they were expected to introduce a variety of measures designed to keep a high level of purchasing power and thereby maintain the momentum of growth. Indeed it has been persuasively argued that in late capitalist society the state sector and state spending may be functioning increasingly as the catalyst for the growth of the private sector and total production.[7]

Once the syndrome of rising expectations was firmly established, wage demands, naturally enough, were aimed not only at preserving real purchasing power but at securing increases in real income on the basis of past and future improvements in productivity. Nor was the mood of self-confidence associated with the psychology of the growth cult confined to employees. It was equally apparent in the behaviour of employers who, rather than provoke industrial unrest or create unemployment, simply passed the higher costs of labour on to the consumer.

The mutually reinforcing inflationary strategy adopted by government, labour and industry was bound in the long-term to have a serious disruptive effect on the economy. The inflationary spiral could not be contained by old-fashioned price competition, for the most dramatic structural development in the advanced capitalist economy has been the increasing concentration of corporate wealth and the consequent globalization of markets and enterprises. By 1970 the top one hundred industrial corporations in the United States accounted for nearly half of all corporate assets.[8] In a situation where a few giant firms dominated most markets, prices could be collectively determined in a manner which cast doubt even on the relevance of the theory of oligopoly. Nor is there any evidence to suggest that the so-called 'battle of industries',[9] as for example between steel and aluminium or between aluminium and glass, has produced the degree of competitive restraints which can prevent the great bulk of commodities and services from entering the market at inflexibly administered prices. Monopoly pricing has been particularly striking in such products as cigarettes, drugs, packaged foodstuffs and petroleum products, all of which exhibit a vast gap between factory costs and consumer prices.

It should not be thought, however, that rising prices are merely the result of profit accumulation. The central objective of modern corporate management is to maximize the profitability and efficiency of production which requires the reinvestment of a high proportion of gross income. Consequently, even costs paid out as profits or dividends to so-called owners may constitute 'a drain on the company's "profitability"'.[10] The large self-financing requirements of the corporation are such that a fall in demand, far from lowering prices, often dictates an upward adjustment in prices in order to offset the possible loss of income. Such an outcome is made possible by the price inelasticity of many consumer goods and the almost arbitrary pricing power of the corporation. Nowhere has this trend been more dramatically reflected than in the oil industry, especially since 1970, with the major oil companies taking advantage of the cost increases imposed by the Organization of

Petroleum Exporting Countries (OPEC) to exact even more exhorbitant prices from the consumer. Close scrutiny of the cost of a typical gallon of OPEC oil, even after October 1973, suggests that the price increases announced by the corporations were far in excess of the new charges levied by the oil producers. According to Tad Szulc, corporate profits in Middle East operations early in 1974 increased on the average from $0.30 to over $1.00 a barrel, and in the case of Aramco, 'from $0.80 early in 1973 to $4.50 a barrel in March 1974'.[11] Clearly, the policy of the multinationals has been to increase their retained earnings in order to promote their ambitious long-term plans in capital spending and thereby further reduce their dependence on fluctuations in demand and changes in fiscal policy likely to affect the availability of external credit.

Given the nature of the corporate economy, it is hardly surprising that the various attempts of governments to control inflation by some form of prices and incomes policy should have resulted in total failure. The levelling of wages, even if it could be enforced, would not necessarily alter the long-term price structure of industry but simply sharpen economic and political conflict, as the British experience under Heath's Conservative government clearly demonstrated. On the other hand, the attempt to moderate aggregate demand by fiscal and monetary measures is no more likely to be successful. Even among orthodox economists, there has been declining support for the view that price inflation stems principally from too much effective demand chasing too few goods and services, especially as, contrary to past experience, prices have continued to rise in spite of stagnant sales and income, tight liquidity and comparatively high levels of unemployment.

If the present inflationary predicament is not susceptible to any simple economic remedy, it is because of the profound structural maladjustment of the capitalist economy. It would appear that periods of prolonged economic buoyancy, particularly in the United States, have come to depend on the operation of one or more of three factors: sustained technological innovation, imperial expansion, preparation for or participation in war. Because of its obvious connection with all three mechanisms, defence expenditure may be regarded as one of the main indicators of the progressive militarization of the growth economy and of its underlying structural imbalance.[12] To cite one example, cumulative missile spending, estimated to have exceeded $250,000 million in 1955–70, provided crucial contracts for the highly specialized science-based aerospace and electronics industries dominated by such giant corporations as General Dynamics, General Electric, AT&T and General Motors. As for the more traditional manufacturing industries, they have been able to capitalize on the Korean and Vietnam Wars and on the resulting demand for food, clothing and textiles, ammunition, artillery and small arms, tanks and vehicles.[13] The dramatic expansion of military aid and of the arms trade since World War II has no doubt fulfilled the same function.[14] Given the increasingly integrated character of the international capitalist system and the dominant role of the United States, the growth of US military spending has also produced a far-reaching stimulus – greatly facilitated by the establishment of military alliances and extensive foreign military installations – on the national economies of Western Europe, and especially Japan which has been one of the major beneficiaries of US military intervention in the Asian rimlands.

Another important attraction of defence spending is its favourable impact on the problem of unemployment. It is calculated that in 1970 the members of the armed forces (2.9 million), the civilian employees of the Defence Department (1.2 million), and those employed in military manufacturing (3 million) constituted nearly 8 per cent of the total US labour force.[15] When one takes into account the additional employment opportunities which result from the demand generated by the military budget, it becomes clear that the continued expansion of the military sector has been vital not only to corporate profits but to the preservation of adequate levels of private aggregate demand. The inability of the civilian sector of the US economy to absorb the entire labour force is underlined by the persistent high level of unemployment, averaging at about 5 or 6 per cent since 1945 and reaching the record post-war level of 9.2 per cent in 1975.

But against the growth benefits of the war industry one has to debit the significant political and social costs stemming from the overt and covert activities of the military–industrial complex. For the moment, however, we need only dwell on the economic cost of war spending and its marked inflationary tendency. The requirements of the nuclear and conventional arms races and of the various wars of intervention have provided American corporations with a cushion of highly profitable business. Given the highly interdependent structure of American industry, it is not surprising that the high profit margins and cost inefficiency characteristic of the military market should have been transmitted to the civilian sector and contributed to a marked acceleration of price increases.[16]

The inflationary spiral which now grips the entire western world and much of the Third World is then the product of several closely interwoven factors. The presence of high rates of growth, however erratic, will normally produce in any market economy inflationary expectations which both labour and industry seek to realize at each other's expense. The increased bargaining power of trade unionism and the monopoly pricing mechanism characteristic of the corporate system of administered competition both tend to feed the cancerous growth of inflation. Like a drug, the growing intervention of the state through credit expansion and public spending often serves to reinforce the economy's addiction to inflation. The high-profit structure of the militarized sector of the economy and the declining productivity of the vast service sector simply accentuate the already intractable problem of inflation, and thereby distort further the economic fabric of society. Nor is inflation amenable to national solutions, for the accelerating integration of the international economy and the mutually reinforcing effects of commercial rivalry have combined to make the contagious inflationary disease a truly worldwide phenomenon.

The new balance of economic power

One of the most significant developments since the end of World War II has been the rapid internationalization of the capitalist system. Some observers have even argued that there exists now a single capitalist world economy, in which the centrally planned economies of the Soviet Union, Eastern Europe, China, North Korea, North and South Vietnam, Cuba, operate as large firms, whose production is 'still geared to trade on a capitalist world market'.[17] Side by side, however, with the progressive integration of the world capitalist system has been the marked trend towards fragmentation resulting from the increased in-fighting among the core capitalist powers.[18] By the mid-1950s Japan and Western Europe were beginning to register significant economic advances in relation to the United States. In the period 1953–69, the annual growth rate in industrial production was 4.0 per cent for the United States, 6.3 per cent for France, 7.1 per cent for West Germany, 8.0 per cent for Italy and 13.6 per cent for Japan. The decline of American industrial dominance was partly reflected in the reduction of the US share in world markets. American exports as a proportion of the total world volume fell from 23.7 per cent in 1948 to 18.5 per cent in 1957 and 15.5 per cent in 1969.

This pronounced shift in the distribution of economic power ushered in a period of intense rivalry and instability. Much of the uncertainty stemmed in fact from the contradictory trends towards greater market integration and a more specialized division of labour on the one hand, and institutional disintegration and economic nationalism on the other. A perceptive analysis of the phenomenon was provided in early 1974 by Helmut Schmidt who likened the pattern of international economic relations to 'a struggle for the world product'.[19] Although the nature of this struggle was considerably complicated by the growing number of protagonists and the intrusion of a new set of complex political, strategic and ecological considerations, its origins clearly lie in two closely related developments: the resurgence of the West European and Japanese economies and the gradual decline of the American economic empire.

As the European and Japanese economies rebuilt their industrial potential, they became major exporters of manufactured goods, successfully competing on the world markets with most American products. A series of company amalgamations in Europe and Japan, the gradual accumulation of capital and the growing sophistication of technological know-how sharply reduced the advantage in productivity held by the American economy. In the case of Japan, the high proportion of GNP which it devoted to capital investment – in excess of 30 per cent throughout the greater part of the 1960s – and the great emphasis placed on heavy industry laid the foundation for sustained long-term growth. Far from becoming neo-colonial outposts, Western Europe and Japan were now serious economic rivals to the United States, not only on the world market but even within the American domestic market. It is estimated that in the ten-year period between 1961 and 1971 United States imports of non-farm processed goods increased 360 per cent from $11,000 million to $40,000 million. In the five-year period 1969–73, West Germany and Japan enjoyed in their bilateral trade with the United States a favourable balance of $4,700 million and $10,200 million respectively.[20] Indicative of the steady deterioration of the US trading position was the progressive recourse, especially under the Nixon administration, to various forms of protectionism – special credit schemes, tax rebates, tariffs, quotas – in the hope of restricting foreign imports and enhancing the penetration of American exports.

At this point, account must be taken of the very considerable advantages that the United States still retains in relation to its principal economic rivals. In the first instance, there remains a very substantial, though diminishing, asymmetry in the flow of capital investment between the major capitalist centres. While the export of West German and Japanese long-term capital to the United States has been continually increasing since the early 1960s, it is still predominantly of the indirect kind, representing investment in US stocks, bonds and government securities. There is still very little of the direct investment in subsidiaries of national companies which accounts for most overseas American investment. The annual sum invested in the Common Market by American companies or their subsidiaries rose from $228 million in 1958 to $908 million in 1965. The sum total of these investments had reached nearly $5,000 million in 1965 and more than doubled by 1969. A study by the European Economic Commission, which revealed that in 1965 80 per cent of Common Market electronics production and 24 per cent of the motor industry were under American control, provided ample confirmation of American overall supremacy in international capital concentration.[21] Of the world's 195 largest industrial corporations in 1971, the United States had 115, Japan 16, the United Kingdom 14, West Germany 18 and France 13.[22]

It is perhaps Japan rather than Europe which has thus far

most effectively challenged, at least domestically, the American advantage in capital concentration. Japan now leads the world in shipbuilding; Nippon Steel is the world's major producer of steel; and Toyota has become the third largest car manufacturer. However, while it is true that foreign assets in Japan represent only 2 per cent of total Japanese corporate assets, American business operations nevertheless exercise considerable control over key sectors of the economy, and especially over the computer, petroleum and rubber industries. Japan's bargaining power may be further reduced by the growing scarcity and higher costs of Japanese labour and by the growing dependence on foreign markets which may eventually force it to open its own domestic market to foreign competition. Japan and, to a lesser extent, Western Europe are also at a disadvantage vis-à-vis the United States in that they both suffer from acute shortages of several strategic materials whose supply is often under the control of their main competitor. The escalation of oil prices following the Yom Kippur War of 1973 has dramatically emphasized their dependence on foreign energy sources and, according to one analyst, effected 'a drastic shift in economic power from Western Europe and Japan to the United States'.[23] These various structural problems facing the European and Japanese economies are compounded by the fact that none of them possesses anything like the military power available to the United States for the defence of its financial and commercial interests. Whatever the underlying motive for the French nuclear deterrent and the rising German and Japanese defence budgets, the enormous disparities in nuclear and conventional capability between the United States and the other advanced capitalist economies are unlikely be bridged in the foreseeable or even distant future.

The costs of empire

Regardless of the persisting inequalities between the main centres of the international market economy, the fact remains that the emerging configuration of forces and conflict of interest represent a rather dramatic shift from the closely integrated capitalist system which had operated in the immediate post-war period under the almost exclusive control of the United

States. As leader of the 'free world' and principal architect of the policy of containment, the United States had arrogated to itself not only the role of international policeman but also that of guardian of the economic viability and prosperity of western capitalism. Underlying the American conception of world order was the commitment to the creation of an all-embracing but tightly-knit political and military structure which would act as an umbrella for the successful expansion of 'free enterprise'. For such an economic project to be realized it was necessary to develop and implement the Keynesian theory of state intervention in economic planning, to provide adequate investment incentives to the private sector, to create expanding domestic and foreign markets which would encourage and sustain increased levels of production, and finally to devise a satisfactory international currency on which to base the expansion of international trade and finance.

To meet the institutional requirements of the new economic order several regional and global organizations were created. Of particular importance was the Organization for European Economic Cooperation, which stimulated the movement towards European economic integration. To reduce tariffs and encourage multilateral trade, the General Agreement on Tariffs and Trade (GATT) was established in 1947. Its principal function was to serve as a focal point of all major tariff negotiations and to exercise restraint on the traditional freedom of national action in commercial policy.[24] The financial framework for economic expansion had already been constructed at the Bretton Woods Conference of 1944 which led to the creation of the International Bank for Reconstruction and Development, better known as the World Bank, and the International Monetary Fund (IMF). The first was to assist in providing private long-term loans for war-damaged and newly developing industries; the second was to make available short-term loans from the contributions of member countries to those members who lacked the necessary foreign exchange to meet their international debts. The monetary system agreed at Bretton Woods terminated the gold standard as the agreed medium of international payment and replaced it with the gold-exchange standard which established the leading position of the US dollar alongside gold, at a parity of $35 an ounce. The new system clearly reflected the dominance of the United States in the world economy accruing from its vastly superior productive capacity and its possession of the greater part of the world's gold reserves. It was then in a position to act as the world's banker and to carry out all financial transactions in gold at the agreed price. For their part, the other countries were expected to maintain stable currencies and to change their value only on the basis of specified regulations to be administered by the IMF. The new system of exchange was designed to produce a stable pattern of growth on the basis of government regulation, inter-governmental cooperation and a degree of international organization.

For more than a decade the Bretton Woods system appeared to be highly successful in achieving the liberalization of trade and payments and the promotion of international financial stability. By the early 1960s, however, the gap between appearance and reality became increasingly obvious. During the 1950s the United States amassed balance-of-payments deficits amounting to $18,000 million, the greater proportion of which had accumulated in foreign hands in the form of short-term investments in the US money market. When deemed no longer profitable, these could be sold and the dollars presented to the US Federal Reserve Bank for redemption in gold. The US balance of payments deficit continued to mount throughout the 1960s and in 1971 reached the all-time record of $22,000 million, by which time the American gold stock had fallen from its peak of $24,600 million in 1949 to $10,100 million, a level lower than the registered at any time since 1936.

What were the main factors responsible for these perennial difficulties in the US balance of payments? The most obvious, though not necessarily the most important, part of the explanation was to be found in the declining competitiveness of American exports in the world market, and hence in the decreasing capacity of the United States to achieve a trade surplus. In spite of a $2,000 million surplus in farm exports in 1971, the United States overall foreign trade registered a deficit of more than $2,000 million.

But the deteriorating trading performance of the United States had merely accentuated the balance-of-payments deficit.

It was not its true cause. The deficit was in large measure attributable to the expenditures incurred by the United States in
order to support its various overseas economic, political and
military activities. A variety of foreign aid programmes (many
of them designed to buttress client governments), a network of
costly military installations spanning all continents, and a
series of expensive military interventions combined to transfer tens of thousands of millions of dollars into the hands of
governments and financial institutions which were likely to
spend but a small proportion on the purchase of goods and
services produced in the United States. The average annual
outflow of dollars resulting from US military and economic
aid had risen from $4,800 million in 1950–4, to $6,900 million
in 1965–9. It is estimated that in its later stages the Vietnam
War alone cost the United States upward of $20,000 million
a year. Other sources of the American deficit included increased
tourist expenditures abroad, rising transport costs payable to
foreign airline and shipping companies, and growing net
capital outflows. American external liquid liabilities, which in
November 1971 were estimated at $63,000 million, represented
to a large extent the costs of empire which the United States
had accumulated since the early 1950s. But if the empire was so
costly, why was the United States not willing to abandon it?
Why was it so intent on living beyond its means?

The first point which needs to be made is that the very substantial burdens arising from US military and economic commitments overseas have not been shared equally by all sections
of American society. While all have contributed to the costs of
empire as taxpayers, only a few giant multinational enterprises
have benefited directly from this global investment. Given their
decisive role in the operation of the American political economy, it is hardly surprising that successive administrations
should have shaped many of their strategic and financial
decisions in accordance with long-term corporate interests.
Apart from the very substantial income accruing from foreign
investments (estimated at $10,000 million in 1970), these
large corporations have developed a major stake in the reinvestment of their foreign profits, the tapping of local money
markets, the exploitation of relatively cheap labour, reliable
procurement of strategic raw materials, the sale of their foreign-

made products to the United States, and the supply of arms and munitions to the large and growing US military establishment. The far-flung American empire has thus served two distinct but overlapping corporate objectives: it has provided almost limit-less opportunities for profitable investment while at the same time affording military protection from hostile forces, whether local or international.

The US balance-of-payments deficit has thus given rise to a strange dichotomy. While creating a major structural im-balance both within the American economy and in its relation-ship with other capitalist economies, it has tended at the same time to promote the geographical and financial expansion of American capital. It is this latter advantage which had dis-suaded the United States from taking any serious steps to eliminate the persistent imbalance in its transactions with the outside world. But why has the rest of the capitalist system been willing to accept such a destabilizing situation? The com-paratively tolerant attitude adopted by the Europeans and the Japanese (except for the brief interlude of opposition offered by Gaullist France) is partly explained by the obvious advantage which an inflationary US economy offers to their export drives on which much of their economic prosperity depends. Any attempt on the part of the United States to restore a balance on the basis of a deflationary strategy could have seriously dis-ruptive effects on the expansion and improvement of Euro-pean and Japanese productive capacity. Another consideration relates to the benefits which are assumed to flow from US mili-tary activities and expenditures. Both Western Europe and Japan continue to host large and sophisticated US military installations and both still operate under the American nuclear umbrella. Moreover, there is some validity to the argument advanced by Sweezy and Magdoff that all capitalist centres have been 'co-beneficiaries' of the success of the US war machine in maintaining in power throughout the Third World 'regimes which are hospitable to capitalist trade and investment'.[25] There can be little doubt that the penetration of Japanese in-vestment in East and Southeast Asia and of West German ex-ports in Latin America has been greatly facilitated by American military supremacy.

The international monetary crisis

In spite of these various domestic and external factors tending towards the institutionalization of the US balance-of-payments deficit, the international monetary crisis steadily deteriorated throughout the late 1960s and early 1970s. The price of gold continued to soar in world markets while the value of the American dollar in relation to gold continued to fall. Following a speculative rush into gold in 1968 and the growing lack of international confidence in the US dollar, a two-tier system for gold was devised consisting of an official price and a free market price. In an attempt to phase out the role of gold from the monetary system, the United States persuaded the IMF, over which it exercised a preponderant influence, to establish Special Drawing Rights (SDR) in the hope of creating the additional international liquidity which gold had failed to provide but which was necessary to meet the requirements of expanding world trade and to provide support for the recurring fluctuations in the balance of national payments. However, the new arrangement which led to the convertibility of the dollar into gold, failed to produce monetary stability. The United States proved unable to maintain the official price of gold; dollar holders continued to convert their paper money into gold; and continuing asymmetries in the value of several national currencies led to a prolonged series of readjustments, notably the decision to devalue the pound sterling in November 1967, and the franc in August 1969, to float the Canadian dollar in May 1970 and to revalue the German mark in May 1971. The crisis of confidence now called into question not merely the future of the US dollar but of the entire world monetary system.

The continuing US deficit and the mounting pressures exerted by speculators, multinational corporations and the Middle East oil producers, finally combined to force the devaluation of the American dollar in terms of other major currencies. In this regard, it should be remembered that the management of corporate finance sees its primary task as placing and recalling funds, borrowing and investing short-term assets so as to earn the optimal yield on available money resources until these are required for long-term investments. Consequently, the search for higher interest rates and the global monetary practices of multinational enterprises caused the movement of thousands of millions of dollars on the short-term money markets in directions that were often contrary to domestic policy, and accentuated the crisis in the balance of national payments.

The manifest impact of these pressures was reflected in the official abandonment of gold convertibility by the United States in August 1971, thus finalizing the collapse of the Bretton Woods system of fixed exchange rates. The Nixon administration complemented this decision with a series of anti-inflationary fiscal measures and the imposition of an import surcharge on all dutiable imports covered by quotas. The Nixon package, designed to relieve the pressure on the dollar and reduce the competitiveness of the other capitalist economies, extracted some of the desired advantage in the Smithsonian agreement of December 1971 which supposedly provided a new set of fixed rates, but which in reality simply ensured the revaluation of the yen and the mark in relation to the dollar. In spite of the impressive claims which were made for it, the agreement proved to be little more than a short-lived exercise in monetary engineering.

After a massive speculative attack in June 1972 on the pound sterling, the United Kingdom decided to float the sterling and within a few months floating rates were introduced successively for the Italian lira, the Swiss franc, the Japanese yen and several other currencies. For its part, the United States opted for a 10 per cent reduction in the par value of the dollar, its second devaluation in the space of fourteen months. Six members of the European Economic Community (Belgium, Denmark, France, Germany, Luxemburg and the Netherlands) as well as Norway and Sweden, agreed to maintain stable rates in relation to one another and to fluctuate only vis-à-vis the dollar. There was no longer a coherent international monetary system but a mere collection of national currencies with rates of exchange likely to fluctuate from one day to the next in response to the disintegrative pressures now operating within the world economy.

The disintegration of the international monetary system

based on the dollar standard was a direct result of the un-controlled monetary expansion within the United States, trans-mitted and amplified throughout the rest of the world by the perennial American balance-of-payments deficit.[26] In the 1960s, the money stock of the ten principal industrial countries had grown at an average annual rate of about 7 per cent, and accelerated to about 12 per cent in the early 1970s. Here no doubt was one of the major contributing factors to the extra-ordinary rate of inflation which followed soon after in all OECD countries and reached in 1974 an estimated average of 15 per cent. The decision of Western Europe and Japan to float their currencies vis-à-vis the dollar and the adoption of restric-tive monetary policies brought a temporary though abrupt end to the expansionary phase of world money supply, thereby contributing to the most severe worldwide recession since World War II. In the United States, the collapse of the money market was reflected in the dramatic slow-down of the motor-car, homebuilding and several other associated industries resulting in greater levels of unemployment and declining real output than those recorded in any of the previous six recessions since 1946.

In the meantime, whatever the eventual outcome of the economic recession which had severely hit not only the United States but also Japan and Western Europe, and however slow or rapid the rate of recovery, the prospect of unified monetary reform remained extremely remote. In a desperate attempt to salvage some order out of the spreading chaos, monetary authorities and the Committee of Twenty devised the principle of 'managed floating' which recognized the inevitability of widespread currency fluctuations for the foreseeable future but sought to define rules for intervention in exchange markets to ensure that national governments did not take unfair ad-vantage of each other.[27] Such an arrangement, however, was hardly likely to provide a durable foundation for the regula-tion of government action and the control of aggregate levels of reserve assets.

In any case, national governments and their credit policies remained highly vulnerable to the enormous and increasingly frequent capital shifts which had so destabilized the world monetary system. The Eurodollar market, expected to carry some $200,000 million in 1976, was clearly beyond the reach of any nation's control mechanisms. The magnitude, speed and unpredictability of capital transactions now exceeded the capacity of national governments and their financial institutions to understand, contain or direct the development of the international market economy.

The oil crisis

Notwithstanding the obvious psychological and economic impact of the fourfold increase in the price of crude oil soon after the Middle East War of October 1973, it should be clear from what has already been said that, contrary to the initial propaganda emanating from official and semi-official American sources, the worldwide inflation–recession phenomenon did not have its origin in the oil crisis. As the OPEC countries have maintained and as several independent analysts and OECD reports have concluded, the drastic escalation in the price of oil contributed at most 1 or 2 per cent to the inflation rate, or less than one-fifth of the overall cost-of-living increase registered by most OECD countries.[28]

Equally exaggerated were the early projections of the accumulated OPEC surplus by 1980.[29] Accordingly, the OECD revised its earlier estimates, reducing them by more than half to $250,000 million,[30] while some financial authorities were even prepared to predict that within a few years the surplus might altogether disappear.[31] Other calculations indicated that by the end of the 1970s OPEC wealth would 'still amount to only 2–4 per cent of the world's capital stock',[32] and the large-scale borrowing from OPEC countries – up to $300,000 million by 1980 – would represent no more than 2 per cent of the fixed assets of OECD countries.[33] The significance of these reappraisals, which themselves remained subject to considerable error given the unpredictability of the crucial variables of price and demand, was that they redefined the parameters of the crisis confronting the world economy.

No one could deny the short-term effect of the abrupt rise in oil prices which was to increase the value of the OPEC surplus from $6,000 million in 1973 to $70,000 million in 1974.[34] Within a year, the international reserves of all the major oil-

exporting countries had risen dramatically. Between the end of
the third quarter of 1973 and the last quarter of 1974, Saudi
Arabia's reserves climbed from $4,081 million to $14,285
million, Iran's from $992 million to $8,383 million, Venezuela's from $1,665 million to $6,529 million, and Nigeria's
from $445 million to $5,629 million.[35] By contrast the combined balance of payments deficit for the oil-importing countries for 1974 rose to $51,000 million, with Britain, Italy, France
and Japan registering deficits of $9,000 million, $7,900 million,
$5,900 and $4,690 million respectively.[36] Many of these countries, and especially the non-oil-producing nations of the
Third World, were thus forced to finance these deficits by
borrowing. But from whom would the consuming countries
borrow? What form would the lending take? What would be
its lasting effects on the relationship among oil-consumers
and between them and oil exporters? These and other questions pointed directly to the profound structural difficulties
in recycling OPEC funds and highlighted the unbalanced and
fragmented character of the international trading and monetary system.

   In the immediate future there was little prospect that higher
import bills could be met by increasing the export of goods
and services to the oil producers, for the simple reason that
the latter, with the possible exception of Iran, Nigeria and
Indonesia, had a limited capacity to absorb the industrial
products of the consuming countries. The rapidly expanding
sales of European, Japanese and North American technology,
manufactured goods and armaments to the OPEC nations
could not eliminate the excess of OPEC income over expenditure. Now it is true that most of this excess tended to flow back
to the importing countries in the form of loans to individual
states and international financial institutions or as investments
in the capital markets of Europe and the United States or in the
Euro-currency market. But the bulk of these investment funds
were placed in short-term deposits and government securities
which could be shifted at any time thereby endangering the
capital–deposit ratios on which banks depend for their viability. American Treasury officials tended to dismiss the succession of small bank failures in Europe and the United States
as minor events which left the banking system essentially intact.

But the losses incurred by several West German banks, Lloyds of London, the Union Bank of Switzerland, the Franklin Bank of New York and the Bank of Brussels all pointed to the declining confidence in foreign exchange dealings and to the diminishing likelihood that the existing network of private and intergovernmental financial institutions could adequately organize the recycling process.

Another obvious problem in the effective recycling of OPEC funds arose from the fact that any allocation of loans which was based on commercial banking consideration of credit worthiness and the relativity of interest rates might not coincide with the needs of those countries whose balance of payments had been most severely affected by higher oil prices. Deficits were likely to be incurred most consistently by nations that were least able to honour their financial obligations. Many underdeveloped countries with relatively large energy imports and even the developed but faltering economies of Italy and Britain were already heavily indebted and might eventually find themselves out of the circle of recycling funds.

As for the more dynamic capitalist economies, though they might succeed in reducing their balance of payments deficit through a carefully conceived strategy combining the rapid expansion of industrial exports to the OPEC nations with the introduction of conservation measures and the development of new sources of energy, they would still have to depend in varying degress at least until 1985 on OPEC oil in order to power their heavy and service industries. Moreover, it should be remembered that the 10 per cent decline in world oil consumption in 1974 had occurred at a time when the major capitalist economies were suffering from high rates of inflation, a steep decline in real industrial output and high levels of unemployment. Were these recessionary trends to be reversed and a high rate of growth to be restored, the demand for oil would undoubtedly rise again and considerably accentuate the balance of payments difficulties of the industrialized world.

With the benefit of hindsight, it has now become abundantly clear that the sustained growth of post-war capitalism was to a large extent fuelled by the abundant supply of artificially cheap oil, 'controlled by an immensely powerful consortium of international oil companies' with the active support of the American

and British governments.[37] In the words of a major study commissioned by the Ford Foundation, 'the world oil market'
became 'the artery of Western European, Japanese and American prosperity'.[38] As a consequence of the cheapness of Middle
East oil compared with the American cost of production, the
search for profitable investments forced American output to
stagnate and even decrease in spite of rising demand.[39] The
manipulation of 'vast profits and fiscal privileges' by the large
oil corporations, often at the expense of the consumer's interest, was tolerated and even encouraged by governments not
simply in order to accommodate the powerful pressures from
the oil lobby, but because the assured flow of cheap oil had become the indispensable engine of growth within the capitalist
economy.

But after 1973 there was no longer any prospect of a return
to the posted price of $1.80 per barrel of crude oil which had
prevailed as late as January 1970. Oil prices might continue to
fluctuate, but the systematic coordination of OPEC strategy and
the absence of any viable alternatives for the western world
would prevent any significant reduction from the market price
of $11.51 for a barrel of Arabian crude agreed at the OPEC
meeting of September 1975, and might actually produce further periodic increases to take account of inflationary trends.
Nor was the threat of economic or military force likely to compel the OPEC countries to comply with western, and particularly American, demands. The emerging OPEC – Third World
alliance was indicative of a renewed determination by underdeveloped countries to achieve their economic emancipation.
In this sense, the oil crisis had been instrumental in accentuating and defining the axis of conflict between those committed to the defence of the status quo and those seeking to
create a new economic order to replace the system which had
ensured wealth at the expense of poverty.

Paradoxically, the oil crisis also introduced additional
friction and tensions in relations among consuming countries.
The decision of both Japan and the European Economic Community to adopt an increasingly pro-Arab line in the aftermath of the 1973 Middle East War, and the readiness of
European nations to reach separate commercial and industrial
agreements with Arab nations, in spite of the vehement op-

position of the United States, were indicative of the growing cleavages between the major centres of the capitalist system. By accelerating the disintegration of the international monetary system, the oil crisis was helping to demonstrate that the failure to agree on a programme of monetary reform was not just a dispute on mere technicalities but the expression of profound economic antagonisms that affected the whole complex network of interrelationships with regard to resource availability, agricultural commodity supplies, money markets and corporate investment decisions.

Far from signalling the return of assured capitalist growth or the stabilization of the world economy, the various American manoeuvres and the consequent Japanese and European counter-measures underlined the desperate expedients to which competing capitalist powers would resort in a vain attempt to resolve their internal problems at the expense of the rest of the world. The increasing incompatibility of the North American, Western European and Japanese economies – compounded by the emerging conflict of interests between oil consumers and oil producers – pointed to a progressively more fragmented and competitive international system with a diminishing capacity to satisfy the interests and objectives of its constituent units.[40]

To the extent that the most highly developed capitalist economies – perhaps one would also need to include the more advanced communist systems – remained committed to a policy of unlimited industrial expansion and GNP growth they were bound to rely on strategies conducive to inflationary trends at home and trade and financial rivalries abroad. The interacting and mutually reinforcing effects of these strategies were reflected in the growing polarization which now typified the domestic as well as the world economy. The policy of unrestricted and unbalanced national growth had given rise to narrow but powerful economic interests whose disruptive impact was likely to outweigh the regulatory potential of existing institutions. Short-term compromises and partial economic recovery might for a time obscure the true nature of the crisis, but could hardly prevent or even arrest the dissolution of the international economic order created by Pax Americana.

5. Underdevelopment and structural dependence

Having examined the disintegrative tendencies operating within the major capitalist centres and increasingly manifested in the wide-ranging interaction of their economies, we may now proceed to an analysis of the profound systemic imbalance which persists between the developed and underdeveloped sectors of the international market economy. The radical nature of this imbalance has been considerably obscured by the use of the 'Third World' label,[1] which suggests that the poor countries of Asia, Africa and Latin America constitute in some sense an economic and political grouping separate from and independent of the advanced western and communist economies. In reality, the vast majority of Third World nations are still experiencing the impact of colonial rule which ensured their integration into the international capitalist system.

But capitalist penetration, far from achieving the industrial development of these societies, has contributed to their pauperization and to the disequilibrium of their economies. In 1970 the per capita gross national product at market prices was $4,760 for the United States, $4,040 for Sweden, $3,100 for France, $2,930 for West Germany, $1,920 for Japan, and an average of $560 for Latin America, $200 for Africa and $150 for Asia and the Middle East (excluding Japan).[2] Every two or three years the developed economies generate additional wealth equal to or greater than the total wealth of the underdeveloped economies, and this additional wealth accrues to those societies which are already consuming twelve times as much as the other two thirds of humanity. It is these sharp and seemingly irreducible economic inequalities within the international system which have led a growing number of theorists and practitioners alike to question the assumptions and conclusions of much developmental analysis which has sought to explain in terms of the tradition–modernity dichotomy the economic underdevelopment, political instability and ideological conflict typical of so many of the emerging states of Asia, Africa and Latin America.

The conception of social change which formed the basis of American mainstream thinking in the 1950s and 1960s[3] was content to abstract the general features of the developed (modern) economy and to contrast them with the equally ideal-type features of the underdeveloped (traditional) economy. Development was thus viewed as the transformation of one type of society into the other. Having identified the gap between traditional and modern societies, most of these theorists proceeded to argue that the gap could or would be closed by the diffusion of knowledge, skills, organization, values, technology and capital from the developed to the underdeveloped world.[4] It is now generally accepted that these attempts to analyse the differences among nations with respect to economic and political development suffered from several defects, notably intellectual ethnocentrism, excessive emphasis on the role of elites as agents of development, selective treatment of historical reality and simplistic concepts of unilinear change.[5]

One of the most striking deficiencies of the various modernization or nation-building models has been the tendency to overlook or dismiss the significance of the colonial experience. And yet it is the process of colonization and the accompanying introduction of new crops and techniques which were largely responsible for the transformation of essentially agrarian societies into commercial economies, and the consequent impoverishment of the peasantry.[6] The progressive accumulation of capital, the revolution of international transport and communications and the development of international finance enabled the European nations to make deep inroads into the colonial economies and to commercialize their land and agriculture. The dominance of the colonial power was achieved by destroying or subverting existing patterns of authority and by substituting a new model of administration which richly rewarded indigenous elites so long as they cooperated in the creation of new structures designed to enhance the industrial and trading interests of the foreign power. To the extent that feudal elites were willing to do the bidding of the metropolis, colonial control often led to the preservation of obsolete social and political institutions. There was moreover a strong tendency for foreign investment to go into mining and plantations, that is into the development of export industries which often created 'modern' enclaves seemingly detached but actually operating at the expense of the 'traditional' agricultural sector.[7] The net result was the creation of lop-sided economies oriented towards the indiscriminate exploitation of natural resources and the export of profits, thereby preventing the necessary flow of industrial investment and impeding the classical capitalist path of economic development.[8]

It is extremely doubtful whether the emancipation of these countries from their former colonial status resulted in genuine economic or even political independence. The experience of Latin America since the early nineteenth century and the more recent emergence of African and Asian states both indicate that the transfer of legal sovereignty has often coexisted with an enduring framework of semi-colonial or neo-colonial economic relationships. The persistence of feudal elements[9] and the continuing heritage of colonial rule have combined to produce truncated and artificial social orders incapable of mobilizing the energies and resources of their respective populations and unable to release their national economies from the constraints imposed by the international system which the advanced industrial nations have continued to dominate throughout the post-war period.

From what has already been said it emerges that the modernization and nation-building models tend to interpret underdevelopment solely in terms of a domestic structural imbalance and to ignore the crucial linkages between the internal and external environment of each national society.[10] It is this simple but radical insight which underlies the contributions of the new school of *dependence* theorists.[11]

Needless to say there are numerous and often considerable variations from one theoretical formulation to the other. But in most general terms, the concept of dependence seeks to analyse the dominance of the rich industrial nations within the international system and the consequent constraints which operate over the internal development of the less developed economies. Dos Santos has defined the dependent economy as that which is 'conditioned by the development and expansion of another economy',[12] while for Osvaldo Sunkel, the concept of depend-

ence links the external pressures and constraints, often operating through 'hidden or subtle financial, economic, technical
and cultural' mechanisms, with the internal process of underdevelopment characterized by the 'self-reinforcing accumulation of privilege' on the one hand and the continued existence
of a 'marginal class' on the other.[13] The great value of the
various dependence models is that they eliminate the artificial
boundaries not only between the national and international
process but also between the political, economic, military and
ideological dimensions of social interaction. The concept of
dependence allows us to grasp the global character of the crisis
of underdevelopment not simply by pointing to a worldwide
phenomenon but by illuminating the whole fabric and
dynamic of human institutions as they operate both in the most
advanced sectors of the capitalist system as well as in the underdeveloped societies of the Third World.[14]

International system of unequal exchange

Essentially, the dependence model postulates a dynamic system of unequal exchange, that is to say, a pattern of asymmetric
relationships such that they consistently favour one party and
disadvantage another, or, at least, favour one relatively more
than the other. As a consequence, there develops within the
international system a pervasive pattern of interaction between
dominant and *dependent* actors, or, to use Galtung's terminology,
between the 'centre' and the 'periphery', or in Frank's imagery
between the 'metropolis' and the 'satellite'. For the purpose
of this discussion these three sets of terms will be used interchangeably. The net result of the network of dependent relationships is economic development for the centre and economic
underdevelopment for the periphery; military ascendancy,
highly developed means of communication and cultural
expansion on the one hand and military inferiority, primitive
means of communication and cultural emulation on the other.
Whereas the metropolis is assertive and largely self-reliant,
the satellite is normally dependent on and submissive to foreign
interests. While this general characterization overlooks many
of the peculiarities and complexities of specific situations, it
does nevertheless express the structural asymmetry that typifies

relations between the most advanced and underdeveloped economies, and highlights the ensuing process of global stratification.

The international system of unequal exchange is most strikingly manifested in the trading patterns which were established during the colonial period and which have since remained in operation in spite of widespread decolonization.[15] The colonial legacy of dependence and the export of raw materials and agricultural products was maintained throughout the 1950s and 1960s. Accordingly, there took place a marked increase in the Third World's production of crude oil, iron ore, bauxite, copper, manganese and natural phosphates. This expansion in the extractive industries was intended to meet the soaring energy and manufacturing requirements of the highly industrialized capitalist economies whose mineral deposits were becoming exhausted or less productive. In 1962 the Third World contributed 92.7 per cent of the tin, 74.1 per cent of the manganese and 64.5 per cent of the phosphates imported by the developed capitalist countries.[16] A similar picture emerges with respect to a large number of agricultural commodities. In 1964, the underdeveloped countries produced nearly the whole of the world's supply of coffee, cocoa beans, palm kernels, bananas, jute and natural rubber, 72 per cent of tea, 77 per cent of timber (excluding conifers), 57 per cent of rice, and 42 per cent of cotton.[17]

The profound impact of commodity specialization in many underdeveloped countries is shown in their marked reliance for export earnings on one or two key commodities. In 1964, cereals constituted 35 per cent of the total value of Argentina's exports, while coffee accounted for 53 per cent of Brazilian exports. An equally dominant role was played by tea in Ceylon (60 per cent), jute and hemp in Pakistan (50 per cent), cocoa in Ghana (65 per cent), groundnut oil in Senegal (70 per cent). In 1968, 90 per cent of all Latin American exports consisted of agricultural and mining products.[18] Hand in hand with this pattern of commodity concentration has been the dependence of many Third World countries on one or two western trading partners. In 1965, Western Europe accounted for 85 per cent of African exports, and the United States and Canada for 47.5 per cent of Latin American exports. While a certain amount of diversification has subsequently occurred, it is noteworthy that by 1973 Bolivia still depended on the United States and the United Kingdom for 77 per cent of its exports, and similarly with South Korea's (70 per cent), the Philippines' (70 per cent) and Indonesia's (66 per cent) dependence on the United States and Japan, Algeria's (64 per cent) dependence on France, Germany and the United States, and Zaire's (62 per cent) dependence on Belgium and Italy.[19]

Far from achieving any of the so-called comparative advan-

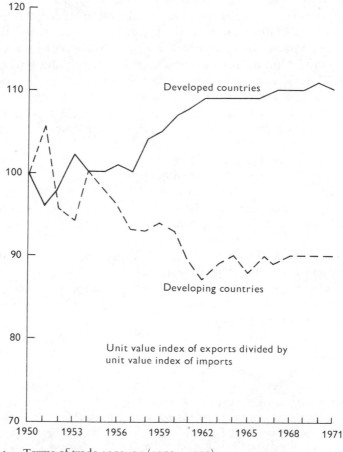

Fig 1.   Terms of trade 1950–71 (1950 = 100).
Source: 'Trends in Developing Countries', *Finance and Development*, Vol. 11, No. 1, March 1974, p. 14.

tages of 'complementary specialization', this high degree of trade and commodity concentration ensured for the Third World unfavourable terms of trade and a declining proportion of world trade. In spite of a few short-lived variations, the general trend after 1945 was for the prices of raw materials exported by underdeveloped countries to rise much less steeply than those of the manufactured products which they needed to import from the developed economies. In other words, the Third World, with the recent exception of oil-exporting countries, experienced a steady deterioration in its terms of trade with the industrialized world. Taking 1958 as a base, it is estimated that in the period 1955–65 the terms of trade improved for the major western economies from 96 to 104 (+8 per cent) and declined for the Third World from 108 to 97 (-11 per cent).[20] This adverse change affected in varying degrees all the major underdeveloped regions. Using 1954 as his base, Paul Bairoch has calculated that by 1965 the terms of trade for the Third World had worsened by 12 per cent result-

T A B L E 5.1 *Export price indices of selected primary commodities and non-ferrous base metals, 1970–2.*

Commodity	Index (1960 = 100)		
	1970	1971	1972
Coffee	146	127	143
Tea	80	79	78
Cocoa	118	93	109
Sugar	118	130	167
Copra	104	88	66
Coconut oil	116	101	72
Ground nuts	121	128	149
Palm kernels	103	87	74
Cotton	102	112	141
Jute	93	91	78
Rubber	51	41	41
Bauxite	191	236	254
Copper	214	167	165
Lead	149	128	151

Source: *World Economic Survey*, 1972, New York, United Nations Department of Economic and Social Affairs, 1973, Table 8.

ing in losses which in 1965 alone amounted to nearly $4,300 million.[21] Fig. 1 gives a clear indication of the relative and growing disadvantage which the prevailing system of trade imposed on the underdeveloped economies, and of the inevitable balance of payments difficulties which it created. Equally detrimental to the prospects of balanced economic development have been the sharp and often unpredictable fluctuations (see table 5.1) in the prices of main commodities from one year or even one month to the next.

These price variations, whether as a result of market forces or corporate policy, have made any form of economic planning extremely difficult, especially as trade constitutes a relatively high percentage of the GNP of most Third World countries. In an effort to offset actual or potential price changes, many underdeveloped countries have sought to increase production, thereby accentuating competition among primary producers and helping to sustain an excess of supply over demand. Far from enhancing the foreign exchange balance of these countries, such a policy has tended to reduce their overall share of the value of world exports, which fell from 30 per cent in 1948 to 20 per cent in 1965 and to 17 per cent in 1971. Nor is there much encouragement to be derived from the periodic increase in non-fuel mineral prices. It is doubtful, for example, whether the gains registered during the short-lived boom of 1973–4 will have significantly improved the trading position of Third World countries or even arrested the downward trend recorded during the 1960s. The dramatic fall in prices for such commodities as cotton, rubber, copper, tin and zinc, which occurred in the second half of 1974 and continued into 1975,[22] was indicative of the vulnerability of Third World exports and in keeping with projected trends pointing to the decline in the price of several non-fuel minerals.[23]

Although the Third World supplies a large proportion of the world's minerals, it processes only a minute fraction of these resources. In spite of the strong commitment of many Third World countries to develop their own iron and steel industries, it is significant that in 1964 their collective output of steel was only 4 per cent of the world's total. In the same year, the Third World's industrial consumption of aluminium, tin, natural rubber and cotton was 3 per cent, 8.6 per cent,

18 per cent and 26 per cent respectively.[24] It is true that in the period 1960–70 the underdeveloped countries increased their exports of manufactures from $3,800 million to $12,700 million, which means that processed goods rose as a proportion of their total exports from 14.6 per cent in 1960 to 23.4 per cent in 1970.[25] But this industrial growth did not necessarily imply the development of independent industrialization.[26] While foreign investment and foreign technology may have helped to promote manufacturing exports, they have tended to favour consumer goods industries at the expense of intermediate and capital goods. In very few instances has Third World industrialization proceeded by relying primarily on the home market or by significantly diversifying the industrial structure. The consequence of this form of industrialization has been vulnerability to sharp fluctuations in the balance of payments and continued dependence on foreign capital.

As for the various efforts of Third World countries to correct their trade imbalances through import substitution policies and the erection of tariffs, they too have tended to encourage the channelling of domestic savings towards investments in inessential production. Moreover, the substitution of imported finished products by domestically produced goods has required the importation of a considerable volume of raw materials and intermediate capital goods, thus defeating the primary purpose of saving foreign exchange.[27]

The net effect of the technological, financial and commercial supremacy enjoyed by the advanced industrial economies has been to create a system of unequal exchange which imposes on the underdeveloped economies a perennial crisis in their balance of payments, marginal or lop-sided industrialization, and, ironically enough, a declining capacity to feed their growing populations. The food crisis confronting the Third World is directly related to the fact that much of the best arable land and a large proportion of scarce water resources are assigned to the production not of foodstuffs but of raw materials and other commodities for marketing in the industrial world. The foreign ownership of large-scale farms, the direct investment, merchandising of commodities and control of credit and port facilities by large foreign agri-business corporations, and the expropriation of the small peasant by the rich landlord in the

name of improved efficiency, have all contributed to the development of an export-oriented agriculture at the expense of
subsistence farming.

It is estimated that in the period 1952–72 food production
in 34 underdeveloped countries failed to keep pace with population growth, and that, if allowance is made for rising incomes,
the increase in food production was able to satisfy less than half
the increase in the demand for food in as many as 53 out of the
86 underdeveloped countries for which data are available.[28]
The long-term defects in the structure of Third World agriculture combined with adverse weather conditions to produce in
1972 the most severe food crisis yet and a 3 per cent drop in the
per capita food production of the Third World. Although the
Far East experienced a substantial recovery in 1973, Bangla-
desh, large parts of Africa and the Middle East continued to
record sharp declines in their per capita food production.
But even prior to these acute food shortages, underdeveloped
countries had become increasingly dependent on food imports,
the volume of grain imports rising from an annual average
of 12.4 million tons in the period 1949–51 to 36.0 million
tons in 1972. It is calculated that in 1973–4 the drain on the
Third World's foreign exchange resources as a result of cereal
imports exceeded $9,000 million.[29]

At this point it is important to note that the steep rise in the
Third World's food import bill was not simply the result of
the increased volume of imports. An equally important factor
has been the dramatic increase in the price of foodstuffs. The
export price of one metric ton of wheat rose from $62 in 1971
to $139 in 1973, with equivalent price increases for maize and
soya beans and a five-fold increase in the price of rice from
1971 to June 1974.[30] While population growth had obviously
contributed to the increasing world food demand, a much
more significnat factor was the sharp rise in per capita cereal
consumption by the advanced industrial countries, whose
population had grown only marginally. In the eight-year
period from 1965 to 1973, US per capita consumption increased
by 16 per cent, with the Soviet Union, the European Community and Japan registering expansion rates of 30 per cent,
11 per cent and 17 per cent respectively.[31] The aggregate
of rich countries (both capitalist and socialist), with 30 per

cent of the world's population, consumed between 1969 and 1971 51 per cent of the world's total grain production, more than half of which was used for animal fodder, a much higher figure than the total human consumption of China and India combined.[32]

The irony of the world food situation was that whereas the developed economies and the upper income groups in the underdeveloped countries had an almost unlimited capacity to increase and vary their food demand, the lowest income groups in the Third World were in no position to create demand for even the most basic foodstuffs. In the meantime, the United States was able to exploit its vast capacity for agricultural production to bring about a dramatic improvement in its balance of payments–US agricultural exports increased from $9,400 million in 1972 to $18,000 million in 1973–and to secure significant economic and political leverage over underdeveloped economies through its various food aid programmes. Transfers of wheat and other cereals had provided the opportunity for American intervention in the investment and financial policies of recipient countries, and for the progressive domination of their agricultural policy by foreign institutions and agri-business firms.[33] Food aid and famine relief thus became additional instruments in a global politico-economic strategy designed to maintain the existing system of unequal exchange.

Domestic inequality and stratification

Enough will have been said to suggest that the inequality and stratification which characterize the international system also describe the internal structure of underdeveloped societies. It is estimated, for example, that during the period 1951–60 the poorest 20 per cent of the Indian population received 3.7 per cent of the national income while the richest 20 per cent accounted for 64.7 per cent of the nation's wealth. Disparities of this order, which are typical of most Third World countries,[34] would suggest that, even in conditions of economic growth as measured in terms of GNP, there has been a steady decline in the relative and perhaps absolute position of lower-income groups.[35] Important elements in this phenomenon of 'structural marginalization' include the lack of adequate educational levels, limited access to the political processes, low levels of savings and consumption, chronic unemployment, and underdevelopment.[36]

The fact that economic growth has been compatible with static or even rising income inequality indicates that post-war industrial and agricultural expansion has given rise to the same type of uneven development which characterized the colonial period. The surviving landed interests, often in close alliance with the emerging industrial capitalist class and the relatively few privileged workers in manufacturing employment, have been the principal beneficiaries of economic growth, usually at the expense of the peasantry and the industrial proletariat. The coexistence of two unequal sectors and the progressive concentration of technological and financial resources within the dominant sector have distorted the development of both the rural and urban economy.[37] Economic polarization between different geographical regions has meant that productive activity and income tend to be concentrated in certain dynamic areas while the peripheral region remains essentially underdeveloped. Stavenhagen has described the polarization of the agrarian sector by contrasting the high levels of consumption, political control and technological leverage available to the 'agrarian oligarchy' with the exclusion of the peasant masses from the modern agricultural sector and from institutionalized political activity.[38]

The numerically small strata of society which dominate the key sectors of the economy, in exchange for foreign financial and military assistance, thus provide the metropolitan power with the institutional means for the exercise of influence and control. By their very nature, foreign interests tend to seek an alliance with the forces of the status quo, for it is they that are most likely to do the bidding of the foreign power. Conversely, these conservative political and economic forces, assured of the support of the metropolitan power, are thereby encouraged to resort to the most repressive measures against peasant rebellions, dissenting students, trade unions, political parties, and the press. The harmony of interests between the metropolis and the satellite is inevitably reflected in the disharmony of interests between the ruling elite and the mass of the population within the dependent society.[39]

The symptoms as well as the underlying causes of dependence are inevitably reflected in the identification of Third World elites with the values, life-styles and institutions of the metropolitan society. The more these elites are involved in a process of interaction with foreign interests and international agencies, the more receptive they become to their cultural and ideological premises, and, therefore, more responsive to their demands. Not surprisingly, the application of metropolitan models to the problems of satellized societies has resulted in alienating structures and the subversion of indigenous values along lines advantageous to the metropolis.[40] Accordingly, 'national communications systems' and the nation's 'cultural ecology' have come to be conditioned more and more by the requirements of foreign governments and multinational interest.[41]

The dependence complex of colonized peoples, so graphically portrayed by Albert Memmi and Frantz Fanon,[42] is a psychological response to the colonial situation which the granting of political independence could not efface and whose far-reaching affects have continued to dominate the political and economic life of the Third World societies. The dysfunctional consequences of uncritically adopting foreign institutional and cultural patterns in the drive towards so-called modernization have been stressed by Ivan Illich, especially in relation to the development of such services as transport, health and education.[43] In this sense, underdevelopment is more than an economic or even political phenomenon. It represents a state of mind which transforms real needs into artificial expectations which the massive intrusion of advanced technology has encouraged but cannot satisfy.

The perpetuation of economic and cultural dependence on the metropolitan centre thus hinders the articulation and organization of the periphery's real interests. The counter-revolutionary military coup in Chile, which overthrew the socialist but legal and constitutional government of Salvador Allende, has provided one of the most dramatic demonstrations of the role of transnational linkages in maintaining and

reinforcing the degree of polarization and inequality characteristic of all underdeveloped societies. The trend towards
authoritarian and repressive rule throughout much of the
Third World – by 1973 18 out of 22 Latin American countries
were controlled by military governments – may be considered
as the natural consequence of a transnational alliance committed to the status quo and hence to the development of order-
maintaining systems responsive to the economic and strategic
interests of the metropolitan power.[44]

Transnational institutionalization of dependence

In the contemporary international system, the continuing
dependence of Third World countries has been institutionalized through a diverse network of both private and governmental economic, political, military and cultural mechanisms.[45]
As we have already seen, the ability of the industrial world to
determine the terms of trade for both primary commodities
and manufactured goods has been one of the most important
mechanisms enabling external economic intervention in the
internal social and political processes of Third World countries. Apart from the impersonal forces of the market, however,
other forms of external intrusion and constraint have gained
momentum as a result of the growing interdependence and
institutionalization of the world economy. Both foreign aid
and foreign investment have significantly contributed to this
process and highlighted not only the political and economic
stratifications of the international system but also the instrumental role of national governments, multinational corporations and international financial institutions.

It should be said from the outset that there exists a very large
gap between the theory and the reality of foreign aid.[46] As
Pierre Jalée has argued, aid has been both 'a pittance and a
mirage',[47] for official aid figures have seldom accurately represented the quantity or quality of the transfer of resources.
It is true that between 1961 and 1970 the total aid provided by
the members of the Development Assistance Committee
(DAC)[48] rose from $8,860 million to $15,166 million.[49] However, this absolute increase, which is calculated at current
prices, conceals the fact that the total transfer of financial re-

sources to the Third World (expressed as a percentage of the GNP of the OECD countries) fell from 0.96 per cent in 1961 to 0.80 per cent in 1965 to 0.74 per cent in 1970.[50] Not only was the total flow of resources falling far short of the recommended 1 per cent of the rich countries' gross national product, but the proportion of official as opposed to private transfers had also steadily declined. Taking the DAC countries as a whole, official development assistance in relation to GNP has decreased from 0.52 per cent in 1961 to 0.35 per cent in 1971.[51]

But quite apart from the relative decline in the volume of aid, some attention must be given to its actual composition. In the first place, there is the important item of technical assistance (valued at about $1,800 million in 1972) of which a very considerable amount is directed to the salaries of technical advisers and assistants provided by the donor countries. Only a certain proportion of these salaries is spent in the assisted country, the remainder returning as savings to the country of origin. A second qualification relates to the simple fact that direct grants from OECD countries have declined as a proportion of total aid from 45 per cent in 1961 to 21 per cent in 1971.[52] The corresponding increase in bilateral and multilateral loans has greatly contributed to the mounting external public debt of the underdeveloped countries, which rose from $37,000 million in 1965 to nearly $67,000 million in 1970. In the same period annual service payments increased from $3,500 million to $5,900 million.[53] Moreover, much that passes for 'development assistance' includes various forms of investment that are not channelled directly into local industry or agriculture but in the creation of infrastructure (i.e. roads, railways, ports, power facilities) designed primarily to service foreign capital and enhance its profitability. American government aid agencies have actively promoted the expansion of foreign investment by providing a variety of services to American businessmen, including contributions towards the cost of feasibility studies, investment guarantees, supply of credit (in dollars and local currency) as well as active diplomatic support.

Severe limitations on the manner in which aid grants or loans are to be used, restrictions on the types of projects that are to be promoted, in-built requirement of cooperation with foreign institutions and of preferential treatment for foreign exports, and crippling debts resulting from interest rates and loan repayments, have combined to ensure paramount external influence on the underdeveloped economy. Considerable political power leverage has also been derived from the allocation of a large proportion of aid to military purposes, often designed to ensure maintenance of the ruling elite or the existing bureaucratic apparatus.

The decidedly negative effects associated with the international transfer of financial resources have been equally apparent in the transnational flow of private foreign investment. The relationship of foreign capital to the structures of dependence will be the subject of a more detailed analysis in the next chapter as part of a wider investigation into the nature and dynamics of multinational enterprise. Suffice it to say that capital inflows into underdeveloped countries have been increasingly offset by outflows which take the form of declared profits and dividends, patent fees, management fees, salaries to foreign technicians and consultants, payments for shipping, insurance, banking and brokerage services, and inflated transfer prices paid to affiliated and parent companies.[54] In the case of Latin America, it has been calculated that the net capital outflow to the United States for the period 1950–1965 was $7,500 million,[55] and almost $7,000 million between 1960 and 1968.[56] Moreover, the ability of the multinational corporation to raise capital in local markets, reinvest from its profits and buy up local firms, suggests that the term 'foreign capital' is somewhat misleading. One writer has estimated that for Latin America foreign capital inflow in the period 1957–65 accounted for only 17 per cent of the accumulation of foreign investment.[57]

Not only has foreign investment been transformed into a mechanism for the transfer of surplus to the major capitalist centres, but it has enabled the multinational corporations to wield far-reaching influence over the political and economic processes of the Third World countries in which they invest.[58] These giant corporations, apart from achieving a position of dominance in key sectors of the underdeveloped economy, tend to promote a neo-capitalist model of development which retards the introduction of urgently needed land reform while advancing the interests of those privileged groups willing to act as intermediaries for the entry of foreign capital.[59] As a broad generalization, it can be argued that multinational investment distorts the underdeveloped economy by subordinating it to the needs of the capitalist system and by creating a new local class of industrialists, managers, bureaucrats and technicians more concerned with the emulation of consumption patterns prevailing in the industrialized countries than with the search for distributive justice or self-reliant development.

It remains to say a word about certain transnational institutions and their growing role in buttressing the existing patterns of trade, aid and foreign investment. The importance of such organizations as the World Bank and the International Monetary Fund has considerably increased with the growth of multilateral aid and the mounting external public debt of most underdeveloped countries. By virtue of the vast resources which they command, they are able to wield considerable influence over the Third World, particularly in relation to monetary and fiscal policies, the flow of foreign capital and the selection of development projects. The magnitude of the balance of payments crisis facing most Third World governments leaves them little option but to depend on emergency action by these international financial institutions whose decision-making processes are largely controlled by the developed capitalist economies.[60] Given that these organizations are firmly committed to 'free enterprise', to the expansion of private foreign investment, and to the creation of western-type consumer societies, the main impact of their strategy is to circumscribe the range of options available to underdeveloped countries and to integrate them as securely as possible into the international market economy.[61]

The main thrust of our analysis so far has been to suggest that almost the entire range of transnational interactions (flow of goods and services and capital transfers, including development aid and overseas investment) and a very large number of transnational institutions have combined to produce a systemic imbalance, that is to say an international allocation of values and resources which maintains and reinforces relationships of dependence between underdeveloped and developed countries. Internal conditions have often consolidated and even intensified these external constraints, but they have seldom

created the structures of dependence. To give additional validity to this conclusion, it may be instructive to consider the
single domestic factor which in popular literature and debate
has been repeatedly misconstrued as the principal determinant
of underdevelopment: the population explosion.

Demographic trends and their implications for underdevelopment

In an earlier chapter, we described the continuing exponential
increase in the world's population which is expected to exceed
6,000 million by the year 2000. If these projections are realized
the underdeveloped regions of the world will need to support
between 4,700 and 5,400 million, that is to say, their contribution to the increment will be in the vicinity of 2,700 million
(or 87 per cent) as against 350 million (13 per cent) by the
richer nations. India is often cited as the classical example of
a country that is being subjected to increasingly powerful
demographic pressures. The rate of population growth, which
was 21.64 per cent for the period 1951–61, climbed to 24.57
per cent in the following decade, resulting in a population
increase from 459 million in 1961 to 547 million in 1971. Because of its large population and its relatively high density
(182 per square kilometre) – the densities of some states are
much higher, e.g. Uttar Pradesh (300), Bihar (324), West Bengal
(507) – India may be said to experience in magnified form the
structural underdevelopment typical of many Third World
countries.[62]

One of the distinguishing characteristics of the demographic
explosion has been the high rate of urban growth. In the case
of India the major cities and conurbations in the period 1961–
71 registered increases of between 31 per cent and 54 per cent,
all above the national average rate of increase. Generally
speaking, this pronounced urban pull has not been in response
to an increased demand for labour in urban areas. Unlike the
previous experience of the developed capitalist economies,
industrialization has not preceded urbanization or provided
the necessary 'transmission belt' for the absorption of the massive exodus from the countryside.[63] Unemployment and underemployment, already fluctuating between 25 per cent and 30
per cent in many parts of Asia, Africa and Latin America, and

still rising, are both the cause and the effect of the migration from the countryside to the metropolitan centres.

Before analysing more closely the relationship between the population explosion and underdevelopment, it may be relevant to delineate some of the factors contributing to the upward demographic curve so characteristic of most Third World countries. As is well known, the present population growth stems largely from a prodigious fall in the mortality rate rather than from a marked increase in fertility. In industrial countries death rates have also fallen to very low levels, but they have been compensated by falling birth rates, whereas in the underdeveloped countries these have remained more or less constant. With the spread of medical knowledge and hygiene, there has been a spectacular improvement in life expectancy. The application of science and technology, however, while it may lower the death rate, cannot of itself control the birth rate. Only now is it being appreciated that mechanical techniques of birth control, used in isolation, are likely to have little effect on the rate of population growth. Social and cultural norms relating to religious beliefs, age of marriage, social class, economic background, or level of education are the factors likely to have the most decisive influence on the size of families and the prestige and economic value that is attached to them.

In most underdeveloped societies, where survival as well as competition is conducted primarily on the basis of numbers, labour represents the main form of wealth, with the result that family planning, which would entail reducing the family labour force, is quite logically regarded as courting economic disaster. Where there is a continuing high rate of death among young children, a large number of births may be a family's insurance policy for economic and even physical survival. Clearly, the problem of changing fertility rates is not essentially biological and, therefore, not amenable to technical engineering. As we shall see, it is inseparably linked with the very structures of inequality and underdevelopment. The attempts of countries such as India to control the birth rate by promoting low-cost contraceptives, massive communications programmes and more efficient administrative methods have yielded disappointing results and at considerable cost. Even in countries like Taiwan, South Korea or Malaysia where fertility rates have fallen, it is now conceded that little of the success can be attributed to official birth control programmes. On the contrary, when governments seek to coerce their citizens into acting against their perceived self-interest, popular resistance, mounting political opposition, and the progressive polarization of society are the most likely result.

What, then, is the essence of the population problem? According to many publicists and prestigious experts, including the president of the World Bank, Robert MacNamara, the present rate of population growth is the greatest single obstacle to the economic and social advancement of underdeveloped countries. In spite of its renewed popularity, this crude neo-Malthusian argument rests on a number of mistaken assumptions. There is, it is true, a limit to the earth's capacity to feed a rapidly rising population. Nevertheless, on the basis of the western standard of consumption and the most advanced methods of cultivation, Colin Clark has projected that the existing area of cultivable land could support a ceiling of 12,000 million people.[64] According to another estimate the world area of potentially arable land could support between 38,000 and 48,000 million people.[65] Now, it is true that these rather optimistic estimates do not make clear how it is proposed to apply the most productive agricultural techniques to all areas of the world. Nor is much account taken of the ecological costs that may accompany the application of these techniques. In any case, if the rate of population growth remains unchecked, the world's population will soon surpass, probably by the middle of the next century, the planet's maximum potential for food production. The point that has to be understood, however is that, set in its widest content, the demographic explosion is a problem of global dimensions rather than as a regional problem confined to Third World countries.

It is now generally accepted that Malthus' law of diminishing returns has been disproved by the success of the developed economies in bringing large amounts of new land into cultivation and by the introduction of major technological improvements in agriculture. Land, technology and capital are obviously not static but variable elements in the food supply equation. Why then has the underdeveloped world not been able to manipulate these variables with the same success? The question is particularly pertinent when it is remembered that only a few Third World countries, such as India, Pakistan or Ceylon, have high population densities, and almost none has a density in excess of 200 per square kilometre. And yet, while the Netherlands, with a population density of 380, is not regarded as overpopulated, countries like Venezuela, Egypt and Ethopia, with much lower densities, are said to have an urgent population problem. Some of the most thinly populated countries are also amongst those experiencing the most serious food shortages. Their difficulties stem not from the large number of mouths to be fed but from insufficient food production or from the inability to obtain imported food in exchange for non-food products. By contrast, several western nations have initiated measures to limit agricultural production and thus maintain the high level of food prices on the world market. The inadequacy of the world's food supply is thus compounded by artificial limitations on production and by uneven distribution. To this extent, the population problem may be regarded as a by-product of the structure of the world economy and its system of unequal exchange.

There are, of course, opposing interpretations of underdevelopment and the demographic explosion, which seek to minimize the relative importance of transnational linkages. Placing much greater stress on the internal environment, they argue that a high rate of population increase impedes development by raising the proportion of resources that must be devoted to investment in order to achieve any given growth rate. By pre-empting more income for food consumption, population growth prevents the accumulation of savings to the level that is required to achieve an adequate rate of investment. For this reason, it is claimed, underdeveloped countries are forced to complement their domestic savings and investment capacity by the import of capital. But as we have already observed, much foreign investment is of local origin and usually channelled into capital-intensive production techniques that fail to absorb domestic surplus labour or to provide the structural foundation for the progressive mechanization of industry and agriculture.

It is here that the success of the Chinese experiment assumes particular relevance. While China, the United States and

Brazil have approximately the same land mass, their population is 800 million, 200 million and 90 million respectively. If deficiencies in the food supply were simply the consequence of population pressure, we should expect China's position to be appreciably worse than that of the other two countries. In actual fact, China is the most successful of the three in ensuring an adequately nutritious diet for all its citizens. The key to this success undoubtedly lies in the structural reconstruction initiated by the communist revolution which has led to a rise in living standards, the almost complete elimination of unemployment, a universal educational system and an extensive programme of social security. It is largely these institutional and cultural changes which have enabled the concept and the practice of family planning to gain widespread acceptance. The creation of a more egalitarian society and an integrated strategy of industrial and agricultural development have fostered the unified political, social and economic infrastructure so essential to any effective and equitable policy of population control.

The same insight into the relationship between development and population growth is suggested by the evidence drawn from an increasing number of Third World countries, such as Taiwan and Korea, where birth rates have experienced a sharp fall despite relatively low per capita income and minimal family planning programmes. A comparison of the economic and demographic trends registered by underdeveloped countries indicate that reduction in the inequality of income distribution and full utilization of the labour force are major factors in promoting development and reducing the birth rate.

Although no attempt has been made to explore in any depth the complexity and diversity of demographic trends discernible in Third World countries, enough will have been said to dispel the myth that a high birth rate is the primary cause of underdevelopment. On the contrary, the weight of evidence suggests that structural underdevelopment is itself a major factor contributing towards rampant population growth. Understood in this sense, the demographic explosion is only one facet of a total situation, a manifestation of the systemic and structural imbalances which distort and retard most Third World economies. The international system of unequal exchange, the resultant structures of dependence and the reproduction of these structural asymmetries and divisions within the under-developed world, have combined to intensify population pressures on the land, while seriously obstructing the more effective utilization of available human and material resources.

In seeking to explain the widening economic gulf between developed and underdeveloped economies, we have placed particular stress on the global patterns of dominance and dependence. It may be argued, however, that the contemporary world is moving increasingly towards an open system characterized by endemic disorder. Widening fissures in the international system are beginning to emerge, which may eventually modify existing international structures and asymmetries. Several clearly discernible trends already point to the rise of new centres of power, new demands and new institutions which may significantly alter the structural relationship between rich and poor nations. The trends pointing towards global polarization on the one hand and domestic revolution on the other may in due course radically alter the future development of the Third World. As yet they represent no more than potential changes to which we shall nevertheless need to return, for their cumulative effect could well produce a dramatic transformation in the international system of unequal exchange.

6. Economic transnationalism: the new imperialism

The rise of multinational enterprise as a major force in the international system may be relatively recent but its far-reaching impact on diplomatic and strategic as well as economic transactions is beyond dispute. In terms of our analysis of the world crisis and of the underlying imbalance in the distribution of power and wealth, two issues are especially deserving of attention. In the first place, it is necessary to examine the impact of the corporation on the processes of political and economic decision-making. Does multinational enterprise enhance or minimize the degree of participation in policy-making? Is the emergence of the corporation synonymous with the gradual demise of the state and with traditional notions of legitimacy and accountability? Has it become necessary to review the state-centric view of international relations? Is the new entity equipped to deal with the complex tasks of economic and political regulation in an increasingly fragmented and polarized world? This last question brings us face to face with a second and equally crucial set of considerations. Are the operations of multinational enterprise conducive to notions of distributive justice and national self-reliance? Do they moderate or accentuate the existing asymmetries and inequalities within the international system? Before examining these and other related questions, it may be helpful to consider, however briefly, the historical and contemporary factors responsible for the rapid and continuing expansion of the multinational corporation.

Historical background

At first sight, modern multinational operations may appear to bear some resemblance to the transactions of the merchant traders of the Italian city-states and the colonial trading companies of the seventeenth and eighteenth centuries. On closer inspection, it is clear that former transnational economic activity was primarily concerned with trading rather than manufacturing, and was located largely within the colonial territories or spheres of influence of the imperial power. During the nineteenth century, very little of British, Dutch, French or German capital, which was exported to the underdeveloped areas of Asia, Africa and the Americas, consisted of direct investment outside colonial boundaries. However, by 1900 several American companies were beginning to produce in Britain a variety of manufacturers, including farming equipment, sewing machines, and printing presses.[1] The rising barriers to international trade significantly reduced the profitability of manufactured exports and even of the sale of patents and technological know-how. Faced with an unfavourable economic environment, the rapidly growing American car industry, especially General Motors and Ford, decided to acquire ownership of several European moter vehicle companies. Within a very short period American corporations were established in the tyre, rubber and other automotive industries. In the meantime, substantial foreign investment had taken place in several extractive industries, especially in petroleum, nickel and copper. Among the earliest multinationals to enter the field were British Petroleum, Standard Oil Company, International Nickel, Anaconda Copper and Kenecott Copper.

The worldwide economic depression of the 1930s and the ensuing world war arrested for a time the expansionary trend in multinational investment. The value of direct American foreign investment, which had stood at $7,500 million in 1929, had decreased to $7,200 million in 1946, but was to rise to $31,900 million in 1960 and to $70,800 million in 1969.[2] After the Second World War, American multinational enterprise experienced a major upsurge in almost every part of the globe. Although the petroleum and mineral industries were still the recipients of enormous investment outlays, the most dramatic growth occurred in the manufacturing industries, where the value of direct US investment increased from $3,800 million in 1950 to $29,400 million in 1969.[3] Parallelling the change in the sectoral distribution of American multinational operations was the geographical shift from Latin America to Canada and Western Europe. In 1929, Latin America accounted for nearly 47 per cent of US foreign investment but for less than 20 per cent in 1962. During the same period, the proportion of US investment in Europe rose from 17 per cent to 32 per cent, and in Canada from 27 per cent to 30 per cent. The multi-national corporation had now achieved a dominant position in the advanced sectors of the most highly industralized eco-nomies. In 1973, it was calculated that business generated by multinational enterprises outside their home countries amounted to $350,000 million a year (three-fifths of it by US companies); that is, the equivalent of one-eighth of the gross product of the non-communist world.[4]

The emergence and accelerating growth of the multinational corporation were directly related to the increasing levels of industrial concentration and monopoly. According to one survey, the 50 largest firms in 1963 accounted for 25 per cent of manufacturing production in the United States. The 200 largest firms had increased their share of total manufacturing output from 30 per cent in 1947 to 41 per cent in 1963,[5] and to more than 60 per cent in 1969.[6] Industrial concentration was greatly assisted by the merger movement which assumed mas-sive proportions during the 1960s, the value of company assets acquired by the 200 largest American corporations increasing from $2,400 million in 1966 to $6,900 million in 1968.[7] In the case of Britain, it is estimated that between 1964 and 1970 ex-penditure on acquiring companies through takeovers and mergers was over £7,000 million, the equivalent of one-quarter of the total capital owned by all commercial and industrial companies.[8]

The growing role of the large corporation relative to the economy as a whole stems from the fact that its very size is such as to assure a higher rate of profit which, in turn, leads to greater growth through the internal accumulation of capital. The primary objective of corporate policy is greater profit-ability precisely because higher profits are 'the sinews and muscle of strength',[9] providing for larger size, a faster rate of growth and increased strength in the sense of a better credit rating and higher prices for the company's securities. But with-in any given industry and the confines of any national economy, cost and demand factors will sooner or later impose strict limits on increased profitability and continuing expansion. The oligopolistic corporation is thus attracted by the prospect of spreading its activities beyond the original field of operation. The availability of surplus capital, the expectation of higher rates of profit from foreign investment, and the possibility of realizing economies of scale provide the necessary incentive for a programme of industrial and geographical diversification.[10] The large corporation is thereby transformed into a multi-national enterprise, a vast conglomerate spanning a large range of industries, with sales running into hundreds of millions of dollars and affiliates spread over several countries.

The dramatic growth of multinational firms in the last two decades – especially those of the United States and to a lesser extent those of Japan and West Germany – has reflected the rapid post-war economic and technological development of these countries and their intensified search for sources of raw materials and market outlets. At the end of World War II, US corporations benefited from a particularly favourable eco-nomic and political environment. Fixed exchange rates and the supremacy of the American dollar provided the stability and predictability within which foreign trade and investment could flourish. The liberalization of international trade, the absence of any serious impediments from either capital-exporting or capital-importing countries, and large foreign aid programmes opened a large number of national economies to multinational penetration.[11] The military defeat of Germany and Japan and the consequent occupation of these countries could not help but open the doors to American capital. The advent of the cold war and the movement towards the economic and strategic integration of the Atlantic alliance system under undisputed American leadership gave additional impetus to the flow of US investment in Europe. As for the Third World, the decaying European empires in Asia and Africa and the failure of the Latin American states to achieve an independent industrial base enabled the progressive invasion of American foreign investment. Within a relatively short period, US multinational enterprise was able to develop the global strategies and organ-izational framework needed to take advantage of the favourable conditions created by Pax Americana. By 1970 the total sales of all US multinational affiliates abroad amounted to $108,700 million, more than double the total value of US exports estim-ated at $42,600 million.[12]

Although multinational enterprise has not been an exclu-

sively American phenomenon – in 1971 direct foreign investment in the United States reached $13,704 million[13] – the
impact of foreign firms on the structure of the US economy
was certainly until the early 1970s, little more than marginal.[14]
By contrast, American corporations took advantage of their
superior organization, their growth and profit orientation and
their more advanced techniques of management, to penetrate
deep into the economies of developed and underdeveloped
nations alike. According to one study, British subsidiaries
and joint ventures of American corporations accounted in
1965 for 10 per cent of the industrial output of the United
Kingdom and for 17 per cent of its exports.[15] What particularly
concerned Europeans was the deep penetration of the high-
technology sectors of their economies. In France, for example,
American firms had acquired a controlling interest in the
photographic film, paper, farm equipment, and telecom-
munications industries. By the mid-1960s IBM had achieved
almost complete supremacy in the European computer industry, having produced at least half of all the computers now
installed in Western Europe.

The multinational corporation and the nation-state

The far-reaching implications of American economic penetration became the subject of increasing European uneasiness and
of Jean-Jacques Servan-Schreiber's best seller, *The American
Challenge*, which argued that technological and managerial
superiority would inevitably spill over into the larger areas
of economics and politics, and eventually give rise to externally
controlled cultural patterns and channels of communication.[16]
Valuable though it may have been in alerting the public to the
magnitude of the American presence in Western Europe,
Servan-Schreiber's analysis of the phenomenon of multinational enterprise remains at best fragmentary and at worst
peripheral, for it fails to distinguish between the interests of
the American corporation and those of the American state.
Moreover, it rests on the rather facile assumption that a federation of European states would, simply by virtue of its greater
size and more rational economic planning, provide an effective
response to the so-called 'American challenge' and match the

technical efficiency and organizational dynamism of the global corporation.

While not disputing the economic and technological superiority of American industry, it is nevertheless true that without the diplomatic or military support of Pax Americana, US corporate interests would not have achieved their widespread dominance in the international economic system. However, once the internationalization of capitalist production has advanced beyond a certain point, its subsequent development need no longer be tied to the fortunes or objectives of any particular state. Corporate strategies and the national interests of capitalist states need not always be synonymous or even compatible. Although a certain tacit understanding may predispose the multinational corporation to be sympathetic to the foreign and domestic policies of its home government in return for some measure of support for its overseas activities, the relationship is likely to prove at best a marriage of convenience. Paradoxically, while an integrated Europe may serve to defend, against American competition, the interests of European multinational enterprise, it may nevertheless leave the state, whether national or supranational, more vulnerable than ever to the financial pressures and organizational strength of the corporation.

As might be expected, the economic power of the multinational company has become most striking in relations with host states, where considerations of sheer size are especially relevant. It is estimated that in 1969 54 corporations as opposed to 46 countries had a gross output in excess of $2,000 million,[17] and that in 1971 the sales of General Motors, which amounted to more than $28,000 million, exceeded the gross national product of 130 countries.[18] Even in such highly industrialized nations as the United States, Britain, Canada, West Germany, Italy, the Netherlands, Belgium, Switzerland, Norway and Sweden, between 20 and 25 per cent of manufacturing output was in the hands of multinational enterprise.[19] This proportion is particularly significant when it is remembered that during the 1960s the 12 per cent annual growth rate of multinational production was far greater than that registered by the world economy or by the main capitalist centres, with the possible exception of Japan. Compounding the magnitude of global corporate production has been its adaptability and geographical mobility, which was reflected in 1970 in some 3,400 American corporations sharing in the activities of some 23,000 overseas companies, including some 8,000 producing affiliates.[20]

It is here that the nation-state is seriously handicapped in competing with the multinational firm, for its jurisdiction is clearly confined to its territorial boundaries. This limitation is especially acute in an age of declining empires and diminishing spheres of influence. To the extent that no single nation-state now enjoys the supremacy reminiscent of Pax Britannica or the more recent Pax Americana, the advantage is even more securely in the hands of the corporation. The presence of foreign investment in the extractive industries and the consequent ownership of land in the host country together with the power to make vital decisions about the extraction and development of non-renewable resources constitute perhaps the most flagrant manifestation of external intrusion into the national decision-making process.

The options for rapid, flexible and yet centralized decision-making available to the global corporation with respect to the location of personnel and capital equipment, and the design, marketing and distribution of goods and services are being constantly multiplied by the application of high-speed communications and information processing techniques. These technological possibilities allowing for the global transfer and rearrangement of information, expertise and product components are, however, beyond the reach of such territorially restricted institutions as the nation-state. While foreign affiliates may choose to integrate their activities with national plans, that choice usually rests not with them or the host government but with the corporation's head office. Foreign subsidiaries are increasingly operating under the discipline and framework of a single global strategy premised on the principles of self-sufficiency and vertical integration.[21]

The trend towards greater centralized control has been particularly obvious in financial policy, where a variety of methods, including dividends, royalty payments and transfer pricing, are used to achieve the desired movement of funds.

The exercise of control has also been reflected in the strong preference of most multinational enterprises for complete or majority ownership. In his study of the 187 largest US-controlled corporations, Raymond Vernon found that in 1967 84 per cent of their foreign subsidiaries were either wholly or majority owned.[22] In any case, control can also be achieved through joint ventures and even minority positions, for such arrangements provide not only a useful avenue for mobilizing local savings and capital, but also the means for creating a dependent and passive local bourgeoisie, and hence the opportunity to expand and diversify corporate operations with a much reduced risk of expropriation or nationalization.[23]

As for the mobility of the global corporation, it is nowhere more conspicuous than in the internal flow of trade and money. A significant proportion of international trade and financial transfers now consists of transactions between different branches of the same corporation. Credit restraint, applied by the host country, can often be bypassed by the foreign affiliate which has ready access to the vast resources of the parent company, while tight monetary conditions in the home country can be circumvented by shifting funds from subsidiaries. The growing financial role of the multinational corporation is also visible in the reverse expedient of investing liquid funds abroad for higher returns, the net effect of which may be to frustrate the attempts of national authorities to stimulate their economy.[24] Massive movements by the corporations in the 1960s and early 1970s against the pound sterling and the American dollar helped to shatter existing parities and to cast serious doubts on the viability of the prevailing system of monetary regulation. Apart from purely speculative activities, multinational companies have affected currency stability by hastening or delaying sales and purchases with a view to minimizing losses and maximizing gains from anticipated revaluations.[25] Destabilizing currency shifts, in which financial institutions and multinational corporations appeared to be involved, were recorded in anticipation of exchange realignments in the United States and Japan in 1971, in Britain in June 1972 and in West Germany in February 1973.

To the extent that many of the most critical issues in international relations have shifted from the military to the economic arena, and that military force has declined as an effective instrument of state policy, the balance of power may be said to have moved even more firmly to the advantage of the multinational corporation. For it is precisely in the economic sphere that the corporation can exert the greatest pressure and where the nation-state is being gradually divested of its power to govern.[26] National control over the economy is being steadily eroded in spite of increased government intervention. As we have already seen, in the case of the most advanced capitalist nations, fiscal and financial measures have failed to achieve the twin objectives of full employment and growth without inflation. Lacking the financial, technological and managerial resources of the multinational enterprise, most governments are gradually discovering that their range of economic options is narrowly circumscribed by well-entrenched relationships of structural dependence vis-à-vis the foreign corporation.[27]

Some writers have attempted to counter the growing evidence of multinational power by laying stress on the wide variety of policy instruments available to governments wishing to neutralize the adverse effects of multinational operations on national economic priorities.[28] In this regard, reference is usually made to the power of governments to insist on quantitative job requirements and the creation of employment opportunities in depressed areas; to oblige firms to carry out locally a significant share of their total research and development; to prohibit any limitations on the distribution of local production by the subsidiaries or on the subsidiaries' use of the parents' technology; to require external financing for foreign investments or to restrict the subsidiary's access to domestic capital; to compel multinational firms to engage in progressively higher stages of processing and assembling and to devote a sizeable share of output to exports or import substitutes; and finally to seek majority or even complete ownership of local subsidiaries of foreign firms, and, where possible, a major share in day-to-day management. It is perfectly true that all these are formal powers within the legal jurisdiction of the state, but there often exists a very wide gap between the prerogatives of states and their capacity to enforce them.

In the first place, governments face a very painful dilemma

when considering the economic costs and benefits of their actions. One the one hand they may recognize that multinational activities are injurious to their development priorities, to their fiscal and monetary policies, or to their balance of payments. On the other hand, they may be strongly attracted by the promise of foreign investment to increase income and exports or raise the level of employment, technology and managerial expertise. In any case, the global corporation has at its disposal a variety of options capable of neutralizing attempts at government control. Host governments may consider imposing drastic unilateral restrictions on foreign investment, but effective action is more often than not impeded by multinational policies based on a judicious combination of inducement, threat and retaliation. Canadian governments have traditionally refrained from severely restricting the entry of American investment so as not to provoke the United States into terminating Canada's preferential status with regard to American regulations on foreign transactions. France's decision in 1963 to impose limitations on American investment, following the action of General Motors in retrenching many of its workers and the acquisition by General Electric of a controlling interest in Machines Bull, prompted US firms to react by transferring their investments to other Common Market countries from which they could still make an inroad into the French market. Not surprisingly, the French government decided after a short period to relax its restrictions. An even more crippling form of retaliation was exemplified in the measures taken by several US corporations, including Kennecott and ITT, to oppose the nationalization of Chilean copper. Their ability to manipulate the international market and financial networks served to undermine Chile's standing with the major national and transnational credit institutions. The deterioration in Chile's balance of payments and the consequent inflationary spiral helped to produce economic collapse and political chaos throughout the country and the eventual overthrow of the socialist but constitutional government of Salvador Allende.

While these may be regarded as exceptional cases, they are nonetheless indicative of the extra-territorial leverage at the disposal of all large multinational firms. Their power to oppose nationalization and other forms of government control, whether by legal or illegal means, represents a direct challenge to the principle of national sovereignty, confirms the increasing permeability of national boundaries, and raises fundamental questions about the accountability of this new transnational institution.

In defence of multinational enterprise and its underlying values, it has been argued that the corporation has achieved a wider and more enduring contractual relationship with its customers, and thus introduced a new element of stability and legitimacy into the social system.[29] The customer, it is claimed, is now committed to the firm or to a whole range of products rather than a single item. The ensuing economies of scale offer the customer a reduction in the price of the commodity while providing the supplier with a large and reliable market. The corporation is said to provide much more satisfactorily than any other organization the fast and efficient service that is required by a vast and complex industrial society. Moreover, by dissociating the managers from the owners, corporate industry has established a much closer relationship with labour, often resulting in the active participation of trade unions in the process of innovation. The final seal of respectability has apparently been gained by the success of the corporation in becoming an active and important partner of the state in the fulfilment of major economic goals.

In spite of their surface plausibility, these arguments are in fact negated by the renewed vigour of economic nationalism in the Third World, as well as by the increasing rejection of consumer values and mounting trade union resistance[30] to be found in many of the advanced capitalist nations. The elimination of cultural resistance to corporate objectives has proven much less successful than the publicists of corporate production would like to suggest. The homogenization of the consumer undoubtedly made great strides during the 1950s and 1960s, but a strong reaction has gradually emerged against the power of the producer to transform the affluent society into a 'want-creating' instead of a 'want-satisfying' mechanism. The accelerated growth of the corporate society is in fact hastening the disintegration of a social order no longer able to support the strain of overgrown institutions that have crossed the threshold of psychological and ecological tolerance.

Multinational enterprise and the international system

In order to achieve assured control over markets and sources of supply, and gain maximum advantage from the national differences in taxation, labour and investment policies, the primary objective of multinational enterprise has been to achieve complete freedom in the location of production and system of distribution. For this reason, all international corporations, irrespective of their natural origins or their specific interests, have shared the common goal of creating and maintaining an international system conducive to the unimpeded development of private capitalist enterprise. In this task they have greatly benefited, especially since World War II, from the foreign policy orientation of the American state and its vigorous opposition to the growth of revolutionary movements and centrally planned economies.[31]

The policy of containment, initiated by the Truman Doctrine and designed to produce the military encirclement of the communist world, was complemented by a strategy of military intervention aimed at maintaining a favourable status quo throughout the underdeveloped regions of Asia, Africa and Latin America. The application of American military power and counter-insurgency techniques against the communist or left-wing governments of Guatemala, Cuba, the Dominican Republic, Chile, China, North Korea, North Vietnam, Iran, Lebanon and several other countries, all reflected the same preoccupation with the defence of the 'free world', by which was understood the protection of uninhibited private enterprise. To secure the compliance of potentially recalcitrant governments, the economic weapon was also used with considerable effect, as in the case of the Hicken Looper Amendment to the Foreign Assistance Act of 1961, which sought to deny aid funds to any country which did not abide by the established rules of foreign investment. The American national interest, as formulated and implemented by the State Department, the Pentagon, the Treasury, the CIA and the other important agencies of foreign policy, thus coincided with the interests of the large corporate and financial empires which had come to be accepted as 'the repositories of national wealth' and 'the organizers of its productive capacity'.[32]

The absolute and relative power of the American empire provided the international order and stability needed by the global corporation to develop a dependable and expanding level of demand for its products. Once a secure environment had been achieved, multinational enterprises were able to turn their attention to the long-term construction of transnational structures linking the economic and political elites of home and host countries, thereby consolidating the new balance of power and the implicit allocation of international resources. The net effect has been to produce a new network of dependent and interdependent relationships with far-reaching consequences for the form and substance of international transactions.

Apart from its direct impact on the international economic system, the global corporation has indirectly affected strategic and diplomatic relations between home and host governments, thereby rendering obsolete the state-centric image of the international system. However, in undermining the sovereignty and efficiency of the state, economic transnationalism can hardly be said to have given rise to more flexible institutions capable of relieving the political and psychological stresses of the technocratic order, the predicament of economic under-development or the crisis of military insecurity. Far from re-dressing the imbalances characteristic of contemporary domestic and international society, the multinational corporation has merely produced a highly centralized and hierarchical form of profit-making transnational organization which reinforces the international division of labour and the inequality between the income, status and consumption patterns of the centre and those of the periphery.[33] When the advocates of multinational enterprise underline its potential to transform world politics from a contest among nation-states into a competition among transnational units for greater and more efficient production, they are, in reality, euphemistically describing the rise of a new type of empire and a new form of empire-building.

Most enthusiastic supporters of multinational activity have actually welcomed the gradual demise of the state and its replacement by the global corporation as the principal regulatory agency in international economic relations.[34] The supposedly independent corporation is said to transcend the conflicts of inter-state relations and to relate more directly to the goals of economic welfare. Transnational production, it is argued, knows no national or ideological boundaries.[35] It transfers raw materials, technology and managerial resources not according to parochial considerations of national interest but in terms of more efficient global economic integration. In pursuing this much larger and more rational objective, multinational enterprise has a direct interest in the prevention of war and the erosion of the great ideological cleavages that divide the world. In support of this contention, reference is made to the presence of corporations in almost every country of the world, irrespective of the nature of its political system. Apart from the sale of several turn-key plants, western corporations have begun to make regular managerial and technological inputs into the economies of several communist states. Some East European governments, particularly Yugoslavia, have taken steps to establish joint ventures with multinationals. The ability of American corporations, among which IBM, Xerox and Standard Oil, to maintain their operations in both Israel and the Arab states, in spite of the continuing hostility between the two sides, has been advanced as further evidence of political neutrality.[36]

Persuasive though it may appear at first sight, the argument which depicts the multinational corporation as an apolitical animal is, in fact, rather tenuous. It is perfectly true that corporate interests, taken individually or collectively, are not committed to any one government or to any specific political elite. But such lack of commitment cannot be equated with indifference to the reigning ideology of different social systems. The advent of centrally planned economies first in Russia and subsequently in Eastern Europe, China and a few Third World countries may have limited the spread but did not significantly affect the main thrust of global capitalist production. Indeed, it can be argued that, because of their more backward industrial development, communist states have been faced with the option of either isolating themselves from the international market economy or maintaining certain trading and financial links on conditions dictated by the major capitalist centres. If western corporations have been willing to do business with communist governments it is not because they are politically impartial but rather because they are able to operate in an international economic environment which provides them with the opportunity and the power to carry out profitable transactions even with potentially antagonistic social systems.

In the light of the rapidly evolving East–West rapprochement since the mid-1960s, the supposed incompatibility between multinational enterprise and centralized state planning would now seem to have been greatly overestimated. Despite the apparent ideological distance separating them, the two systems have experienced a strong and growing mutual attraction. By their very nature, communist bureaucracies are well placed to carry out transactions with the disciplined and centralized organization of the global corporation, while the latter is attracted by the prospect of 'orderly markets, strike-free factories and predictable five-year plans'.[37] Moreover, the Soviet and East European elites have had to contend with increasingly powerful demands for greater and more immediate consumer gratification. In so far as the satisfaction of these demands is dependent on the import of western technology, multinational penetration may be said to have become the *sine qua non* of the stability of bureaucratic socialism. What we are witnessing is the progressive fusion of two large monoliths, the conjunction of the centralized Soviet super-state with centralized capitalist enterprise.

It is precisely the input of advanced western communications technology into the communist unified planning systems which holds for both sides the promise of larger and better controlled markets undisturbed by economic competition or political opposition. The fusion of corporate interests and the underlying objectives which it serves explains the progress of diplomatic détente as well as of technical and scientific cooperation.[38] The introduction of multinational operations into the socialist bloc and the accompanying expansion of mutual trade, which are but the most visible economic linkages between the two systems, are the product not so much of convergence as of parallel and, in some cases, intersecting lines of development.[39] They represent the accommodation of two distinct modes of production on the basis of their shared commitment to functional rationality, economic growth and political stability.

Economic transnationalism, as reflected in the tacit under-standing between corporate capitalism and bureaucratic col-lectivism, may be interpreted as a global enterprise committed to the preservation of the status quo both nationally and internationally.

Multinationalism and economic stratification

Although the larger proportion of multinational investment still remains within the industrialized world, it is now generally recognized that global corporations wield far-reaching in-fluence over the economic and political institutions of the underdeveloped countries in which they invest. Significantly, while the share of total US direct foreign investment located in the Third World was little more than 27 per cent in 1971, the corresponding share of earnings was 42 per cent. Taking the category of 'interest, dividends, and branch earnings', which more accurately reflects total earnings repatriated to the United States, in 1971 the amount originating from developed coun-tries was $3,100 million or 42 per cent as opposed to $3,700 million or 51 per cent from underdeveloped countries.[40] In other words, the proportion of earnings from foreign invest-ment reinvested in the host country has been much smaller for the underdeveloped than for the developed countries.

Perhaps the most important effect of multinational opera-tions in most Third World countries has been to weaken the state's powers of control over the national economy. The in-tegration of underdeveloped economies into the private inter-national money market has increased their vulnerability to external constraints and severely restricted their ability to control their monetary and foreign exchange policies. The resulting pattern of economic dependence and political in-stability has often led the indigenous capitalist class to reinforce its alliance with foreign capital and, where necessary, to es-tablish a system of political repression financed, at least in part, by foreign aid.

How, then, is one to reconcile this reading of the facts with the claim that the multinational corporation offers the best possibility for the 'greater equalization between rich and poor nations'[41] through the transfer of capital, technology and management skills? Is one to conclude that the erosion of national sovereignty is simply the price that has to be paid for the sake of economic development. In reality, far from reducing inequalities, the multinational corporation has tended to preserve and exacerbate domestic and international disparities in both income and wealth. The introduction of foreign investment in underdeveloped countries has often stunted the growth of local capital, subordinated their political, cultural and technological development to multinational interests and, thereby, caused severe damage to the structure of their economies.

To the extent that multinational enterprise operates in a context of uneven development and that greater profitability is its primary objective, it tends to concentrate on continuous innovation in consumer goods. The unavoidable outcome of this strategy in an underdeveloped economy is to inhibit the mass production of cheaper consumer goods and to limit consumption of corporate products to a relatively small fraction of the population. By its emphasis on product development and marketing, multinational intrusion in Third World countries tends to create a dualist structure in the national economy. The highly profitable corporate sector with its bias towards high technology, high wages and capital-intensive methods of production, inevitably grows at the expense of the much larger, more labour-intensive domestic sector geared to small-scale production, low productivity, low wages, low profits, and much less advanced technology.

The fragmentation of the national economy resulting from corporate activity is equally evident in extractive investment, which in 1969 represented more than half the value of US direct investment in the underdeveloped countries. Most of this investment enjoys a very high rate of return, and operates as an enclave, directed primarily to the export market and largely insulated from the rest of the economy.[42] While it is true that certain benefits usually accrue to the host government in the form of taxation and royalties, the magnitude of these benefits is closely related to the political autonomy and bargaining power of the government in question, thus providing an apt reminder of the logical and practical nexus between national independence and economic development.[43]

But if extractive industries, whether in mining, smelting, or petroleum, are detached from growth in the local economy, does not manufacturing investment have a direct stake in the expansion of the domestic market? More than one writer has laid stress on the multiplier effect of foreign manufacturing investment, its capacity to create a local managerial and entre- preneurial class, and to provide economies of scale, employ- ment opportunities and foreign exchange earnings.[44] Regret- tably, little of the available evidence would appear to support this rather optimistic assessment.

In many instances the substitution of capital for labour has intensified rather than diminished the problem of unemploy- ment. Multinational investment automatically places village industries, often located far from the big cities, at a serious disadvantage. Unable to compete with the organizational or technological resources of the large corporations, they lose many of the former outlets for their productivity. The neglect of traditional arts and crafts and the abandonment of local production facilities are but the logical consequences of the employment–displacing function of private foreign invest- ment.[45] It is perhaps significant that between 1925 and 1960 the manufacturing sector was able to absorb only 5 million of the 23 million people who migrated from the countryside to the urban centres of Latin America, and that, while total manu- facturing output increased its share of national product from 11 per cent in 1925 to 25 per cent in 1970, the proportion of the work force which it employed during this period decreased from 14.4 per cent to 13.8 per cent.[46]

As for the transfer of capital, it is a well-established fact that a large proportion of foreign investment is financed by local capital. Indeed, if it were not for the foreign acquisition of local firms and the repatriation of multinational profits, one could envisage a greater contribution from local profits to local con- sumption and savings and possibly a less acute shortage of foreign exchange. It is perhaps not coincidental that Latin America, which is at a much more advanced stage of multi- national penetration than Asia or Africa, should also be ex- periencing the severest difficulties in its payment of foreign debts. One study has shown that, although US corporations accounted for about 40 per cent of Latin America's manufactured exports, these constituted only 16 per cent of the region's total exports, and well over half of these exports were produced in three countries: Argentina, Brazil, Mexico. Moreover, much of the export trade was directed to other subsidiaries or to the parent of the multinational company at prices lower by some 40–50 per cent relative to the prices obtained by local firms.[47] Export underpricing, import overpricing, inflated royalty payments and a variety of other multinational devices have compounded the already acute balance of payments problem confronting most Third World countries.[48]

If no strong case can be made in favour of the global corporation as an instrument for the transfer of capital, may it not be argued that its most valuable contribution lies in the transfer of managerial expertise and technological know-how? Here again the evidence is not very encouraging, for subsidiaries are often instructed by the parent company as to the uses which may be made of imported techniques and are prevented from adapting products or processes to local conditions. Such limitations on the use of foreign technology reinforce the technological dependence of underdeveloped countries on foreign sources and often lead to the absorption of the domestic firm by the multinational corporation, or subordination to its licensing restrictions.[49] Moreover, the heavy cost attached to the acquisition of patents, licences, know-how and trademarks as well as management and service fees, represents an additional drain on the scarce foreign exchange resources of these countries.

Apart from its impact on the financial and technological structure of the underdeveloped economy, the intrusion of foreign private investment is also conducive to psychological and ideological dependence. It is now increasingly acknowledged that the transfer of capital equipment and technical know-how is not a neutral process. The cultural influence of foreign corporations in Third World countries may be gauged to some extent by the magnitude of the sums allocated to advertising, which in many cases represent a very significant fraction of the total educational budget of national governments. In the case of Brazil, one estimate suggests that advertising expenditures by American manufacturing affiliates have equalled over one-third of recurring public expenditures on all forms of education.[50] The function of this flow of foreign values and standards is to produce public tastes and consumer wants which bear little relationship to the needs of underdeveloped societies. Thus, for example, in Latin America the production of facilities of the car industry, which are ten times greater than the demand of the local market, restricted in any case to a small and privileged minority, absorb many of the resources which could otherwise be made available for the production of more universally accessible means of transport such as bicycles, buses and trains. The transmission of imported standards of consumption invariably results in a misallocation of resources and unbalanced development.

Another deleterious consequence of multinational investment is the natural inclination of the indigenous personnel, who are directly or indirectly involved with the foreign corporation, to absorb its cultural package for the purpose of personal advancement. A dual process results in which the foreign management input from the parent company is complemented by the socialization of the local elite. Gradually there emerges a new class of entrepreneurs highly dependent on the foreign firm, predisposed to accept its ideology but indifferent and even hostile towards any concept of power sharing or distributive justice. The function of the multinational corporation, therefore, is to widen the traditional gap between the political and economic elite and the predominantly peasant population, thereby weakening the legitimacy of the political system and hence its capacity to mobilize the energies and resources of the society around a coherent and long-term programme of national development.

Although we have argued that corporate interests need not always be considered as identical with those of the major capitalist states, it was only to be expected that the objectives, strategies and underlying philosophy of multinational enterprise should have found their most hospitable environment in the industrialized nations of the western world. By contrast the relationship with underdeveloped countries has been much less harmonious as multinational operations have repeatedly had to confront political systems conscious of their vulnerability to foreign economic pressures and at the same time anxious to maintain at least a measure of national independence. But even in relations with the First World, one could begin to discern by the early 1970s a trend towards increasing divergence between multinational strategies and the policies of both home and host governments. The uneasy and pragmatic compromise which has prevailed until recently may not be able to contain indefinitely the contradictions implicit in opposing perspectives, conflicting loyalties, contrasting structures and distinct sources of power. It remains to be seen, for instance, how the diplomatic and military resources of the nation-state will contend with the economic leverage of the corporation in any future confrontation. Equally uncertain is the likely development of relations with the communist state where the ideological and institutional interests of the party bureaucracy may at some point dictate a reversal in the current trend towards the fusion of technocratic interests.

In the more immediate term, however, the general impact of the global corporation on the international system is likely to be one of fragmentation and polarization. By taking the philosophy of free enterprise and the concept of the division of labour to their ultimate and logical conclusion, multinationalism has helped to create a global political economy based on hierarchy and inequality. But already numerous voices, disadvantaged or outranged by the establishment of these transnational feudal structures, are beginning to mobilize public opinion in support of new concepts of equity and world order.

7. The energy crisis

In his perennial struggle with scarcity, man has developed over the years ever greater skills and ingenuity enabling him to complement his manual labour with energy derived from solar radiation, and from the earth's internal heat as well as its rotation and other mutations. Inputs of available energy, in the form of water power, fossil fuels and sunlight, have helped to transform the material world from the non-economic to the economic realm; that is, from a less valuable to a more valuable state. These various sources of energy have been utilized to achieve not only a much higher level of industrial activity but also greater agricultural productivity, through the application of machines, fertilizers, pesticides and new methods of irrigation.

The most dramatic evolution in both the sources and the uses of energy has probably occurred in the last hundred years. In 1800 the burning of wood was still the principal means of generating energy, but by 1910 coal was supplying 75 per cent of total energy consumption. In the ensuing fifty years, coal gradually lost its preeminence to liquid and gaseous fossil fuels, namely oil and natural gas. By the mid-1960s construction had already begun on a number of nuclear plants, although the full potential of nuclear energy was not expected to be realized until the 1980s or 1990s. The accelerating demand for energy, especially for purposes of heating, transport and industry, has reached its most frenetic pace in the last two or three decades. World energy consumption, which stood at 2,700 million tons of coal equivalent (mtce) in 1950, reached 6,000 mtce by 1968, thus registering an annual increase of 5 per cent. At this rate, world consumption would be expected to rise to 19,000 mtce in 1990 and to 36,500 mtce by the year 2000.[1] Significantly, since 1950 the consumption of oil and natural gas has grown at the much faster rate of 7.8 per cent a year, the contribution of these

113

two fuels to total energy needs rising from one-third in 1950 to two-thirds in 1970. As Table 7.1 indicates, the dependence of some European countries on these two sources of energy became ever more pronounced. Similarly, by 1970, 70.8 per cent of Japan's energy consumption was generated by oil,[2] and in 1972, petroleum and natural gas accounted for 77.8 per cent of the US energy supply.[3]

It should be added that by the late 1960s the ten leading industrial countries of the world were consuming three-quarters of the world's energy production. Total US per capita energy consumption was two to four times greater than that of most other developed economies and some 25 times greater than the average per capita consumption of the underdeveloped countries.[4] In the light of projections envisaging the quadrupling of energy requirements by the end of the century, an explosive situation had developed by the early 1970s in terms of both the exponential growth of total energy consumption and its disproportionate concentration in the advanced economies of North America, Europe and Japan. The oil crisis, which erupted in the wake of the Yom Kippur War, thus served to crystallize the many critical problems relating to the future structure of the energy economy, notably the issues of resource scarcity, economic growth, systemic inequality, and the environmental impact of technology.

TABLE 7.1 *Proportional dependence on primary fuels (1973)*

	Oil	Natural gas	Coal*	Other†
	%	%	%	%
Italy	78.6	10.0	8.1	3.2
France	72.5	8.1	16.1	3.2
Belgium Luxembourg }	62.1	13.8	23.7	0.4
Netherlands	54.2	42.3	3.4	0.1
W. Germany	58.6	10.1	30.1	1.3
Britain	52.1	13.2	33.6	1.2

* Including lignite and brown coal.
† Including nuclear energy, hydro-electricity and geothermal energy.
Source: BP Statistical Review of the World Oil Industry, 1973

The oil crisis and its immediate consequences

There can be little doubt that the use of the oil weapon by the Arab states after the Middle East War of October 1973 considerably strengthened the militancy of oil-producing nations. On the other hand, the short-term disruption caused by the oil crisis must not be exaggerated. The embargoes imposed by the Arab countries, principally against the United States and the Netherlands, did not reduce their total production by more than 25 per cent. In fact, the major oil companies, with the covert approval of most western governments, reallocated the available oil to ensure that no country would suffer disproportionately from the oil shortage. Moreover, Iraq, Iran, Oman, Nigeria and Venezuela did not participate in the embargo and continued to direct their flow to the countries hardest hit by the restrictions. As for the quadrupling of oil import prices within the space of one year, there was no disputing its widespread repercussions for a number of national economies as well as for the entire international monetary system.

In many cases, balance of payments difficulties were compounded by the prohibitive cost of new investment required to develop other sources of energy or to move away from existing energy-intensive forms of production. Moreover, such a rapid transfer of financial resources could not be rectified by a simple recycling device whereby the funds accumulated by the oil producers returned to the capital markets of advanced industrial countries or were spent on goods produced by them. This financial mechanism did not necessarily ensure that petrodollars would flow to the countries experiencing the most acute deficits, nor was there any guarantee that the burden of debts would eventually diminish, even if spread over a number of years. Moreover, there were serious doubts as to the ability of some consuming countries to absorb, not only economically but politically and psychologically, large investments from the oil producers. In any case, the countries hardest hit by the oil crisis were the underdeveloped consuming nations, such as India, which had to pay the higher prices but could expect little by way of capital inflows or export orders from oil producers. According to one estimate, the quadrupling of oil prices added about $10,000 million a year to the import bills of these countries and another $5,000 million for fertilizers.[5] While disputable, the figures point nonetheless to the magnitude of the problem confronting Third World oil importers.

In spite of this dramatic transformation in the nature of international economic transactions and the seemingly arbitrary power wielded by OPEC governments, it would be a serious mistake to consider the oil crisis as an unexpected exercise in price-rigging, politically engineered by a few Middle-Eastern despots. The trend towards higher oil prices, which preceded the Yom Kippur War, was essentially a response to the continuing importance of oil in the world economy and the perceived gradual depletion of oil reserves. For more than two decades, the main western economies had predicated their policy of unfettered growth on the assumption of continued access to secure and seemingly inexhaustible supplies of energy. By keeping Middle East oil below its true scarcity value, in terms of production costs in other parts of the world or equivalent costs for other sources of energy, the industrialized world had discouraged the growth of new sources of supply, helped hold down the prices of such substitutes as coal and hydroelectricity, prevented or retarded the development of new sources of energy, and above all contributed to the incredible waste and inefficient use of the world's fossil fuels.[6] The capitalist economic miracle, as reflected in the dramatic rise in industrial production, the export boom and the vast accumulation of international reserves, had been subsidized by the oil-producing countries 'at the expense of their limited irreplaceable assets'.[7]

The oil crisis then was not simply the by-product of artificial upward changes in the price of the commodity, but the manifestation of a more profound crisis within the global energy economy, seriously calling into question the feasibility and desirability of the projected fourfold increase in energy consumption by the end of the century. Although oil might continue to be available in abundant supply for some years to come and new reserves might be discovered, it was generally accepted that, at the current exponential rate of increased consumption, this resource would be exhausted at the latest by the year 2050. However, well before the actual date of exhaustion, the world economy would need to have acquired effective access to other energy inputs in order to satisfy desired growth objectives.

No doubt, nuclear, solar and geothermal energy, oil shales, tar sands, and coal gassification would in due course make their contribution to energy requirements but they could not be expected to replace oil in the immediate future. By 1985 nuclear power would still satisfy only 10 per cent of US energy demands, while the projected proportion for natural gas was 15 per cent. One might expect a greater contribution to be made by coal, which now supplied some 20 per cent of total US energy consumption. Similarly, it might be possible to devise the required technologies for the extraction of oil from shale, but it was doubtful whether any or all of these substitute sources of energy could be developed on a scale sufficiently economic or comprehensive to achieve a drastic reduction in the current dependence on oil. Such a critical transitional stage in the evolution of the energy economy was bound to be characterized by a series of economic, political and strategic realignments, as the major actors vied with each other to gain immediate or long-term advantage.

Axes of conflict

In a daring bid to strengthen their bargaining position in relation to both the Palestinian issue and the return of Arab lands occupied by Israel after the June 1967 war, Arab countries decided to use the oil weapon as a means of bringing pressure to bear on Israel's traditional friends and allies, thereby isolating their arch enemy. The policy, aimed principally at the United States and Western Europe, sought to demonstrate the importance of oil to their respective economies. While recognizing the role played by Arab solidarity in cementing a united front comprising such diverse political systems as the conservative Saudi Arabian monarchy and the revolutionary Libyan government, the fact remains that in the wider context of OPEC, unity was maintained by the common interest to increase oil revenue, by the integrated structure of the international oil industry, and by the common perception that the retaliatory options open to the United States was severely limited by its adversary relationship with the Soviet Union, and by the increasing divergence of interests within the western alliance system. It appears, therefore, that apart from intensifying superpower rivalry and magnifying the existing asymmetries between the resource-poor and resource-poor regions of the Third World, the oil crisis gave rise to a conflict between consumers and producers and to new lines of division among the major oil-importing countries, as well as between the large oil corporations and their home states.

In order to understand the evolution of the oil crisis, it may be useful to identify, however briefly, the underlying strengths and weaknesses of the OPEC phenomenon. Apart from the political benefits deriving from the strategic stalemate between the two superpowers and the unifying effect of Islamic hostility towards the Jewish state, the Middle Eastern oil producers enjoy the incomparable advantage of controlling nearly 60 per cent of the world's proven crude oil reserves.[8] As an oil-bearing area, the Middle East is geographically and strategically unique, in the sense that its dominant position in the supply of this key commodity cannot be significantly altered by future additions to reserves either from new discoveries or revisions of past discoveries. Reinforcing the strong position of the Arab oil-exporting countries, and of the OPEC group as a whole, has been the increasing dependence on oil of the major western economies. European net imports of oil had increased from 183.3 million metric tons in 1960 to 596.8 million metric tons in 1970, when indigenous production, mainly in the form of coal and natural gas, accounted for only 39 per cent of Europe's primary energy requirements.[9] The increase in Japanese dependence has been even more dramatic with imports of crude oil rising from 49 million barrels in 1955 to 1,569 million barrels in 1972.[10] Although much less acute, the position of the United States was moving in the same direction, with the trend in the late 1960s and early 1970s indicating that US imports of oil, which represented 35 per cent of total oil consumption in 1973, might reach 10 or 11 million barrels a day by 1980, or the equivalent of 50 per cent of the projected US oil consumption in that year.[11]

In proposing his energy programme to Congress in 1975, President Ford had to admit that domestic oil production had fallen from 9.2 million barrels a day in 1973 to 8.8 million barrels in 1974, while total consumption had continued to increase, though at a slower rate as a result of higher prices.

Moreover, natural gas shortages had led to the curtailment of supplies for both industrial and residential use. Coal production was at the same level as in the 1930s, and nuclear energy still accounted for only 1 per cent of the total energy supply. Various economic and environmental difficulties were causing the construction of new atomic plants to be delayed, postponed or cancelled.[12] Similar difficulties were hampering Japan's atomic energy programme, which, even by 1985, was not expected to fulfill more than 10 per cent of national energy needs.[13]

In the light of these indicators, one could not easily accept the conclusions of an OECD report which forecast that member countries would achieve 80 per cent self-sufficiency in energy by 1985, and that dependence on oil would decrease from 55 per cent to 45 per cent over the next decade.[14] Previous estimates had in fact projected a decline in self-sufficiency from 65 per cent in 1972 to 55 per cent in 1985. The optimistic findings of the report were based on the dubious assumption of a much higher degree of energy conservation than was previously anticipated or was currently contemplated by any major government. The OECD projections were also premised on a vast and universal programme of energy diversification which would require a major shift of resources into the energy sector, a shift, moreover, which would almost certainly come into conflict with other stated economic and environmental objectives.

Enough will have been said to suggest the circumscribed range of choices open to the advanced capitalist economies. Yet the freedom of action available to the oil producers was also limited. It is now generally understood that oil wealth is not synonymous with economic development. As the case of Iran has clearly shown, the sudden additions in foreign revenue may simply lead to asymmetrical growth and the expansion of one sector at the expense of the rest of the economy. The relatively small domestic market may help to accentuate the dependence on exports, while capital-intensive industrialization is likely to lead to the neglect of agriculture and raise the level of unemployment in urban areas. National wealth is thus directed towards a small fringe of society, and much of it may be apportioned for military purposes. There are, moreover, physical limits on the capacity of the oil-producing economies to absorb the vast inflow of petrodollars, hence the necessity for large-scale foreign investments, over which they are likely to have less than total control and little recourse in the case of nationalization or expropriation.[15]

These considerations help to explain, at least in part, the change of mood which was clearly discernible within OPEC by the beginning of 1975. Even Iran and Algeria, considered to be among the more assertive members of OPEC, were now mainly concerned to protect their purchasing power against the monetary policies and inflationary conditions of the consumer nations. It was perhaps not altogether coincidental that this new element of moderation on the Arab side should have been introduced so soon after the provocative statement by the American secretary of State in which he hinted at the possibility of US armed intervention in the Persian Gulf.

Other factors tending to weaken the united front of oil-producers were the worldwide downturn in economic activity and the internal divisions within OPEC. Excess oil production and reduced western consumption were adding strains to relationships among OPEC countries, many of which were suspicious of revolutionary objectives. The governments of Iran, Saudi Arabia and Indonesia might welcome the flow of additional revenue but they had little enthusiasm for the contruction of a new international economic order. By February 1975, the real price of crude oil appeared to be falling. Some of the smaller producers were by-passing the official price by offering extended credits which effectively reduced the price from above $11 to as low as $8.50 a barrel. Although oil producers had been forced to cut production by 10 to 20 per cent, the surplus in world supply was now estimated to be in excess of 2 million barrels a day. Aramco was reported to have stopped pumping oil through its major pipeline in Saudi Arabia, and Venezuela was considering cutting its production from 3.0 to 2.4 million barrels a day. Was the Western, or more precisely, the American response to the oil crisis beginning to pay dividends? Was a new stable equilibrium about to be reached, resulting in lower prices and assured sources of supply?

In spite of some preliminary successes, there was little reason to believe that the energy diplomacy of the United States would be able to resolve the main economic and environmental pro-

blems raised by the energy crisis. Notwithstanding their inter-
nationalist guise, US objectives and strategies were essentially
preoccupied with short-term national advantage. As a direct
consequence of OPEC policy, Japan and Western Europe were
attempting to secure unilateral benefits through separate
arrangements with the various oil-producers. Such a trend,
which would spell the demise of US hegemony within the western
alliance system, had to be opposed at all costs. Equally crucial
to American interests was the need to prevent the international
financial system from collapsing under the strain of widespread
and chronic balance of payments deficits. When publicly
defending its policy, the United States was careful to stress the
cooperative thrust of its approach,[16] but there was no disguis-
ing the overriding objective of American resources diplomacy
which was to force a reduction in oil prices and use the oil crisis
to demonstrate the determination of the United States to maintain guaranteed access to strategic raw materials, especially
those in which it was deficient. Consumer solidarity was to
provide the necessary conditions for the implementation of this
policy. Dialogue with producer nations would simply confirm
and ratify the acceptance of American proposals.

The task of creating a consumer bloc under the leadership of
the United States was greatly facilitated by the inability of most
other consumer governments to develop a coherent energy
policy. Even after the Teheran and Tripoli agreements of 1971
had made it clear that oil prices would no longer stay at their
extraordinary low levels and that restrictions on production
might endanger the security of supplies, the European Economic
Community had done very little to prepare itself for the events
of October 1973. Apart from an agreement in October 1972 to
stockpile the equivalent of 90 days consumption of oil, and the
introduction of legislation for petrol rationing in case of
emergency, there had been little progress towards an overall
energy policy. Community members appeared to be divided on
a wide range of questions, including relations with oil-exporting
countries, the organization of a community oil market, the
development of nuclear power, the future of coal, the use of
gas, environmental safeguards and energy conservation.[17]
France, which was perhaps the only European country with
anything approaching a well-defined energy policy, saw the oil

crisis as an opportunity to reaffirm its pro-Arab position and possibly to erode the American political and commercial supremacy in the Middle East.

American plans were given their first institutional expression in the Washington Conference of February 1974, attended by all the major western oil-consuming countries. The United States had convened the conference as part of a larger programme intended to promote the coordination of national policies in relation to energy conservation, the diversification of existing sources of energy, the development of an emergency system of allocation and the acceleration of energy research projects. The combined effect of these measures was aimed at moderating the demand for oil and thus lowering its price. Significantly, France was the only country to dissociate itself from several conference resolutions, especially from those which sought either to discourage competitive devaluations and trade monetary restrictions, or to promote a united front of industrialized consumer nations likely to create a confrontation between producer and consumer governments. Accordingly, in October 1974, the French President, Giscard d'Estaing, while reaffirming France's refusal to participate in the deliberations of the International Energy Agency created as a result of the Washington discussions, proposed instead that a conference be convened in 1975 at which would be represented a small and equal number of oil-producers, highly industrialized oil-consumers, and under-developed countries. The French proposal appeared to gain some momentum after the Franco-American summit meeting of December 1974 and the favourable response which it elicited from the OPEC ministerial meeting in January 1975, but a preliminary meeting in April 1975 proved abortive as the United States rejected the OPEC demand that the producer–consumer dialogue be extended to cover not only oil but all other raw materials.

In order to strengthen its position in this intricate web of diplomatic manoeuvring, the United States had already decided to launch 'Project Independence', a domestic energy programme designed to exert pressure directly on the oil-producers by reducing the demand for oil, and indirectly by providing other major consuming nations with a lead in energy conservation and energy diversification. The immediate aim of the conservation programme launched by the Ford administration was a reduction in the growth rate of energy consumption.[18] The strategy was to reduce oil imports to no more than one-fifth of total energy requirements and then to ensure that the demand for imported oil remained static. It was projected that oil imports could be reduced by one million barrels a day by the end of 1975 and by two million barrels a day by the end of 1977. By 1985, imports would have fallen to 3–5 million barrels a day, which could be replaced immediately in case of emergency from the strategic storage system. Vulnerability to an embargo would thus have been eliminated. Beyond 1985, the policy envisaged the development of energy and technological resources which would meet not only American needs but a significant share of the free world's energy requirements. Well before this stage was reached, the fall in demand and the availability of new sources of energy would have forced the OPEC countries to apply deeper and deeper cuts in supply in a vain attempt to prevent a reduction in their oil revenue. The energy economy would have been transformed into a buyer's market, compelling the oil-exporting nations to resume full-scale production though at much lower prices. Conservation measures were to be introduced not as a means of restricting the engine of growth but simply to restore the situation which had prevailed prior to the oil crisis and thereby maintain the energy-intensive character of western economies.

Precisely the same commitment to economic growth governed United States plans for energy diversification. Apart from encouraging the exploration and production of petroleum in Alaska and the outer continental shelf, the US administration was prepared to expand coal production and to accelerate the nuclear programme by expediting the selection and licensing of sites with only minimal regard for environmental problems. Within the next ten years, the new policy envisaged the construction of 200 major nuclear power plants, 250 major new coal mines, 150 major coal-fired power plants, 30 major new oil refineries and 20 major new synthetic fuel plants.[19] It was readily conceded that Project Independence would require an investment of hundreds of thousands of millions of dollars, both public and private, and substantial participation in joint projects with other advanced western economies in such fields as coal technology and uranium enrichment.

But, as several studies indicated, even the most aggressive

energy policy and the most complete neglect of environmental considerations could not guarantee the maintenance of past rates of growth in energy consumption on the basis of self-sufficiency.[20] Logical though it might appear from a short-term perspective, the American energy programme was in fact riddled with inconsistency. Far from encouraging energy conservation, it was premised on the expectation of unlimited energy consumption. Far from preserving the quality of the environment, it risked producing unprecedented ecological degradation. Far from promoting consumer solidarity, it was predicated on the pursuit of narrow self-interest.

If American diplomacy had met with less than total success in mobilizing the industrialized oil-importing economies into one united front against OPEC, it was even less successful in exploiting the balance of payments difficulties of the resource-poor countries of the Third World to weaken the position of the oil-producing cartel. The American proposal for the creation of a separate trust fund to complement regular IMF facilities was hardly sufficient to persuade underdeveloped countries of the sincerity of American intentions. After all, it was the United States which had strongly opposed their inclusion in the proposed international energy conference. Predictably, at their Dakar meeting in February 1975, Third World nations decided to give strong support to the OPEC position which had sought to link the oil problem to that of other raw materials. Once again and for obvious reasons, the United States reacted unfavourably but the proposal could not be easily dismissed for the OPEC nations had developed an interest in promoting Third World objectives because of the additional leverage with which such a policy provided them in their relations with the industrialized western world. For example, by encouraging the Third World's agricultural production, OPEC might be able to reduce its own food dependence on the United States. It is noteworthy that, apart from contributing about $3,000 million to the IMF oil facility and lending $1,000 million to the World Bank, the total flow of OPEC assistance to underdeveloped countries during January–September 1974 amounted to $8,600 million.[21] This gradual convergence of interests between the oil-exporting and oil-importing members of the Third World could not but reinforce the unity and assertiveness of underdeveloped countries and further polarize the already divided international economic system.[22]

The various economic and diplomatic initiatives outlined so far are particularly instructive because of the light they shed not only on the true nature of American policy, but also on its declining power and diminishing range of options. It was partly in order to offset this emerging gap in capability that the American diplomacy felt it necessary to allude to the possible use of armed force in the Persian Gulf area. Such action, it was argued, could not be excluded 'in the event of actual strangulation of the industrialized world by the oil producers' cartel'. The threat of force was probably intended as an intimidating tactic rather than as a serious statement of intention, for such a course of action, however swiftly executed, would incur the avowed hostility of the Arab world and provoke large-scale protracted guerrilla activity. Only the most reckless optimism and some rather dubious assumptions about Soviet interests and capabilities would confidently preclude the possibility of a Soviet counter-intervention.[23] Moreover, a favourable response could not be reasonably expected from either Western Europe or Japan, since none of these countries would wish to risk the drastic deterioration of relations with the Soviet Union and the Arab world for the sake of a few more years of assured oil supplies. As for the underdeveloped countries, they would hardly be favourably disposed to the use of American military power as a means of breaking the petroleum price structure. The past record of American actions and the acute difficulties of Third World nations in securing adequate prices for their primary commodities would be far more likely to strengthen their resolve to create a new international economic order.

Nor was there much likelihood that confrontation strategy would receive the support of the large oil companies. Throughout this period, they remained less than lukewarm to the notion of consumer solidarity, for the implementation of such a proposal would inevitably necessitate increasing interference by consumer governments in the affairs of multinational oil interests. Until the late 1960s the oil companies had steadfastly resisted the various efforts of producing countries to increase their share of oil revenue and their participation in the management of the industry. However, once OPEC members had demonstrated, singly and collectively, their determination to use their newly found bargaining power to advantage, the major oil corporations accepted their diminished role in the Middle East and adopted a policy of cooperation with OPEC, relying primarily on their size, technical competence and financial strength to maintain and improve their profitability.[24] Indeed, much of OPEC's success in affecting the dramatic increase in the price of oil had been made possible by the structure of the international oil industry whose exercise of monopoly power helped to shelter crude markets from excessive competition. Moreover, by the early 1970s, the oil companies had been able to complement their vertical control of the oil industry, from the mining of crude petroleum through the refining, transportation and marketing process, with the horizontal integration of their main energy competitors. It is estimated that in 1970 the oil corporations controlled 84 per cent of the oil refining capacity, 72 per cent of natural gas production, 20 per cent of coal production and 50 per cent of uranium reserves in the United States.[25] As a result of these various factors, the 'oil crisis' had been extremely valuable to the oil corporations for the increased payments to the OPEC governments had been more than offset by deductions from US taxes and the much greater prices paid by the consumer for oil and a whole range of other energy products.

The strong market position of energy suppliers and the impracticality of the use of force thus combined to produce a change in American strategy and a greater degree of accommodation with political reality. The United States was now willing to discuss the possibility of commodity agreements between the producers and consumers of industrial and agricultural raw materials. The new tactical direction in American policy was designed not so much to present a further increase in the price of oil – a decision to raise its price by 10 per cent was in fact taken by OPEC in September 1975 – as to deflect Third World pressures for a 'new economic order', delay the defection of Europe and Japan towards 'special relationships' with the producer countries and secure from Saudi Arabia a commitmet to impede the further radicalization of OPEC behaviour. It remained to be seen, however, whether such a strategy would successfully stem 'the new dispersion of economic power' or prevent the underdeveloped countries from using the energy crisis as a lever with which to challenge the sustained expansion of the industrialized capitalist countries.

The limits of energy growth

Over the last two decades, thanks to a major expansion of Middle East production, oil has provided a cheap and plentiful source of energy for the major industrial nations of the western world. It is now generally accepted that oil is a finite commodity whose supply will reach a peak in 1990 and disappear almost completely by 2050. In the early 1970s the total proven reserves of crude oil were estimated at 570,000 million barrels and ultimately recoverable reserves at 1,600,000 million barrels.[26] Although these estimates may have to be revised in the light of recent discoveries in Alaska, the North Sea, Brazil and Southeast Asia,[27] the higher costs associated with greater technical difficulties of exploration in remote areas are likely to diminish the marginal productivity of new reserves. Moreover, one must expect future additions of reserves as a result of underestimating past discoveries to decrease as a result of improved evaluation techniques. It has been calculated that if the world demand for oil were to continue to grow at the annual rate of $7\frac{1}{2}$ per cent, the ratio of proved reserves to annual production would fall to 10 by 1978, and that by the year 2000 some 1,100,000 million barrels would have to be found if the ratio were not to fall below 10.[28] The temporary slackening in demand and the discovery of new deposits may alter this projection, but only slightly. The fate of natural gas will be similar, although its life expectancy may be a little longer.

The gradual depletion of oil reserves is likely to result in greater reliance on coal, which is the most abundant of the fossil fuels. Measured world reserves of hard coal (i.e. anthracite and bituminous) have been estimated at 460,000 million metric tons and reserves of soft coal (i.e brown coal and lignite) at 270,000 million metric tons. At present consumption rates, these reserves are likely to last for more than 100 years. Moreover, total reserves are known to be much greater than proven reserves, and in the case of the United States alone they are thought to exceed 3,000,000 million metric tons, which, even with an exponential growth in demand, are not likely to be exhausted for another 200 or 300 years. According to one estimate, coal will remain a major world source of energy for another 340 years and production will continue to increase for another 140–200 years.[29] Clearly, the use of coal as a source of energy for the foreseeable future will not be limited by dwindling physical reserves but rather by rapidly rising extraction and transportation costs. It is this economic factor which made coal less and less competitive in relation to gas and oil during the 1950s and 1960s. Coal production could be significantly expanded in the Soviet Union, the United States, Australia and South Africa, but it remains to be seen whether these reserves can be developed economically, especially in the case of remote coal deposits which are likely to depend for their exploitation on high voltage electricity transmission, high speed coal trains and super-tankers for shipping.

An important consideration with all fossil fuels is that costs will rise as scarcity increases, which is to say, well before the complete exhaustion of known reserves. This process will be markedly accelerated should the world's population continue to grow and energy consumption increase at the same rate as in the 1960s. Moreover, when liquefaction and gassification processes for the conversion of coal into oil and gas have become fully competitive, the much greater reliance on coal for all fossil fuels will drastically reduce the life expectancy of coal reserves. Heavy oils, tar sands and oil shales may provide an additional source of energy, but they are unlikely to become economic until further technological developments occur and even higher prices for conventional fossil fuels are reached.

In the search for cheap and readily available energy, hydroelectricity, tides and wind can be expected to make a useful but limited contribution. Although theoretically inexhaustible, the practical potential of these sources is likely to be restricted by geographical, financial and environmental considerations. In underdeveloped countries the low level of industrialization is bound to militate against the large-scale expansion of hydroelectric power. Tidal energy, severely limited by the suitability of sites, can have only local significance, while wind energy suffers from the disadvantages of low concentration and unpredictable intermittency.

Far more speculative but also much more promising are the possibilities of solar energy and thermonuclear power. In spite of the serious technological problems posed by the irregularity of the sun's energy flow and its low concentration, it may be eventually possible to devise relatively efficient solar-electric power facilities. But much more immediately effective are likely to be thermal applications – low temperature heat for water heating, for space heating and cooling, for industrial processes such as drying (timber, fruit and other foodstuffs) and possibly for many of the uses to which steam produced from coal, oil or natural gas is now put. As regards transport fuels, it has been suggested that these can be derived from vegetation. Plants absorbing the sun's energy process the carbon dioxide in the air to produce cellulose, carbohydrates and other organic materials. If vegetation is gathered in very large amounts it can be processed to yield hydro-carbon fuels, although the economics of large-scale harvesting and processing has hardly begun to be considered. Moreover, the enormous area of land and water that would be required indicates that the feasibility of the proposal may be limited to countries with a large land mass and a low population density.[30] Solar energy no doubt holds much promise for the future, both because of the long duration of its source and its obvious environmental advantages, but it is most unlikely to replace fossil fuels within a foreseeable time span.

Much has been written in recent years about the potential of controlled thermonuclear fusion to provide an almost inexhaustible supply of energy with little radioactive waste.[31] However, the technological feasibility of the fusion reactor has yet to be demonstrated. The fuel costs would be low, given the abundance of hydrogen, but the cost of constructing a reactor which can contain the fuel in the required density and in temperatures of tens to hundreds of millions of degrees remains an unknown quantity. It is these doubts about the technical and financial prospects of nuclear fusion and the difficulties associated with the various other sources of energy which have led most western governments to plunge headlong into massive dependence on nuclear power from fission reactors, and given rise to projections of 900 nuclear plants in the world by 1985 with a capacity of 800,000 to 1,000,000 megawatts. The US Atomic Energy Commission has predicted that the United States alone would construct 900 nuclear plants by the year 2000 capable of satisfying nearly 50 per cent of the nation's power needs.

However, the difficulties surrounding the development of nuclear energy are many and varied. In the first place existing fission reactors use uranium very inefficiently, extracting only one or two per cent of the potential energy of this rather scarce fuel, which is eventually fissioned, either as uranium-235 or as plutonium made from uranium-238. According to a 1971 estimate, about 275,000 short tons of $6.00 to $10.00 per pound uranium oxide would be required to fuel reactors now on order to 1980, and another 400,000 tons to sustain them until the turn of the century.[32] However, it has been calculated that to meet all future requirements additional reserves of more than a million short tons will have to be discovered and developed by 1985.[33] Thus unless large new discoveries of low-cost uranium ore are made or unless it becomes economic to recover uranium at much higher prices (up to $30 or even $50 per lb), it is difficult to see how it will be possible to meet the rapidly accelerating targets in the production of nuclear energy.

The only other alternative is to develop a functioning breeder reactor which can transform fertile material into fissile fuel faster than it consumes fissile fuel itself. However, it is doubtful whether such reactors will be able to enter into commercial use before the late 1980s.[34] Apart from the substantial environmental costs of both the burner and the breeder reactor, of which more later, it is clear that nuclear power will not be cheap; that underdeveloped countries are unlikely to be able to make use of large plants and that small nuclear plants are much less economical than small plants operating on fossil fuels; that nuclear installations are designed to produce mainly electrical energy and are not, therefore, an easy substitute for many other forms of energy. In conditions of rising energy consumption, nuclear power can relieve but not eliminate the pressure on fossil fuels.

Although brief and highly simplified, the preceding discussion has attempted to show that while the current levels of known reserves do not set physical limits on energy consumption, they do give rise to several other limiting factors. Even if inexhaustible sources of energy can be harnessed, limitations on energy may nonetheless result from considerations of environmental and financial cost.[35] It is now widely accepted that the extraction, processing and use of most forms of energy create ecological and economic costs which may become increasingly intolerable. Unlimited resources cannot by themselves ensure sustained growth in the world system, if the application of technologies produces unacceptable levels of pollution.

Atmospheric pollution as a result of emissions of carbon monoxide, sulphur oxides, hydrocarbons, nitrogen oxides and solid particles has been the subject of growing concern and has led to increasing pressure for restrictions on the burning of fossil fuels. It is estimated that currently more than 20 billion tons of carbon dioxide are being released into the atmosphere from fossil fuel combustion each year. The discharge of these air pollutants and other solid wastes inevitably contributes to the pollution of rivers, lakes and oceans. Another closely related side effect of energy use is thermal pollution. The transfer of waste heat into streams often results in the disruption of the balance of aquatic life. Similarly, atmospheric waste heat can cause the formation of urban 'heat islands' leading to weather irregularities.[36] It has been argued that these are localized effects from which it is not possible to extrapolate on a global scale. However, if world energy consumption were to increase at 4 per cent a year for the next century, the heat released could begin to have a lasting impact on the temperature of the atmosphere and perhaps bring about a major climatic transformation.[37]

There are, of course, many other environmental costs resulting from energy use, of which despoliation of the countryside is an obvious example, but to complete this rather brief survey, we need dwell only on the twin factors of radiation and waste disposal associated with nuclear power. The release of radioactivity into the environment may occur through the mining or processing of the nuclear fuel or through the generation process itself. The mining of uranium is dangerous because it decays naturally into radon 222, a heavy gas which, on entering the body, can cause devastating effects through the emission of alpha ray particles. A disproportionately large number of uranium miners are known to have died from lung cancer.

An even greater risk arising from energy conversion through nuclear fission is the production of large quantities of extremely toxic radioactive materials which require infallible and prolonged isolation from the biosphere. Procedures for handling these very dangerous wastes, which contain strontium 90 and cesium 137 with hazard lives of 600 to 700 years, involve storage at the reprocessing plant for a period not to exceed 10 years, conversion to solid form, and shipment to a designated repository. Adequate safeguards must therefore be maintained not only during storage, conversion and shipment but for the whole period of disposal. However, most present methods for storage and disposal do not appear entirely satisfactory in terms of biological risks even for the present quantities of radioactive wastes, let alone for the much higher quantities expected in the relatively near future.[38] The other material produced in nuclear reactors employing uranium fuel is plutonium, which has a half life of 24,360 years and whose hazard life may extend beyond the duration of the human species. And yet large quantities of plutonium, much of it in the form of the isotope Pu,[239] could be in use and in transit by the end of the century if present plans for breeder reactors materialize. Any site of accidental dispersal would be contaminated for about half a million years.

Apart from the still unresolved problems of storage and disposal there remains the very real possibility of an accident at a nuclear plant. In the United States, the safety standards of the Atomic Energy Commission have come under increasing attack from numerous academic circles and environmental groups. In contrast to the comforting conclusions of the Rasmussen Report prepared for the US Atomic Energy Commission, a series of well-researched public disclosures in 1971 provided considerable evidence that the Emergency Core Cooling System, or basic safety system, of several nuclear reactors was faulty. In several areas, techniques for dealing with cooling problems were completely missing, while in others, existing techniques were described as incomplete, unverified, inadequate, imprecise or preliminary.[39] It has been calculated that in the event of an accident, the escape of radioactive gas from a major nuclear plant could kill everyone within a radius of 60 or more miles. The long-term effects of radiation would be felt for a considerable period over a much larger area. In order to provide the public with appropriate and fully tested safeguards against such hazards, it would be necessary to slow down the development of nuclear power generation and significantly increase its financial cost. However, prevailing trends pointed in the opposite direction, as western governments, and particularly the United States, were attempting to use the energy crisis to justify a far more liberal approach in the licensing of new power plants, with the emphasis on speed and economy rather than safety or foresight.

Equally dangerous was the prospect of nuclear proliferation arising from the vastly increased role for nuclear technology. As the Indian nuclear explosion of May 1974 has already demonstrated, aspiring nuclear powers will be able to rely increasingly for their nuclear weapons capability on fissionable material obtained from their civilian programme. It was estimated that in 1980 the world's nuclear reactors would be producing 350,000 kilograms of plutonium, one-third of which was likely to be located in the non-nuclear-weapon states, sufficient for them to develop some 12,000 nuclear weapons.[40] Nor were the possibilities of diversion from civilian industry to weapons-grade nuclear material likely to be confined to national governments. Several subnational and transnational organizations might in fact wish to acquire such material whether by overt or covert means. Given the necessary motivation and the technological feasibility of constructing a private bomb, it would not be surprising if at least a small fraction of the increasing volume of fissionable material in international transit were to find its way into the hands of persons or groups intent on nuclear sabotage, theft or blackmail.[41]

So far we have confined our discussion of the costs of energy growth to the depletion of non-renewable resources and the creation of environmental hazards. We have made no more than passing reference to the extensive investments that are required to finance the development of alternative forms of energy. Technical advances, whether they be in relation to transportation, storage or power generation, require the outlay of massive financial resources. Mention has already been made of the vast sums that would need to be expended on Project Independence. Large diameter pipelines, bulk liquefied natural gas tankers, underground refrigerated storage, enrichment uranium plants, all represent highly expensive technologies which have yet to be subjected to a thorough cost-benefit analysis from the perspective of the public as opposed to the private interest.

But even more far-reaching in its implications is the science of energy impact analysis, which raises the fundamental yet largely ignored question of the energy costs of energy technologies. For example, it is not outside the realm of possibility that the proposed sale of manufactured products by the oil-consumers to the oil-producers may involve the export of greater amounts of energy than oil imports. In this regard, one need only consider the shopping list of the Shah of Iran, which includes such items as nuclear power stations, gas liquefaction plants, liquid gas tankers, steel and petrochemical complexes, synthetic rubber as well as the most sophisticated military equipment. By way of another example, one may cite the search for oil and gas in previously neglected regions, which invariably necessitates the development of new techniques and new capital investment. The discovery rate may be maintained for some considerable time but probably at the expense of growing energy inputs. An energy economy that is reliant on coal conversion, oil-shales, tar sands and other marginal technologies may turn out to be a net consumer of energy. The main thrust of this argument is to highlight the gap between the monetary expression of an energy technology and the actual energy balance in terms of inputs and outputs. For instance, Project Independence, which would require capital investments over the next decade in excess of $1,000,000 million, might carry spectacularly large hidden energy costs, among which one would include the operation of on-site machinery such as pumps and cooling towers; the extraction of fuel as in the mining and milling of uranium ore; the construction of support facilities such as enrichment uranium plants and transport systems; research and development; administrative costs; and environmental safeguards. It is by no means certain that an accurate addition of all these energy costs would show fission technology to be a net producer of energy. Paradoxically, the nuclear programme might require a continuing subsidy from fossil fuels. Whatever the validity of this argument, the inescapable problem of all energy consumption which many economists and politicians have refused to face is that all forms of energy use must ultimately involve a degree of environmental decay. The very process of recycling involves the dissipation of additional matter and energy resources. To be viable, a long-term energy strategy must be made compatible with acceptable levels of pollution and resource depletion.

Social and ethical considerations

The first important conclusion which readily suggests itself is that energy accountancy, if it is accurately to reflect material and human reality, must be expressed in other than purely monetary terms. What is required is a holistic model to ensure that all resource costs, many of which are often disregarded by conventional bookkeeping methods, are subtracted from the gross energy output to determine net output. For this reason one cannot but welcome, whatever their technical limitations and oversights, the recent attempts to bring together forecasts of population growth, resource depletion, food supply, capital investment and pollution into one general model of the earth's ecosystem.[42] The value of such a perspective is that it brings to light the hidden costs of energy growth and exposes facile economic calculations which conceal the true nature of man's energy economy. Fundamentally at issue is the conflict between the finitude of man's material environment and continued exponential growth, between the unlimited expansion in energy consumption and the stability of the earth's energy cycle.

To the extent that matter and energy cannot be destroyed, it follows that the process of production must inevitably lead to a measure of depletion and pollution. Viewing the earth as a complete thermodynamic system, some have described this phenomenon in terms of the entropic nature of the economic process which transforms *available* or *free* energy, over which man has almost complete command into unavailable or bound energy, which man cannot possibly use.[43] Thus, for example, when coal is burned, its initial free energy is dissipated in the form of heat, smoke and ashes which man cannot readily use. It has been degraded into bound energy. This is not to argue that the burning of coal may not be a valuable activity but simply that the benefit has a corresponding cost. Similarly, if one were to take the world economy as a whole, it is clear that the very attempt to maintain or enhance the existing human and material stock involves a trade-off between different benefits or different costs. The precise point at which such a trade-off should occur may be illuminated by economic and ecological considerations but is ultimately determined by ethical values and judgments.

At this point a few examples of the hidden costs of energy growth may clarify the underlying social and normative implications. It may be true that the mechanization of agriculture permits an increasing proportion of arable land to be allocated to food production, but by replacing the draft animal with the tractor, man is also replacing the use of solar energy through photosynthesis with terrestrial energy (normally derived from some fossil fuel). The same process is at work in the replacement of manure with synthetic fertilizer. Both of these economic shifts may be valuable and even necessary in the short-run, but they undoubtedly represent a long-term cost in so far as the production of food is increasingly made to depend on the scarcer of two energy resources.

A somewhat different but closely related argument may be made in relation to the growing consumption of electrical energy. Herman Daly has shown that the exponential increase in the generation of electricity, with a doubling rate every decade, may not serve the objectives which have been ascribed to it.[44] He examines in some detail four benefits frequently cited as flowing from higher levels of energy consumption: increased living standards, more adequate recycling, higher levels of employment and a more adequate military capability for purposes of security. His analysis demonstrates that these four interrelated aims are an integral part of the concept of open-ended growth. The first two are obviously complementary since greater industrial production leads to greater pollution which necessitates more adequate recycling of waste, which in turn will require more energy inputs whose costs may be greater than the pollution they are designed to neutralize. On the question of employment the inescapable fact is that the increased supply of non-human energy is intended to substitute human labour. Electrical energy may raise productivity per worker but is unlikely to increase the level of employment unless it is assumed that the total output is growing faster than the rate at which energy is replacing human labour. Clearly, the assumption is one of limitless growth based on infinite wants and the development of massive advertising techniques. Increased per capita consumption is not an end in itself but the mechanism necessary to perpetuate the growth syndrome and keep rates of return on investment sufficiently high to maintain the continuing expansion of production. In the case of the military sector, the arms race provides the obvious catalyst for unlimited growth, which depletes the civilian economy of valuable resources and technical personnel. Greater energy inputs in the military sector thus reduce civilian productivity while achieving diminishing levels of security.

Far from being universal or permanent, the benefits of higher rates of energy consumption may prove to be severely limited in both space and time. The economic affluence which a minority now enjoys may have been gained at the expense of the less privileged regions of the world, but also of entire generations yet unborn, for the vital question is not simply how many energy growth can help to feed, but how long it can feed them. Increasingly, man's condition may be one of scarcity because he has reached the limits not of his physical but of his political and moral resources. The growth structure of advanced industrial society is such as to make adjustment to a stable or moderately declining gross national product almost impossible without accompanying sharp falls in investment, soaring levels of unemployment, and intensified social and political conflict. As for the victims of underdevelopment, the prospect of energy growth has offered the hope or at least the illusion of progress. It has been the function of the energy crisis to shatter these hopes and illusions and to highlight the conflicting demands of growth and distributive justice. It remains to be seen how overdeveloped and underdeveloped countries will respond to this challenge, and whether they will reassess the philosophy which has made economic growth the overriding objective and supreme justification of social organization.

8. The security crisis

Whatever adaptive function organized violence may have played in the early stages of human evolution,[1] no one can dispute the increasing destructiveness of war which has resulted from the much higher levels of organization and technology achieved by man since the advent of the bronze age. Man's failure to develop effective mechanisms for the prevention of war may be ascribed in part to his inability to evolve adequate responses to the international environment and to the inescapable fact of scarcity. Given the limited nature of the world's resources and the often mutually exclusive character of conflicting value-systems, societies have tended to operate in conditions of scarcity or, at least, perceived scarcity. It is precisely in these terms that several theorists of international relations have sought to explain the incidence and intensity of war.[2]

In a systematic analysis of the dynamics of international conflict, Choucri and North have argued that the antagonistic competition between national or imperial interests is largely a function of population, resources and technology.[3] They begin by making the obvious point that, within any finite environment, an increasing population will lead to rising demands for food and other essential resources. Similarly, the more advanced the level of technology, the greater the variety and the quantity of resources needed by that society. In other words, a growing population and a developing technology are both important factors contributing to the perception of scarcity. In order to satisfy the needs or demands of their respective population, governments and economic elites will allocate a certain production of the available human and material resources of society in order to develop specialized capabilities, enabling them to expand beyond their original boundaries. This phenomenon, which the authors describe as 'lateral pressure', is the essence of all imperialism or empire-building and underlies the contemporary struggle among great powers for strategic bases, control of the seas, and access to raw materials, markets and investment opportunities.

In a system of sovereign states, scarcity, whether measured in absolute or relative terms, need not always refer to territory or to material resources. It may involve such intangibles as status, prestige or ideology. Either because of the actual scarcity of resources and their uneven distribution or because of the fear of potential scarcity, states tend to develop an ethnocentric orientation whereby the external environment is often pictured as threatening and hostile, and the values and achievements of domestic society become symbols of exclusive loyalty.[4] In this sense, a fragmented international system, although not necessarily conducive to zero-sum outcomes, may nevertheless produce zero-sum perceptions which distort inter-societal images, breed international mistrust and suspicion and contribute to the generalized feeling of insecurity. It is not possible to analyse here the complex psychological and cultural origins of this state of mind, but its net effect has been to reinforce and universalize both the general assumption of future violence and the state of constant military preparedness.

One of the great paradoxes of the contemporary system of international relations is that war has frequently resulted not simply from the perception of insecurity but from the very initiatives taken by states to preserve their security. Traditional solutions to the problem of war, far from achieving their purpose, have frequently produced the very state of affairs they were intended to prevent. The strategy of meeting force with force, whether unilaterally or through the agency of some collective security arrangement, has been a self-defeating exercise, at least from the point of view of the maintenance of peace. On the other hand, disarmament proposals for the total or even partial abolition of the means for waging armed conflict have proved equally unavailing. No more successful have been the efforts to regulate or minimize the level of international violence through the operation of international law or the development of international organization. As for the establishment of a balance of power, the outcome has usually entailed relatively short periods of order punctuated by intermittent outbreaks of violence, eventually leading to large-scale war. Conceptual fallacies and structural deficiencies have either invalidated or hindered these traditional approaches to the search for security, and helped to maintain the system in a state of constant disequilibrium.

The use of force

International relations have often been described in terms of the interacting policies of states, each seeking to safeguard its sovereignty and independence. Accordingly, the international system is represented as a fragmentary structure whose constituent units operate largely in a context of actual or potential rivalry. Each state can ultimately count only on itself. Thus, it is argued, in a world of sovereign states security must rest on the availability of force, by which is meant those resources already converted or readily convertible into military power. Paradoxically, it is the very reliance which states have placed on armed force as a means of ensuring their security which has been one of the major factors responsible for the occurrence of wars.

It is of course in the very nature of a great power to regard its military capability as a useful instrument for modifying an otherwise hostile environment and removing what are considered to be actual or potential dangers to security. A case in point is the behaviour of the United States, especially since the development of the cold war in the late 1940s. In accordance with the policy of containment, American policy-makers tended to interpret any communist success, whether achieved by revolutionary or parliamentary means, as a long-term threat to American security, or, at the very least, as a challenge to the kind of economic and political world order which the United States was determined to create. In order to deny victory to these communist movements – often thought to be directed from Moscow or Peking – the United States has engaged in a long series of overt and covert military interventions in the rimlands of East and Southeast Asia, the Middle East, Africa and the Western Hemisphere.[5] It is doubtful, however, whether any of these military actions have made a positive contribution to security, although it is probably only in relation to Indochinese war that the total futility and unprecedented human and material cost of American interventionism have been clearly and widely appreciated.[6]

However, it is not merely the actual use but also the very possession and deployment of military power which has proved counter-productive in terms of the security objective. Once a state accumulates a large arsenal of destructive power, a situation is invariably created in which other states feel their security to be threatened. The mutual feeling of insecurity is then intensified by the self-reinforcing mechanism inherent in an arms race. Measures taken by one state to increase its defensive power are interpreted by another state as offensive in intent. The latter will seek to meet this threat by increasing its own military capability, thereby inciting the former to expand further its plans for military preparedness. Competing policies of escalating armament and rearmament eventually produce an explosive situation in which each of the conflicting parties, convinced of the inevitability of war, is left with little choice but to determine the most appropriate time for initiating hostilities. If war is deemed unavoidable, then it only remains for each state to decide on the political, strategic and psychological conditions most conducive to victory.

For a classical contemporary example of a regional arms race, one need simply examine the development of the Arab–Israeli dispute. The competition in armaments, which began with the arming of Zionist settlers in Palestine and the creation of the Jewish state in 1948, soon produced the anticipated Arab attack. Although a large influx of arms enabled Israel to bring the combined Arab armies to a standstill, the subsequent injection of Soviet military hardware into Egypt and other Arab states demonstrated once again the inherent instability of the prevailing equilibrium. The escalating tension of the mid-1950s prompted Israeli leaders to take advantage of the Suez crisis by striking first in October 1956 in order to remove the alleged possibility of an Arab strike. However, far from putting an end to the state of mutual mistrust, the war was soon followed by an intensified arms race eventually leading to another Israeli preemptive attack in June 1967 and to the occupation of several Arab territories. Unable to force Israel's withdrawal from occupied territory, Egypt launched a war of attrition along the Suez canal in the hope of raising the manpower costs of the conflict beyond the enemy's endurance. The Israeli air force retaliated by carrying out several punitive expeditions deep into Arab territory, thereby encouraging the introduction of additional Soviet weaponry and a new phase in the Arab–Israeli arms race. The ensuing war of October 1973 inflicted heavy casualties and severe military losses on both sides but did little to improve the prospects for a Middle East settlement.[7] In spite of this fourth major Middle East confrontation in the space of twenty-five years, the Arabs and Palestinians were still deprived of the territories which they regarded as theirs, while the Israelis still had no guarantee that the Arabs, encouraged by the increasingly effective use of their oil power, would not resume hostilities at a time and in circumstances of their choosing.

The foregoing discussion has served to illustrate the argument that the attempt to achieve security by relying on the use, the threat, or the acquisition of military force may simply serve to prolong or magnify rather than resolve the conflict. In reality, dependence on armed force as a major instrument of foreign policy has not only increased the probability of inter-state violence but also diminished the capacity of military power to guarantee a state's territorial integrity.

In elaborating this argument, we may briefly refer to the concept of declining 'territoriality' as developed by John Herz.[8] In the European state system of the sixteenth to the eighteenth centuries, states would quarrel and attack but seldom annihilate each other. Their fortress-type shells of defence could normally survive a frontal assault, and provide them with a considerable degree of external security. Since the nineteenth century, however, several political and economic developments have severely diminished the state's capability for unconditional survival. Among the more important we may list: the shift from limited to total war characterized by national conscription and the increasing destructiveness of weapons; the enhanced effectiveness of economic warfare (e.g. economic blockade); the growing recourse to ideological–political penetration (e.g. subversive techniques of persuasion and intimidation); the development of air warfare; the advent of nuclear force; the production of chemical and biological weapons; the rising tide of urban terrorism and aerial piracy.

These combined trends have sharply reduced the degree of state defensibility and contributed to the mounting sense of insecurity in international relations. As states feel less and less secure, they double and redouble their efforts to accumulate an arsenal of military force sufficiently terrifying to deter the enemy. But the accumulation of large military capabilities merely intensifies the feeling of insecurity and thereby produces a never-ending spiralling arms race. Applied to the relations of the great powers since the late 1940s, this phenomenon has come to be known as the 'balance of terror'. The two super-powers and their respective military blocs, motivated by a feeling of insecurity derived from the immeasurable power of destruction available to both of them, as well as from mutual fear and suspicion reinforced by the ideological gap, have felt compelled to compete for ever more power in order to find security.

At the time of the Cuban missile crisis, the US and Soviet nuclear stockpiles were calculated at 35 kilomegatons (35,000 million tons of TNT) and 20 kilomegatons (20,000 million tons of TNT) respectively, their joint nuclear arsenal amounting to some 16 tons of explosive power for every human being on earth.[9] But gross megatonnage and even the available number of missile launchers are no longer regarded as the decisive indicators of destructive capability. The most meaningful and realistic measurement of nuclear deterrence is said to be the number of separate warheads that can be delivered accurately on individual high-priority targets with sufficient power to destroy them. After taking into account the provisions of the SALT agreements, it is expected that by the end of the 1970s the United States will have more than 10,000 such warheads, while the corresponding number for the Soviet Union is likely to be in the vicinity of 5,000. Clearly, both powers will have several times the capacity to destroy each other's total population and industry. In 1974, the US defence budget amounted to $85,800 million while the corresponding figure for the Soviet Union was $33,056 million.[10] According to estimates published in 1972 by the US Department of State, combined Soviet and American expenditure on defence since World War II had already exceeded 2,000,000 million dollars.[11]

On what grounds are such vast expenditures and destructive

capabilities justified? Why are states so anxious to acquire lethal weapons, when their use would obviously result in a total war which would destroy all semblance of national life? In pre-nuclear times, there was at least some plausibility to the proposition that, where peaceful means failed, war might, at least in certain circumstances, be a rational instrument of policy with a reasonable expectation of gains exceeding the costs involved. By contrast, rather than help to preserve or attain anything of value, nuclear weapons now threaten to destroy everything that is valuable, for in a major nuclear exchange there would be no survivors let alone any victors.

These self-evident considerations have led policy-makers and strategists to conclude that the principal function of the nuclear weapon is not defence but deterrence. The potential aggressor will not dare strike if he is threatened with a retaliatory blow which would result in unacceptable damage. However, for the threat to be credible, the opponent must demonstrate his resolve as well as his capacity to retaliate by inflicting intolerable destruction. Faced with the risk of virtual suicide, a nuclear power will therefore desist from attacking since the price to be paid will almost certainly be greater than any possible gain. The logic of deterrence thus appears to be perfectly rational, but it is here precisely that the strategy is most vulnerable for it depends for its success on the rationality of the protagonists in the conflict. Is there, however, any guarantee of such rationality? Can one rely on decision-makers operating in situations of severe emotional stress to make cool-headed, dispassionate calculations of the relationship between ends and means? Is the political and military leadership of every nuclear power capable of making the same rational choices that one expects of players in a game of chess? Several exponents of the deterrence strategy have insisted that the dangers of the nuclear era must be faced calmly and realistically. Herman Kahn, among others, has continually emphasized the need to think and prepare for 'the unthinkable'.[12] Peace and war, conventional and nuclear weapons are not, strictly speaking, separate phenomena. They are all elements of a complex diplomatic and military game, which the contestants can and must use to advantage.[13]

The attempt to revive the Clausewitzean philosophy of war and portray nuclear violence as a continuation of politics by other means has given rise to such concepts as 'flexible response', 'limited nuclear war', and the 'diplomacy of violence'. According to the notion of 'graduated response', which is designed to bridge the gap between nuclear warfare and conventional military strategy, the principal military objective, even in an atomic exchange, should be the destruction of the enemy's military forces, not of his civilian population.[14] More recently, the US administration has inclined towards a 'counterforce' strategy which, it is claimed, would offer a much wider range of options in response to potential action by the enemy, including a capability for precise attacks on both soft and hard targets, while at the same time minimizing unintended damage to industrial sites. It is difficult to understand, however, how the new military projects required by the adoption of the counterforce strategy (e.g. procurement of more Minuteman III missiles, refinement of existing guidance systems, development of a terminally guided manoeuvrable reentry vehicle (MARV), construction of new-generation intercontinental ballistic missiles) would actually limit civilian damage, given a substantial nuclear strike.[15]

In spite of the most ingenious intellectual gymnastics performed by strategic analysts, these and other endeavours to harmonize the use of nuclear power with the specific requirements of military and political objectives have remained unconvincing, for they overlook the simple but fundamental attribute of nuclear weapons, which is to unleash devastating violence on the enemy, without nevertheless achieving military victory in any accepted sense of the word. Nor can nuclear weapons, however effective or destructive, prevent the enemy from inflicting unendurable damage by way of retaliation. This is the inevitable outcome of a situation of mutually assured destruction, as now prevails in the global strategic balance, in which both superpowers enjoy a second strike capability. It is because nuclear war is essentially a contest in national destruction that the use of military force can no longer achieve its original objective. It is now impossible to remove the threat to one's own military security without at the same time destroying the enemy nation, thereby inviting massive retaliation. In the nuclear era the power to hurt has vastly outdistanced the power to defend.[16]

Not only does nuclear violence offer little prosepct of military success, it precludes the possibility of political control over military operations. By comprising the most catastrophic devastation into an almost momentary span of time, nuclear weapons drastically affect the politics of war, the process of decision-making, the opportunities for control and restraint. The very speed with which the nuclear weapon can reach its destination and fulfil its purpose creates an insuperable barrier between war and politics. The increasing computerization of nuclear strategy clearly indicates that once it begins, nuclear war will have been taken out of human hands. Nor can one reasonably expect anything like the restraints on violence that have usually operated after a conventional military test of strength since a major nuclear contest is, by its very nature, a massive exercise in civilian violence in which restraint and moderation may not be feasible either after or during the actual exchange.

Now it is true that the rationale of nuclear deterrence lies not so much in the use as in the threatened use of the nuclear weapon. It is the threat of nuclear holocaust which ensures its prevention. Despite the surface plausibility of this premise and the apparent ability until now of the two superpowers to maintain their adversary relationship below the threshhold of nuclear violence, it is nonetheless difficult to avoid the conclusion that far from promoting international stability and security, the balance of terror, which is an exercise in competitive risk-taking based on brinkmanship and bluff, has considerably accentuated the conditions of hostility, suspicion and tension which dominate the existing international system. Indeed, it is because the nuclear deterrent does not result in a lasting sense of security that nuclear powers are constantly revising their nuclear strategies and expanding their nuclear capabilities. Given that a state can never know exactly the intentions of its opponent, it feels constrained to prepare for the worst plausible rather than the most probable case. Indicative of this tendency was the decision of the United States in 1961 to undertake a major build-up of its Minuteman and Polaris forces in anticipation of a hypothetical Soviet strategic build-up which did subsequently materialize, but only in response to the American initiative which threatened to endow the United States with a possible first-strike capability. The futility of the action–reaction phenomenon which fuels the nuclear arms race underlines the supreme irony of nuclear power which, for all its awesome destructiveness, remains essentially non-usable power since its use would negate the very notion of deterrence.

The crisis of national security which confronts the world's nuclear powers is now greater than at any other time for the simple reason that the accuracy and destructiveness of the arsenals available to their opponents have vastly increased. The enormous strategic superiority which the United States enjoyed during the 1950s did not make the American nation feel more secure. It merely encouraged the Soviet Union and China to develop their own nuclear capabilities and strengthened the conviction that vital national interests could be defended only by reliance on nuclear weapons. It is doubtful whether the nuclear threat, which was brought into play during the Berlin crises of 1958 and 1961, the confrontation over Cuba in 1962 and the Middle East conflict of 1973, safeguarded any vital American interests either in Europe, Latin America or the Middle East. On the contrary, these crises have contributed to a far more pervasive climate of fear and mistrust in which great and small powers alike continue to suffer from a profound sense of insecurity. The trend towards so-called stability in the balance of terror does not point to a new era of peace and security but to a more equal strategic relationship, as a result of which both superpowers as well as lesser nuclear powers are trapped in an arms race which they dare not abandon for fear of allowing their rivals to establish an unbridgeable gap in destructive capability. Nuclear stalemate is no more successful than nuclear superiority in achieving psychological security.

In conditions of 'atomic plenty', nations and political elites have a much chastened confidence in the logic of nuclear deterrence. For, while they realize that security depends on the hope of never using the very weapons they are constantly threatening to use, they also know that deterrence is credible only so long as there exists a real possibility of all-out nuclear war. They understand that deterrence relies on the commitment to retaliate even when retaliation is likely to result in even greater devastation and unacceptable damage. They are obliged, therefore, to prefer a nuclear exchange to surrender even though surrender may be preferable to a nuclear exchange. They can barely avoid the conclusion that the balance of terror depends for its effectiveness on a piece of incredible bluff, since it seeks to make credible an incredible threat, and the more incredible it becomes the more convincing it needs to be. Nowhere is the problem of credibility more acute than in those situations where nuclear retaliation is threatened in response to a conventional attack, or where one member of an alliance serves notice on the potential aggressor that aggression against any other member of the alliance will be opposed, if necessary, with the aid of nuclear weapons. In conditions of nuclear parity, can one reasonably expect the United States to use its nuclear weapons in defence of Europe, were it to be attacked by Russian conventional forces? Differently expressed, would Washington be willing to sacrifice New York for Paris or Chicago for London? It is on this critical yet ultimately unstable pillar that rests much of the edifice of nuclear strategy.

It has been argued that, however shaky the foundations of this edifice, it is nonetheless thanks to it that the world has been spared a global military confrontation. It is perfectly true that since 1945 the United States and the Soviet Union have not faced each other on the battlefield. By the same token, it is not possible to infer from this fact that it is solely or even primarily the nuclear deterrent which has prevented a nuclear holocaust. In the enthusiasm to prove their case, strategic theorists often lose sight of the rather obvious point that without nuclear weaponry any conflict involving the great powers would be fought at a much lower level of violence. In any case, deterrence is one of those circular conceptual constructs which by definition cannot be invalidated since it interprets the absence of the postulated threat as evidence not of the irrelevance but of the eficacy of the policy. Deterrence thus becomes a self-fulfilling prophecy and a self-perpetuating phenomenon which continues to thrive long after the threat has ceased to exist – assuming that it existed in the first place. Indeed, the greater the original commitment to the policy, the greater the financial and psychological investment necessary to sustain it and the greater the reluctance to abandon it. No cost is considered high enough when compared with the magnitude of the threat which is supposedly deterred. With the passage of time there develops within society a complex web of powerful economic, political and military interests with a stake in the continuation of the balance of terror. In due course, the dynamic of deterrence spreads to more and more countries, all eager to take advantage of the benefits presumed to derive from this form of military preparedness. In reality, nuclear proliferation simply complicates strategic calculations and further diminishes the predictability of state behaviour. The consequent randomness of the strategic system is but one more sign of its essential irrationality and of its considerable and steadily rising vulnerability to human or technical error.

The foregoing analysis of the logic of nuclear deterrence is not intended to suggest that the world is set on an irreversible course towards extinction, but simply to indicate that the balance of terror heightens the feeling of insecurity, exacerbates and enlarges existing local and regional conflicts, and reduces the scope of diplomacy. The conditions, in which any arms race – a fortiori a nuclear arms race – is likely to develop, are seldom conducive to peace. It is precisely because the risks and costs inherent in the feverish competition for nuclear sufficiency have become so painfully evident in the last twenty or thirty years that the impulse to disarm has remained alive even among the most realistic and hard-headed military and diplomatic circles.

Disarmament

Disarmament proposals have traditionally come to the fore after the conclusion of great wars. After the Napoleonic wars the Tsar of Russia led a movement for disarmament as part of a larger plan for a European system of state relations based on Christian principles. A more concrete proposal was made by Tsar Nicholas II who, in 1898, invited the sovereign states of the world to send representatives to a conference at the Hague to consider the possibility of mutual agreement on the reduction of armaments. However, the Hague Conference of 1899 did little more than express the desirability of disarmament by general agreement. The second Hague Conference of 1907 adopted a code of regulations for the more humane conduct of wars, although it is doubtful whether any power felt itself bound by them in those cases when observance of the law might mean defeat. On the question of the limitation of armaments, a resolution was passed which proved as ineffective as that of the first conference. A renewed impetus for disarmament negotiations came after the end of World War I and was personified by the more enthusiastic supporters of the League of Nations. The more conciliatory atmosphere in international relations engendered by the conclusion of the Kellogg Pact was reflected in the agreements on naval limitation signed in 1922 and 1930 by Great Britain, the United States, France, Italy and Japan. The Geneva Disarmament Conference of 1932 considered several proposals, including the suggestion of a proportional reduction of the existing forces of all powers by one-half, one-third or one-fourth; the prohibition of certain types of warfare such as submarine attack; a financial agreement restricting military expenditure within the agreed limit. None of these proposals was adopted and the conference adjourned to 1933. Germany, now increasingly bellicose in its attitude, withdrew from the conference, and, although it returned for a short period, finally withdrew from both the conference and the League of Nations. After another session in 1934 the Conference acknowledged its failure, as indicated by the feverish arms race which ensued.

In the post-1945 period, the record of disarmament negotiations has been equally unimpressive. In spite of the formulation of several proposals such as the Baruch plan, neither the United States nor the Soviet Union acted as if it believed general and complete disarmament to be a feasible policy objective. In spite of the Soviet and American common purpose in preventing a nuclear exchange, essential disagreements arose between Moscow and Washington in relation to central political issues as well as to the seemingly more technical questions of inspection and timetable. Throughout the 1950s and 1960s, the two superpowers participated in negotiations covering such diverse proposals as nuclear disarmament, conventional disarmament, the creation of a centralized military force, the reduction in the production of fissionable materials, a partial or total test ban, various forms of inspection to prevent surprise attacks, the establishment of nuclear free zones, the removal of overseas military bases, the reduction of defence expenditures, the prohibition of the use of space or the seabed for military purposes. However, the adversary relationship between the two great powers and the lingering mistrust of one another's intentions have thus far constituted a major stumbling block to any substantive agreement.

The explanation for the failure of these numerous disarmament initiations may be found, at least in part, in the very nature of the fragmented international system in which states have to operate. In the nuclear age, perhaps more than ever before, states are reluctant to abandon their military capacity which they regard as the ultimate protection of their interests and, above all, of their security. Given the prevailing climate of ethnocentric suspicion, ideological rivalry, and the expectation of future violence, the policy-makers of most great powers have little confidence that any disarmament arrangement will preclude the possibility of its violation.

Doubts as to whether any disarmament agreement would be respected by all the signatories arose in some instances out of the belief that the resources of concealment were greater than the resources of inspection. In the early years of nuclear deterrence, reference was often made, especially by US administrations, to the opportunities for diverting hidden atomic bombs, building secret process plants and secretly detonating underground atomic devices.[17] Although subsequent improvements in detection equipment significantly neutralized the techniques for concealing strategic operations, the problem of control and inspection remained a complicating factor in relation not only to nuclear weapons but also to chemical and biological warfare which holds even greater possibilities for secrecy and camouflage.

In any case, the issues of concealment, inspection and enforcement are themselves manifestations of the much deeper and more serious phenomenon of mutual mistrust and hostility. As the SALT talks have recently demonstrated, the great dilemma of all disarmament initiatives is that they can succeed only when the situation they are attempting to bring about is already in existence. This is not to suggest that disarmament can never eventuate until states competing in an arms race have settled all their outstanding disputes. On the other hand, the political conditions prevailing at any given time will determine to a large extent the concessions which each state is inclined to make and the trust it is prepared to place in the formal affirmations of other states.

A closely related factor which has consistently militated against substantive disarmament is that proposals for arms reductions or arms limitations are usually interpreted as favouring one state at the expense of another. Disarmament measures are likely to be universally acceptable only when they are of equal benefit to all states. But such a situation is unlikely to arise as long as states have different or contradictory perceptions. A case in point has been the refusal of both China and France to subscribe to the limited Test Ban Treaty of August 1963. Obviously, China and France were opposed to any agreement which would perpetuate their position of military inferiority vis-à-vis the two superpowers. Similar considerations have prompted several countries to retain the nuclear option and to refuse to sign or ratify the Non-Proliferation Treaty (NPT) which came into force in 1970, and in which nuclear members pledge not to transfer to non-nuclear states – and the latter not to accept from the former – any nuclear materials or technology to be used for military purposes. The treaty is ultimately unenforceable, and signatories may in fact withdraw from its obligations upon three-month notification, by informing the UN Security Council of the 'extraordinary events' which have precipitated such a course of action. China, France and several non-nuclear states have objected to the treaty on the grounds that it is primarily a Soviet–American device designed to consolidate their strategic superiority by institutionalizing their unique ability to offer and withdraw the nuclear umbrella. It is, therefore, hardly surprising that the NPT should exclude two nuclear powers and many states within reach of developing a nuclear capability. India's detonation of its first nuclear device in May 1974, the continuing atmosphere tests by France and China, the Nevada underground tests by Britain, the American offer of nuclear power reactors and enriched uranium to Egypt and Israel, and France's decision to sell five nuclear power reactors to Iran are indicative of the trend towards escalation and proliferation in the nuclear arms race.

All disarmament proposals face the almost insuperable difficulty of reconciling the principle of the equality of states with objective conditions of strategic inequality. Any effective disarmament must rest on one of two assumptions. Either it envisages the transformation of the international system from an unequal to an equal balance of military power, in which case the stronger states are unlikely to accept such an arrangement since it deprives them of their major instrument in the coercion of weaker states. Or it aims at a general but proportional reduction of armaments; that is, at the maintenance of the existing relation of forces, in which case opposition is likely to arise from states which, though militarily weaker for the moment, are not prepared to see their position of military inferiority frozen into a state of legal permanence.

In response to the above difficulties governments have been increasingly attracted by the prospect of arms control as opposed to disarmament. The arms control school subscribes to the view that, since disarmament lacks feasibility for a variety of military, political and psychological reasons, emphasis should be placed on the control rather than the abolition of arms.[18] Proponents of this approach are essentially concerned to reduce the risk of a general war, whether by accident (human error or technical fault), by the escalation of a local conflict, or by the strategic miscalculation of one or other of the major nuclear powers. At face value, arms control would appear to have had in recent years a measure of success, as indicated by the Antarctica Treaty which forbade the militarization of Antarctica and prohibited nuclear testing there (1959), the Limited Test Ban Treaty (1963), the Latin American Denuclearization Treaty (1967), the Outer Space Treaty prohibiting the stationing of nuclear weapons in interplanetary space (1967), the Non-Proliferation Treaty (1970), the Soviet–American Treaty on Anti-Ballistic Missiles and the Interim Agreement on Strategic Offensive Missiles (1972), the Soviet–American Agreement on the Prevention of Nuclear War (1973), the Agreement on the Limitation of Underground Nuclear Weapons Tests, as well as the continuing negotations on Mutual Force Reductions in Europe. Impressive though it may appear at first sight, this series of agreements may ultimately do little more than diminish the sense of urgency and crisis over the continuing arms race and thereby produce a false sense of security. Even if one were to regard arms control as a worthwhile development, it would be difficult to avoid the conclusion that it succeeds only at the periphery of the problem and leaves unresolved the central question as to how nations may achieve lasting security in a world still dominated by a precarious balance of terror.

Thus far, in examining the obstacles to disarmament, we have confined our attention to the structure of the international system, that is, to the diplomatic and strategic environment in which states have to operate. But the impulse to arm or disarm is as much a function of domestic pressures as of external constraints. Recent history would suggest that the very fabric of the modern industrial state gives rise to a complex network of pressures conducive to high and rising military expenditures. It is in order to describe and analyse this phenomenon that several studies have developed the concept of the 'military–industrial complex'.[19] Significantly, in his farewell address to the nation in January 1961, President Eisenhower recognized the existence of a permanent armaments industry of vast proportions, and of powerful economic and political pressures tending towards the creation of a 'garrison state'.

As one would expect, the military services play a vital role in shaping the US military budget. Locked in fierce competition amongst themselves for a greater share of the budget, the army, navy and airforce are all constantly trying to win support for their particular doctrines, projects and long-term requirements. The services go to considerable pains to maintain a close relationship with the legislature and particularly with the Armed Services and Appropriations Committees. It is estimated that in fiscal year 1967 the lobbying effort of the Defence Department and of the military services had cost nearly $4 million.[20]

Complementing these pressures are those emanating from the defence contractors and especially from those large companies which depend for a large proportion of their business on military contracts. An analysis of the 38 major defence contractors for the period 1961–67 showed there were 15 companies that derived more than half of their income from military production.[21] In fiscal year 1967, McDonnell Douglas received $2,125 million in defence contracts, while the other four largest Pentagon contractors, General Dynamics, Lockheed Aircraft, General Electric, and United Aircraft were also awarded contracts totalling in excess of $1,000 million.[22] Despite the heavy concentration of major awards among a few companies, extensive sub-contracting ensures that research expenditures, employment and profits are spread far more widely through the economy.

It is calculated that Pentagon spending has involved awards to 22,000 prime contractors and some 100,000 sub-contractors, that 76 industries are oriented primarily towards military production, and that the shipbuilding and aircraft industries owe more than half their income to defence contracts. In the years 1966–7, the Vietnam War is estimated to have provided employment for one million people, representing 23 per cent of the total increase in the workforce during this period. While these statistics are by no means conclusive, they do provide solid evidence in support of the proposition that a vast network of economic, political and military interests within American society has an ideological or material stake in a large military establishment. In this sense, the military–industrial complex may be said to consist of a very loosely structured coalition of converging or overlapping interests, in which are represented the armed services, private industry and finance, the legislative and executive organs of government, trade unions, the scientific and technical professions, colleges and universities.

At this point, it should be stressed that the military–industrial complex is not a phenomenon peculiar to the United States. Its existence is also evident, though somewhat less pervasive, in the highly industrialized societies of Western Europe and even in some of the underdeveloped societies of the Third World. However, it is in the Soviet Union that one is likely to find the other most striking manifestation of a network of interlocking interests with a high stake in defence spending. The armed forces, the defence industries, heavy industry in general and important elements of the Soviet Communist Party and of the scientific and technocratic community are obviously linked by a tacit understanding regarding the interdependence between security, ideology, heavy industry and professional competence.[23]

It would appear then that the internal pressures emanating from the growth of the military–industrial complex, however uncoordinated they may be, are often capable of engendering or accelerating an arms race. The long-standing efforts of the US military establishment to identify and bridge such fictitious gaps in American defence capability as the bomber gap and the missile gap, and the more recent campaign for the deployment of an anti-ballistic missile system, are indicative of the capacity of the domestic environment to condition perceptions and responses to imaginary external threats. Any large military–industrial complex must inevitably have repercussions far beyond its national boundaries. Indeed, the cold war may be said to have resulted from the interaction of two rival complexes, each seeking to gain an advantage over the other, yet each indispensable to the other in order to justify its own existence, its actions, strategic doctrines and procurement policies.

The large military establishments of the great powers have also made their presence felt through arms transfers either as commercial transactions or in the form of military aid. It is no coincidence that countries with the largest defence expenditures, such as the United States, the Soviet Union, France and Britain should also be the greatest beneficiaries of the arms trade. According to a recent study by the US Arms Control and Disarmament Agency, US arms sales abroad from 1963 to the end of 1973 totalled $29,700 million while Russian sales during the same period amounted to $15,600 million. Even more striking is the rate of growth in arms transfers. In 1963, American and Soviet weapons sales amounted to $1,190 million and $1,200 million respectively; in 1968 these exports had risen to $2,680 million and $1,370 million and in 1973 to $5,000 million and $2,500 million respectively. By 1975, US sales of weapons, support equipment and training services to foreign governments totalled $9,500 million.

Apart from the substantial contribution made to private profits and to the national balance of payments, arms transfers are an important source of political influence, since the recipient country becomes increasingly dependent on the supplier country for the procurement of the most up-to-date weapons, for training and guidance in their proper use as well as for spare parts. In fact, it is the military–industrial complexes of the great powers which have been responsible for training and equipping the military elites of most Third World countries and which have, therefore, a direct stake in the outcome and, in some cases, the perpetuation of many regional conflicts, as suggested by the Soviet, American, French and British roles in the Middle East, the Indian subcontinent and Indochina. Given the nature of these diverse but powerful and closely intertwined incentives, it should come as little surprise to the student of international affairs that disarmament should have made until now such mediocre and spasmodic progress.

Collective security

Conscious of the obvious dangers stemming from the unilateral use of force and aware of the general failure of disarmament negotiations, states have become increasingly attracted to the notion of collective security. Central to the concept are two conditions: firstly, that all states participating in the treaty system will consider the prevention of aggression as the overriding objective of foreign policy; and secondly, that states will be ready to oppose aggression with measures adequate for the preservation of peace.[24] In a system of collective security peace is to be enforced by the police action of peace-loving, sovereign states against recalcitrant, aggressive states, while the police force is to be provided by the collective organization of states which, ideally, would have a universal membership. The Covenant of the League of Nations and the Charter of the United Nations represent to date the two most comprehensive experiments in collective security.

The first and most fundamental difficulty encountered by all experiments in collective security relates to the definition of aggression. Several committees appointed by the United Nations for the specific purpose of defining aggression have not been able to bring their work to a satisfactory conclusion, and such agreement as they have reached represents more a theoretical compromise between competing great power interests rather than a practical guide for identifying actual aggression in complex international disputes.[25] In protracted conflicts, as in the Middle East, where the original antagonism has been obscured and complicated by new tensions and a spiralling arms race, identifying the aggressor becomes extremely problematic. A similar problem arises from the distinction to be drawn between the threat of force and its actual use. Prior to the Yom Kippur War of 1973, some observers may have wished to ascribe to Israel a greater share of the responsibility for the repeated outbreak of hostilities. On the other hand, several Arab states as well as the Palestinian liberation organizations had publicly stated their intention of physically destroying the state of Israel. Which party, if either, could legitimately be described as guilty of aggression?

Another complicating factor has emerged with the increasing military, economic, diplomatic and ideological involvement of outside powers in the internal affairs of Third World countries. The great power presence in various areas of internal tension and conflict (e.g. Korea, Vietnam, Congo, Dominican Republic, Middle East) has often served to blur any distinction that may have existed between the initiator and the victim of aggression. But even in those cases where aggression is explicitly identified, it does not follow that a collective security arrangement will result in the punishment of the aggressor, especially if the aggressor is a great power. When the United States intervened in the Dominican Republic in 1965, neither the United Nations nor the Organization of American States was in a position to take effective counteraction. Similarly, when the Soviet Union invaded Czechoslovakia in 1968, there was no policing action which could have been undertaken under the aegis of either the United Nations, NATO or the Warsaw Pact. The very power of the United States and the Soviet Union precluded any feasible military response on the part of these collective security organizations.

To the extent that the UN Charter has recognized the futility of coercive action against any of the great powers, it represents a repudiation of the very notion of collective security. The powers and functions assigned to the Security Council and the accompanying provision that no substantive decision may be taken without the concurrence of the five permanent members have ensured that no punitive action can be directed against a permanent member.[26] The UN Charter represents at best an international enforcement mechanism capable of functioning only in certain limited areas of peace-keeping where the conflict of interests among the great powers is minimal or non-existent. The weakness of the United Nations system of peace enforcement is that it is predicated on the assumption of solidarity between the great powers, whereas it is precisely the absence of such solidarity which has given rise to the need for an international peace-keeping structure. The inability of the international organization to act as a peace-keeping agency even in such limited but destructive conflicts as the Indochina War or the India–Pakistan dispute, and the failure of its operations in Cyprus and the Middle East to preserve the peace are indicative of the profound institutional and conceptual difficulties which militate against the establishment of a viable system of collective security.

In addition to these practical difficulties, the idea of collective security is also vulnerable to criticism in relation to its theoretical adequacy and ultimate desirability. Collective security, whether embodied in a universal organization (e.g. United Nations) or a defensive alliance (e.g. NATO), does not abolish war but rather attempts to enforce peace through war or the threat of war. For a system of collective security to succeed, it must have at its disposal sufficient armed force to coerce deviant states. In this sense, collective security does little or nothing to obliterate the differences and antagonisms dividing states. By attempting to minimize the ensuing violence, by forcing the aggressor to pursue a policy of peace it may simply beget new violence. Had NATO responded by military action to the Soviet intervention in Hungary in 1956 or in Czechoslovakia in 1968, or had the Soviet Union reacted more forcefully to the American involvement in Korea or Vietnam, a global confrontation would have been the almost inevitable outcome. If collective security is to be based on the principle of armed coercion, then it is quite possible that in certain circumstances the whole diplomatic system would be reduced to a state of violent anarchy.

The polarizing impact of regional collective security arrangements on the international system became painfully obvious during the height of the cold war. Each of the two blocs, which consisted of an integrated network of bilateral and multi-lateral agreements on the establishment of bases, the stationing of troops and the adoption of joint strategies, existed to meet the threat allegedly posed by the other bloc. The creation of the

Soviet and American security systems thus culminated in the rigid political, military and economic division of Europe. Once the 'iron curtain' had fallen on Europe, almost the entire world appeared to become the theatre of cold war rivalries. Neither side was willing to tolerate the slightest deterioration of its strategic position. A minor border violation, a change in the status of a particular territory, the deployment of a new weapon system, all these were viewed as events capable of unleashing a major crisis. Confronting each other in a context of ideological bipolarity, the two security systems precluded any possibility of accommodation or compromise and engendered instead a self-fulfilling expectation of suspicion and hostility, which transformed relatively minor incidents into high tension crises. It is perhaps revealing that the era of détente should have followed rather than preceded the development of polycentric tendencies within the two blocs. Indeed, the progressive decrystallization of the cold war since the Cuban missile crisis of October 1962 may be attributed, at least in part, to the relative decline of the superpowers and the erosion of their respective security systems.

The other dangerous aspect of the bipolar security structure, which had emerged by the late 1940s, was the tendency of the two giants, particularly of the United States, to engage in police actions on a global scale. The American military presence in Germany and the rest of Europe became a springboard for military intervention in Korea, Indochina, the Middle East, the Congo and various parts of Latin America, as the NATO alliance, based on North America, Western Europe and the Mediterranean, was expanded into a global security system, encompassing the American–Japanese Security Treaty, the ANZUS treaty, the mutual defence pacts with the Philippines, South Korea and Taiwan, the Southeast Asian Treaty Organization (SEATO) and the Central Treaty Organization (CENTO). This vast network of security links was to provide the United States with the necessary legal justification as well as the strategic and logistic base from which to launch its numerous and often costly military operations. These painful experiences tend to suggest that a world order in which 'peace-loving' states enforce the peace on aggressive states may soon degenerate into a situation of universal intervention and global violence.[27]

The imposition of peace by force may also place additional

strains on the international system by virtue of the fact that peace is identified with the preservation of the status quo. Systems of collective security, in their efforts to maintain their military effectiveness, often prove unable to make adequate allowance for change. The collective security system of the League of Nations, for example, committed to perpetuating the world order prescribed by the peace settlement of 1919, was essentially an expression of the interests of the victors, against which the defeated enemy was sooner or later bound to rebel in an effort to recover its former rank as a great power. In this sense, the collective security system established by the victors at the conclusion of World War I was perhaps one of the critical factors contributing to World War II.

Collective security may be considered even more inadequate in the contemporary world of revolutionary change where existing political systems and national borders are under constant challenge, particularly in the fluid situation which prevails in many parts of the Third World. In this regard one need only refer to the border disputes between Israel and the Arab states, India and Pakistan, India and China, China and the Soviet Union; to the numerous wars of national independence that have brought the colonial era to an end; to the continuing wars of liberation in Southern Africa, the Middle East, Southeast Asia, and various parts of Latin America; to the territorial and political divisions which separate East and West Germany, Mainland China and Taiwan, North and South Korea, Greek and Turkish Cyprus. In the face of so many national and international antagonisms and so much dissatisfaction with the existing world order, it is difficult to envisage how any system of collective security can adequately deal with the underlying causes rather than the mere symptoms of insecurity.

Ultimately, the theory of collective security, which advances the self-defeating principle that it is the duty of peace-loving states to punish aggressive states for their immorality or irrationality, is based on the rather facile assumption, invalidated by so much recent history, that some states are endowed with superior moral or rational judgment. Such an unwarranted assumption, far from encouraging peaceful processes, merely serves to diminish the scope of neutrality and non-alignment, to impede the possibilities of mediation and conciliation, and to exacerbate international tensions by transforming the conflict of national ambitions and sectional interests into a moral struggle between competing ideologies and military blocs.

International law and organization

The painful deficiencies of the approaches to the problem of security that we have so far examined have led several jurists and other students of international affairs to the conclusion that the quest for a secure and warless world can be satisfied only through the institution of a universal and comprehensive legal order.[28] The appeal of various models of world government lies principally in the possibility of replacing national security systems based on deterrence with a global security system based on universal disarmament and enforced by an international peace-keeping force under the control of the world government. The added attraction of the proposal is the promise of a more just economic order which would eliminate many of the grievances of the poorer nations and thereby remove or at least attenuate one of the chief motives for war and revolution.

Some of the proposed schemes, such as the Clark–Sohn plan, provide for a world authority capable of controlling international conflicts, but on the basis of an extremely limited form of government. The authors envisage a world organization which would be restricted to issues directly related to disarmament and war prevention so as not to pose an unacceptable threat to national loyalties and national sovereignty. But by so limiting the scope and power of the international legal authority, the proposal would, if adopted, do little to reduce the competitiveness of interstate relations and their propensity to violence. All notions of world government ultimately suffer from the common defect of mistaking the symptoms for the causes of insecurity or of proposing such radical measures as to put them beyond the realm of feasibility. It is, in any case, doubtful whether a world government could, in practice, coerce states that violate world laws without resorting to the very violence it is seeking to prevent. Nor have the various schemes for world government taken sufficient account of the essential differences with respect both to legitimacy and to the possession of the means of violence between international society and domestic society, and their implications for the maintenance of law and order.[29]

Conscious of the obstacles preventing the creation of powerful and authoritative central institutions for the management of international relations, sovereign states have been more attracted to the possibility of a less structured system of international regulation which would depend for its functioning on the degree of consent received from the obligated states. Such consent may be given explicit expression in the shape of formal treaties, or it may be tacitly reflected in the conduct of diplomacy and the accepted conventions governing trade and other commercial, and cultural actions. In this sense the recent development of several new international governmental organizations may be said to constitute an additional and significant source of international legality.

While not disputing the valuable contribution of legal arrangements to the maintenance of cooperative relationships, especially at the cultural, scientific and technical levels, international rules and regulations have been far less effective in mitigating violence, and most notably when the need for such restraining influence has been most acute. For example, in the years immediately following World War II, international law seemed powerless to regulate the profound Soviet–American antagonism which had emerged with respect to their strategic and ideological relationship and their competition for status and spheres of influence. The United States was willing to support the United Nations only in so far as it was able to exercise a predominant role within the organization. Its enthusiasm soon evaporated once its supremacy in the General Assembly was challenged by the voting power of the non-aligned states. As for the Soviet Union, at no stage did it consider the United Nations as anything more than a limited treaty, certainly not as the legal base for a future world government or as the foundation of a comprehensive body of international law.

Several writers have argued that, in spite of the cold war, a considerable number of unwritten accords nevertheless emerged.[30] The acceptance of the very principle of bipolarity, the willingness to refrain from intervening in each other's sphere of influence, the gradual elaboraton by both sides of a deterrence strategy that took account of the opponent's interests and capabilities, these and other reciprocal arrangements have been advanced as evidence of the tacit understanding which gradually developed between the two superpowers. However, apart from the doubtful validity of interpreting every minor agreement between two states, no matter how provisional, vague or informal, as a positive contribution to international law, it would seem unreasonable to neglect the contrary effects of such agreements on third parties and, more specifically, on the polycentric tendencies which soon emerged within both blocs, underscored by the increasingly antagonistic attitudes of China and France towards the leadership of their respective camps.

International law has been further hampered in the post-1945 period by the marked blurring of boundaries between domestic and international law. Progressively more sophisticated techniques of overt and covert political, economic and armed subversion have considerably aggravated the problem and have often paralysed all efforts to deal with a dispute at the level of legality. The cold war, as manifested in the Asian rimlands, in the Middle East and in Latin America, has been conducted in such a way as to render the application of legal norms either impracticable or irrelevant. Both the Soviet Union and the United States have sought to promote their external objectives by creating extra-diplomatic agencies whose main functions are to collect information, dispense propaganda, organize agitation, establish links with local political or economic groups, train foreign agents, and direct subversion. Few would wish to dispute the considerable and at times decisive role which the US Central Intelligence Agency has played in advancing American interests in almost every corner of the globe. By capitalizing on local conditions of political unrest and economic instability, great powers are often able to obscure the illegality of their actions and manufacture a situation of legal chaos in which it is no longer possible to apply, let alone enforce, the provisions of international law.

Among the obstacles encountered in recent years by international law, mention must also be made of the increasing number of conflicting jurisdictional claims with respect to territories, seas and populations. In the era of ideological polarization, such disputes have been further complicated by diametrically opposed attitudes to diplomatic recognition. Traditionally, states have accepted the existence of an independent state and an effective government as the necessary and sufficient criterion for the establishment of diplomatic relations. But since 1945, a situation has arisen in which some governments have tended to extend recognition in accordance with their particular concepts of legitimacy and their own ideological evaluation of the acceptability of the regime in question. It is on such grounds that the United States refused to recognize the governments of East Germany, North Vietnam and North Korea, and maintained for nearly a quarter of a century the absurd fiction that the legitimate government of mainland China was to be found on the island of Taiwan. As the protracted Indochinese conflict has indicated, international law can make little positive contribution to the resolution of conflicts when there is not even agreement on the identity or the credentials of the political entities constituting the international system.

The inherent weakness of international law appears, then, to be its acceptance of the principle of state sovereignty, and the consequent inability to define the boundaries of its jurisdiction from those of municipal law. International law, as presently formulated, faces the almost impossible task of reconciling the particular interests of nation-states with the general interests of the world community. States will seldom defer to the demands of international law (e.g. France's refusal to abide by the decision of the International Court of Justice prohibiting further atmospheric nuclear tests in the Pacific) when these are deemed to conflict with the national interest, a principle that is invariably invoked when issues of security are at stake.

In an attempt to refute the notion that international law lacks any real power of enforcement, many legal theorists have argued that the element of force is not actually necessary to ensure compliance with the law.[31] In many domestic legal systems governments do obey court decisions even when there are no supra-governmental forces at the disposal of the judiciary. Laws are obeyed because the consequences of obedience are preferred to those of disobedience. Similarly, it is argued, in the international context, the attitude of any state towards international law is likely to depend on the assessment that is made of the possible reactions of other states. Customary law and treaties are often respected because of the fear of possible retaliation – military, economic or diplomatic – by other states. The likely intervention of third parties, the imposition of international sanctions, or simply the creation of an unfavourable climate of world opinion, are likely to impose additional restraints on potentially deviant state behaviour.

Respect for international law, it is claimed, is also the outcome of the existing respect for domestic law. Since governments are themselves dependent on the maintenance of laws, they must to that extent have an interest in obeying, or at least appearing to obey, laws applicable to themselves. Moreover, governments may prefer to have certain disputes referred to an independent and impartial judicial authority, in order to get out of an impasse reinforced by the fear of appeasing the enemy or losing prestige. Plausible though these arguments may be, the fact remains that states have repeatedly broken existing agreements. Even when a dispute is referred by one or more of the protagonists to the United Nations or to other international organizations, more often than not the purpose of the exercise is not to have the dispute resolved by peaceful means but to gain some diplomatic or psychological advantage over the opponent. The legal institution becomes simply another arena in which states contend for power and influence.

As for the United Nations, while in no way belittling its efforts or the tactical successes it has frequently achieved in securing ceasefires or initiating a process of mediation, one may justifiably argue that the organization has failed to bring about a lasting political settlement in any of the crises or disputes in which it has intervened. In reality, all the investigating, mediating or supervisory activities of the United Nations have been aimed primarily at limiting or containing the hostilities rather than at resolving the underlying conflict. In the Korean case, the United Nations flag provided merely a convenient umbrella for the United States military operation against North Korea. The stated objective of bringing about the peaceful reunification of the country remains unfulfilled to this day. Similarly, in the peace supervisory functions undertaken in Kashmir, the Middle East and Cyprus, in the sanctions imposed against

Rhodesia, and in the measures directed against the South African government's illegal occupation of Namibia, the United Nations has not secured a settlement or compromise outcome, much less constructive peaceful change. Even where violent conflicts have been frozen for a period, as in the Middle East and Cyprus, UN forces have been powerless to prevent the subsequent resumption of hostilities, often at a much higher level of intensity.

In explaining the relative ineffectiveness of the international legal order, it cannot be stressed enough that the juridical homogeneity expressed through the United Nations is but a mask for the profound heterogeneity which characterizes the international system. Within the global diplomatic universe marked differences exist between states and societies in relation to their size, wealth, military power, level of political and economic development, ideological orientation and cultural traditions. The growing disintegration of the two blocs, reflected in the increasing bitterness of the Sino–Soviet dispute and the gradual loosening of the bonds tying the Soviet Union and the United States to their respective European allies, has already affected the pattern of international decision-making in the twin spheres of strategic and economic relations. But it is especially the non-aligned nations of Asia, Africa and Latin America which have, by their sheer voting power, highlighted during the last fifteen years the fundamental conflict of interests between the industrialized western world and the under-developed economies of the Third World. As a result of the increasing oppostion to colonialism and neo-colonialism, it has become increasingly obvious that the prevailing international legal system is essentially the creation of modern European civilization and the projection of the cultural values and economic interests of the major industrial powers. It is no coincidence that until recently international law tolerated and legitimized the colonial systems of domination established by the European powers. However, as we have already seen, the system of direct political control has in many cases simply given way to much less formal but equally and perhaps more far-reaching mechanisms of economic and military domination. These forms of unequal exchange have been ratified and reinforced not only by military arrangements but by the vast network of legalized relationships involving aid, trade and investment. If international law is to become a viable instrument in the regulation of the international system, it will need to express not only the interests and ideological pretensions of the great powers but also the mood and aspirations of the Third World. So long as international law remains the embodiment of the dominant economic and political interests within the international system, so long as it is incapable of translating demands for radical change, it is likely to multiply and exacerbate conflict situations rather than minimize the incidence and intensity of international violence.

The balance of power

Probably no other concept in the theory of international relations has been responsible for so much confusion and misunderstanding. Different theorists have made use of the notion of the balance of power to describe different situations, processes and policies.[32] Some have viewed the balance of power from the perspective of the international system as a whole, while others have analysed it from the viewpoint of individual actors within the system. The balance of power concept has been employed, often interchangeably both to describe and prescribe. It assumes the constancy of force, and yet seeks to deter aggression by confronting it with superior force.

Contrary to the conclusions of certain writers,[33] balance of power principles are not the immutable and universal laws of international politics but at best the policy guidelines which some statesmen have consciously or unconsciously adopted in order to preserve the security and independence of their particular state. The balancing of power has normally rested on the premise that there exists within the framework of interstate relations an essential dispersion of power, and that this fragmentation feeds the interaction of competing and conflicting wills. Given the permanent tendency towards international anarchy, balance of power policies seek to create a world in which some measure of order and predictability is restored in interstate relations.

According to the theory of the balance of power, the most effective method of neutralizing the destructive effects of military might is for all states to engage with vigilance and perseverance in a balancing act, thereby preventing any one among them from achieving hegemony through force. States must forever be preoccupied with shifts in the nature and distribution of power, that is, with changes in the capabilities – military and otherwise – of other states. Once shifts in power have been perceived, states must be able to respond flexibly and rapidly so as to reestablish an adequate balance. To achieve this objective, states will need to maintain their military defence preparedness under constant review, and resort to such other balancing techniques as the formation of alliances, agreements on compensation and spheres of influence and, in some cases, military intervention. It is on the shoulders of the great powers and their enlightened statesmen that lies the principal responsibility for achieving and maintaining a stable equilibrium. Minor states and regional balances are little more than subsidiary weights in a global balance in which the major states predominate.

It has often been suggested that for a stable balance to prevail there must exist a large and, preferably, odd number of major powers.[34] Emphasis on the need for a multipolar system derives from the belief that a small number of states is likely to militate against an equilibriated balance because of rigid alliances and sharply diminishing diplomatic manoeuvrability. In a bipolar system, such as that which prevailed at the height of the cold war, the balancing of power may continue for some time, but the actual balance is likely to become increasingly fragile and ultimately inoperative. Some observers have nevertheless maintained that the two opposing alliance systems, based on the principle of nuclear deterrence, constituted a balancing mechanism, designated as the 'balance of terror', which enabled both superpowers to contain each other's expansion.[35] With the rise of polycentric tendencies within the two blocs and the emergence of new centres of military and economic power, the gradual progress towards East-West détente, and the continuing attachment of much of the Third World to a policy of non-alignment, balance of power concepts have regained some of their former prestige and appeal. Indeed, United States foreign policy in the Nixon–Kissinger era was explicitly formulated in terms of a new global (pentagonal) balance of power said to comprise the United States, the Soviet Union, Western Europe, China and Japan.[36] Two closely related questions immediately arise: To what extent are balance of power principles applicable to the transitional international system which appears to have emerged in the late 1960s? Would the application of these principles enhance the capacity of states to solve the problems of security and reduce the incidence of international violence?

In answering these two questions, it is necessary to emphasise that the validity of many of the central assumptions underlying the balance of power concept has always been open to question. For example, the proposition that potential aggressors will be deterred as soon as they are confronted with superior force is not supported by the available historical evidence. To cite one contemporary example, Palestinian political movements and Arab states have refused, in spite of successive defeats on the battlefield, to be intimidated by the superiority of Israel's military power or by the very considerable American support on which it was able to rely. In any case, coalitions against states striving for a preponderance of power may fail to achieve their objective because of insufficient strength or internal divisions. The notion of confronting aggression by superior force is even less feasible in the context of the present global balance. As we have already observed, in a situation of nuclear parity in which both sides possess a second-strike capability, the function of military power is not defence but deterrence. The 'balance of terror' depends for its effectiveness on the principle that nuclear power is essentially 'non-usable' power. It is, therefore, extremely difficult for the Soviet Union and the United States to make use of their awesome military might to prevent each other from maintaining or expanding their sphere of influence. The meteoric growth of the American empire in the twentieth century, particularly since 1945, occurred largely as a result of the global supremacy of the American capitalist economy. The unchallenged economic and military dominance which the United States achieved in Western Europe, Japan and much of the Third World, was to some extent obscured by the cold war and the ideological terms which were used to justify the conduct of American foreign policy. Given the relation of forces prevailing at the conclusion of

World War II, there was little possibility of successfully resisting the expansion of American power. Although spatially more restricted, the extension of the Soviet Empire into much of Eastern Europe appeared equally immune to counteraction.

But apart from the limiting factor of geopolitics, the balancing process often fails because the power calculations on which states base their policies are in fact inaccurate. The assessment of a state's power is little more than a subjective judgement, for what is involved in an intricate and often inextricable nexus of military capability, diplomatic skill, cultural cohesion and psychological advantage. Moreover, the constituent elements of state power are often dynamic rather than static, that is to say, subject to unexpected change (e.g. a technological breakthrough, the rise of a new political movement, the emergence of a powerful personality). Perhaps the most serious recent error of judgment was evidenced in the Vietnam War and in the repeated miscalculation which prompted American military and political decision-makers to escalate the level of US involvement in a futile attempt to contain the steady advances of the revolutionary forces in Indochina.

Because of the uncertainty and ambiguity surrounding power calculations, each state seeks to achieve not a genuine equilibrium but a favourable margin of power. States generally do not feel secure unless they are more powerful than all their potential enemies, but the very attempt to achieve this superiority increases the feeling of insecurity, for one state's margin of security is another state's margin of danger. Alliances are thus likely to lead to counteralliances and armaments to counterarmaments. In this sense, the balance of power system serves to exacerbate the conflict of competing interests. The Soviet–American adversary relationship, which developed soon after the Potsdam agreements, and the subsequent establishment of the NATO and the Warsaw Pact alliance systems followed exactly this pattern. The two superpowers were engaged in a grim contest for prestige and strategic advantage, which established their presence in almost every corner of the globe and involved them in almost every major crisis of the post-war period.

But perhaps the major conceptual weakness of the balance of power model is its internal contradiction. On the one hand, the balance of power presupposes a sense of community, a consensus as to the rules of the game, while, on the other hand, it functions in a framework, which it claims to recognize, of permanent rivalry between states. The system will remain in stable equilibrium only so long as states comply with the rules of the game. But when a state is radically dissatisfied with its position within the international system, when it is eager to expand beyond its existing boundaries, and when its dissatisfaction and desire for expansion cannot be accommodated within the system, it may well be prepared to break the accepted rules of the game. Once the grievances and ambitions of Napoleon's France and Hitler's Germany had exceeded a certain threshhold, no amount of balancing could have prevented the outbreak of hostilities or the subsequent collapse of the existing framework of interstate relations.

In the contemporary world, a similar break in continuity appears to have resulted from the Russian Revolution of 1917, the subsequent eclipse of the other major European powers and the demise of their colonial empires. The resulting unpredictability of international behaviour, so dramatically manifested in the era of cold war rivalries, has acted as a major obstacle to the operation of the balance of power and precluded the common observance of essential rules and the standardized practice of diplomatic intercourse. With the passage of time, it is true, the cold war gradually gave way to a process of détente between the United States and the Soviet Union. The fears aroused by the Cuban Missile Crisis appeared to give a powerful impetus to the establishment of a whole series of new channels of communication. Regular diplomatic contacts, periodic summit meetings, and a hot-line connecting the highest levels of Soviet and American decision-making, provided the institutional background, even in the face of continuing competition, for far-reaching consultations on such intractable issues as the nuclear arms race, the Middle East conflict and the Vietnam War.

By the early 1970s a new era of negotiations was inaugurated with the successful conclusion of the European Security Conference and the decision to proceed with the Strategic Arms Limitation Talks and the discussions for mutual force reductions in Europe. The attempt to stabilize the global strategic relationship was complemented, however hesitantly, by an increasing number of cultural contacts, a growing volume of two-way trade and an expanding flow of western capital and technology into Eastern Europe and the Soviet Union. Once the two protagonists had recognized the legitimacy of each other's claims for superpower status and accepted the boundaries of each other's spheres of influence, the danger of a violent confrontation between the two alliance systems appeared to diminish.

The Soviet Union, for its part, notwithstanding its ideological pretensions, was increasingly committed to the maintenance of the status quo and the preservation of the very considerable diplomatic and military gains it had achieved since 1945. The converging interest of the two superpowers, strengthened by a common desire to retain the international duopoly of power, enabled the United States to secure in several instances tacit Soviet cooperation in limiting the advance of revolutionary movements in Third World countries. Soviet and American diplomacy appeared to be moving towards a consensus centred on the continued operation of a conservative international system and the elaboration of the techniques of crisis management. It is precisely this new community of interests, reinforced by the gradual disintegration of the two blocs, which, in the view of several writers, has provided the opportunity and the incentive for a return to balance of power politics.

But the new elements of accommodation and flexibility, significant though they are, do not encompass the whole globe or the entire spectrum of international relations. The measure of consensus which unites the two superpowers separates them, in fact, not only from other aspiring great powers but also from much of the Third World where there has recently emerged a marked trend towards the rejection of both the Soviet and American models of development, the adoption of more assertive policies on matters of trade and control of national resources, and the withdrawal from military commitments and alignments. Apart from the actions of governments and governmental organizations, account must also be taken of the role of revolutionary and national movements in eroding the position of colonial or neo-colonial powers. In this fragmented international system, the most advanced industrial states can no longer rely on a common cultural heritage or a cosmopolitan diplomatic ethos to impose an international normative consensus. As the division between status quo and revisionist interests gains additional momentum in the years ahead, the applicability of balance of power theory will largely disappear.

Because the international system now constitutes a closed system, attempts at compensation or allocations of spheres of influence are much less manageable. So long as there existed vast territories and populations which imperial powers could colonize and exploit, differences between them could be settled by compromise and negotiation, with each imperial centre able to apportion for itself a corner of the world. But in the modern era, where almost the entire planet is divided into a number of independent states, each claiming sovereign jurisdiction over its territory, private arrangements among great powers, as have operated since the sixteenth century, are now much less likely.

Paradoxically, the opportunity to exercise economic, diplomatic and military dominance appears to be diminishing precisely at that moment in history when major national and transnational actors have developed the most powerful and sophisticated economic and military techniques yet devised. But this capacity for global intervention appears to be neutralized by the prospect of rising costs and diminishing returns. The net effect of these trends is to reduce the scope of imperial expansion and seriously limit the degree of manoeuvrability so crucial to the effective operation of the balance of power. The Indochina War, the Indo–Pakistani conflict, the Middle-East confrontation and the impending collision in Southern Africa, all exemplify the decline of established spheres of influence and the practical impossibility of harmonizing the global strategic balance with regional balances of power.

The foregoing examination of state responses to the external environment has sought to highlight the continuing problem of security, and the relative failure of these responses to achieve their stated objective. The traditional principles and procedures by which states have sought to regulate their relations have proved incapable of preventing or restraining interstate violence, either because the principles themselves were not valid, or because the means chosen to implement them were inappropriate for the task. The attempt to achieve security through force, whether by unilateral or collective action, is manifestly self-defeating since it resorts to means that negate the end. The balance of power model, on the other hand, depends for its success not only on far-reaching assumptions of doubtful validity but on a specific set of conditions which may not currently apply, given that the international political economy is characterized by environmental scarcity and progressively sharper lines of jurisdictional demarcation. As for disarmament and international law, while they may offer a rational and conceptually elegant solution to the problem of international violence, they do not appear compatible with the existing structure of the international system or of its constituent units.

While international insecurity and its concomitant, war, may be considered as an expression of the systemic imbalance in human relations, it does not follow that the solution to the problem will be found exclusively or principally at the systemic level. It may be more valid to attribute the systemic disruption resulting from the permanent expectation of violence and preparation for violence to the wide gap between the almost unlimited objectives of states and the limited capacity of the international environment to satisfy them. But sight must not be lost of the fact that the international environment is ultimately no more than the sum of its parts, which simply means the totality of national and other actors which comprise the international system. Though the parts may be susceptible to varying arrangements, no amount of engineering, whether violent or peaceful in design, can hope to cancel or neutralize the impact of a state's internal environment. In other words, the various approaches to security that we have analysed, whether taken together or in isolation, tend to ignore the dynamics of the structural and psycho-social imbalances which underlie the organization of national societies, and hence overlook some of the crucial factors which influence the nature and direction of global interaction.

No macrocosmic model of the world order can lay the necessary foundations for an international community of interests without at the same time giving serious attention to the structural and ethical implications of the microcosmic economic and political institutions which govern the life of national communities and smaller socio-cultural units. A realistic evaluation of alternative world futures must therefore consider not only the structural defects of international organization and communication but the very basis of contemporary individual and social pathology.

9. The claims of morality and utopia

In the preceding chapters we have attempted to isolate and explain some of the factors which account for the contemporary crisis in human relations. We have sought to illuminate this crisis by pointing to four pervasive and mutually reinforcing imbalances in existing patterns of social interaction. We have designated as the psycho-social imbalance the large and widening gap which separates the individual from society and drastically reduces his prospects of exercising any meaningful influence over decisions that vitally affect him. Obliged to comply with the requirements generated by the bureaucratic state, the multinational corporation, the military–industrial complex, or simply the technological society, human life is increasingly made to conform with the dictates of anonymous, arbitrary and irrational authority. The marked tendency towards bureaucratic centralization, technical rationality, higher energy consumption and the concentration of industrial and financial power inevitably produces within society a preoccupation with immediate consumptive pleasures, a retreat into a private and atomized world of personal gratification and a sharp decline in the quality of ethical discourse. The dimensions of space, time and complexity in social organization are now so divorced from ordinary human experience as to undermine the foundations of the normative order and heighten the vulnerability of the individual to physical and psychic manipulation.

Mirroring this disorder is the structural imbalance which expresses in institutional terms the disparity between the power of the few and the impotence of the many. The internal disintegration of traditional culture and the rapid collapse of moral and religious belief systems are laying bare new depths of social conflict and polarization which centralized decision-making structures can neither conceal nor resolve. The modern state, committed to the twin goals of economic growth and military security, has had only limited and intermittent success in achieving its objectives and then only at the expense of stability and equity. The acute and costly political, economic and diplomatic crises to which overdeveloped and under-developed societies alike have been exposed this century are indicative of the institutional deficiencies in both domestic and international society. The global pattern of cultural, political, economic and military stratification has thus created a systemic imbalance which perpetuates, both materially and psycho-logically, relationships of dominance and dependence. The colonialism of the past has given way to new and expanding forms of metropolitan domination and to a new system of un-equal exchange which condemns a large fraction of humanity to a precarious and captive existence. Apart from its mani-festation in the transnational institutionalization of under-development, the systemic imbalance is reflected in increasingly sharp inter-capitalist rivalries and in the emerging conflict between resource-exporting and resource-importing countries. A closely related incompatibility of interests is developing between national political units and transnational organiza-tions as evidenced by the growing rift between states and multinational corporations. These instances of global in-equality and institutional breakdown are compounded by the escalating use of violence in inter- and intra-state relations, and by the proliferation of the means of nuclear destruction, which further weaken the prospects of international regulation and the equitable allocation of values and resources.

The disharmonies that have come to permeate the whole fabric of human relations and human institutions are no lon-ger confined to man's cultural environment; they vitiate his entire relationship with the natural order. The resulting eco-logical imbalance, which is a function of the uncontrolled growth of technology and population, reflects the other three imbalances and the failure of social organization to distinguish between short-term and long-term advantage and between private and public interest. Unlimited and unplanned expan-sion violates the basic principles of ecology and threatens to transform the illusory search for abundance into an economy of dire and permanent scarcity, thereby accentuating the asym-metry and polarization of the international system and its pro-pensity to violence.

Underlying our whole conceptual approach to the general crisis of survival and to the specific imbalances which typify it has been the assumption that in the current phase of human evolution man's response to his cultural and natural environment is essentially maladaptive. In an effort to dramatize and interpret this tendency towards maladaptation, some writers have developed the concept of social pathology by applying directly and analogically the principles of individual pathology to an analysis of social organization.[1] The failure to develop normally, which stems principally from the wasting of human potential (understood in its widest cultural sense) and the creation of artificial wants, is inevitably accompanied by suffering and the desire to overcome it. As with pain in the physical organism, suffering can function as a signal to the individual that a pathological condition has arisen and that for health to be restored some change must occur within the psyche itself or in its external environment. To the extent that the various imbalances which we have outlined can be considered as primary sources of contemporary social pathology, they are suggestive of the changes needed to achieve a healthier society.

Among the most common forms of pathological behaviour in modern industrial society one would include the preoccupation with having and acquiring rather than with being or becoming; the obsession with the power to dominate rather than liberate; the profound sense of alienation from rather than participation in the wider social reality; the attitude towards work and leisure as means of killing time rather than creatively living in time; the predisposition to an in-group rather than an out-group psychology which discriminates on the basis of sex, race, creed or nationality; the tendency to resolve conflicts through the use or threat of force. It goes without saying that these pathological strivings are by no means confined to advanced technological societies. They are to be found in varying degrees throughout history and are compatible with different types or stages of political and economic organization. Nor can it be argued that those who live under the technocratic order are all or equally affected by pathological inclinations. However, what distinguishes the super-industrial system – and the global spread of its empire – is the high degree to which social pathology has become institutionalized through the pyramidal stratification of wealth, power and knowledge, but above all through the growing monopoly of industrial production over the satisfaction of human wants. It is the industrial institutionalization of values which has progressively obscured the distinction between health and pathology, normality and abnormality, reason and unreason, illusion and reality.

The institutional integration of pathological behaviour has now reached such proportions that it is not merly the quality but the very survival of human life which is at risk. We may define then the twentieth century crisis as a function of growing social pathology and a declining threshold of psychological and ecological tolerance. The rapidity of transport and communications systems and the global scale of industrial, commercial and military operations have ensured the increasing standardization of cultural styles and the fusion of several imbalances into a crisis of planetary dimensions. If this is an accurate diagnosis of the serious and deteriorating condition of our civilization, then no piecemeal, provisional, or parochial remedy is likely to prove efficacious. It would appear that in order to sustain the organic evolution of the human species it will be necessary to develop perspectives and responses that are both radical and global in inspiration.

The utopian vision

Our discussion of pathology, imbalance and crisis presupposes, at least conceptually, the possibility of health, balance and stability. In fact, basic to our entire analysis has been the tacit assumption that in order to elucidate, explain and appraise empirical reality it is not enough to consider observable facts. It is necessary to contrast the 'empirically given' with the 'potentially possible'.[2] The actual or empirical world cannot be considered an absolute world from which are derived all normative criteria, but simply as one world which should be compared and contrasted with other possible worlds in order to explicate and evaluate the flow of historical reality. By relying exclusively on so-called objective processes of deduction and derivation, empirical theory risks becoming an ideology which serves, whether consciously or unconsciously, to justify and perpetuate the status quo. It is, then, the task of critical theory and, therefore, of all utopian thinking to conceptualize the actual in terms of the potential and to indicate how it may be possible to bridge the gap between the present and a preferable future.

In spite of the scorn with which speculative and idealistic writings have come to be regarded in recent scholarly and political discourse, it has become increasingly apparent to many, both inside and outside the utopian tradition, that visions of a more desirable natural and cultural milieu are an integral part of the human condition and an essential motivating force for social change.[3] Though differing greatly in their assumptions about human nature and in their practical recommendations, all utopias are ultimately based on the view that the selection of appropriate facts for political action implies value choices and that such choices can be directed towards the creation of a more acceptable social order. Some utopian thinkers have concentrated their attention on the establishment of small-scale model 'towns' or 'communities', while others have elaborated proposals for a universal system of peaceful interaction.[4] Both the microcosmic and macrocosmic approaches belong to the long-standing tradition which seeks to integrate empirical and normative theory, and both have experienced a dramatic revival over the last few decades.[5] The rebirth of utopian thinking may be understood, at least in part, as a reaction against the dominant ideological systems and their failure to diagnose, let alone cure, the deep-seated sickness afflicting both industrialized and underdeveloped societies.

The appeal of utopian thinking has become increasingly evident not only in the writings of a few 'romantic' philosophers and the aspirations of a youthful counterculture, but also in the changing attitudes of even such conservative religious institutions as the Roman Catholic Church. In a major statement on social ethics, Pope Paul VI described utopia as a kind of criticism of existing society which 'provokes the forward looking imagination both to perceive in the present the disregarded possibility hidden within it, and to direct itself towards a fresh future; it thus sustains social dynamism by the confidence that it gives to the inventive powers of the human mind and heart.'[6] This perspective, which has become especially noticeable in those parts of the world where the Christian churches are attempting to express the aspirations of oppressed peoples and social classes, has given enormous impetus to the theme of *liberation* and to profound theological reflection on the relationship between human liberation and the salvific process. Man is seen as assuming conscious responsibility for his destiny, for the gradual conquest of freedom and hence for the creation of a new man and a qualitatively different society.[7]

It may appear a little strange that utopian insights should be reemerging within the confines of a seemingly moribund theocracy, whose mythical–supernatural worldview, ritual symbolism, conceptual apparatus and even moral framework are now considered to have little relevance to contemporary social reality. On the other hand, it is well to remember that by the very depth and scope of its eschatological perception, religious faith, as distinct from institutional religion, is able to bestow purpose and coherence on man's role in the cosmic environment. Thus, for all their obvious differences, one can discern the common ground shared by the religious and utopian impulses, for both are ultimately ready to place their faith in the power of the 'image-creating' wish. It is this 'longing for *rightness*', whether 'experienced as revelation or idea', this faith in human potentiality which animates as much the eschatological vision of the perfection of creation as the utopian unfolding of the possibilities latent in mankind's communal life.[8] It is this same faith which has motivated all genuinely progressive movements throughout history, and which constitutes the radical assumption in democratic and socialist thought. In this sense, the theories of progress developed in the age of the Enlightenment and their historical continuation in the writings of Marx and other socialist thinkers may be interpreted as the secular translation of the Judaeo-Christian concept of messianic salvation.[9]

Faith in man, the cornerstone of every utopian edifice, is the force which has normally provided the daring and enthusiasm that men need to break with the past and overcome the powers which enslave them. It is only on the basis of such faith that it has been possible to affirm and extend the power of human will and the efficacy of self-sacrifice. Realizing that human

knowledge is less than absolute and human reason more than
fallible, many modern thinkers are consciously stressing the
role of faith in the search for a politics and religion of human
survival. But is commitment to the desirable and the possible
to be rooted in mere blind faith? The authors of *Gestalt Therapy*
are forced to pose the question:

> ... by what criterion does one prefer to regard 'human nature' as
> what is actual in the spontaneity of children, in the works of heroes,
> the culture of classic eras, the community of simple folk, the feeling
> of lovers, the sharp awareness and miraculous skill of some people in
> emergencies? Neurosis is also a response of human nature and is
> now epidemic and normal, and perhaps has a viable social future.[10]

It is clear, as the authors readily acknowledge, that this question is not susceptible to a purely rational answer. Ultimately,
the choice between a hopeful and despairing view of human
nature rests on faith. For its part, the utopian faith asserts that
human nature can be understood in terms not of immutable
facts but of potentialities which are progressively actualized in
the course of history.[11]

The eschatological perspective and the closely related biblical
themes of hope and promise are central to the Judaic and
Christian interpretation of history and have recently found expression in one of the most important movements in contemporary Christian theology.[12] For Moltmann, the Christian
hope in the resurrection liberates man from the present and
enables him to act in accordance with the reality which is coming.[13] Significantly, the belief that hope can fulfil a mobilizing
and liberating function in history is common to both religious
and secular faith. According to Ernst Bloch, hope is a state of
mind uniquely experienced by men and uniquely fitted to subvert the existing order.[14] It is this utopic and transforming
function of hope which no doubt animates Marx's assertion
that 'philosophers have only interpreted the world in various
ways; the point is to change it'.[15] The value of the utopian impulse lies then in its power to set men free from their docile
acceptance of the grim reality which surrounds them and to
provide them with a map of a world which, though not necessarily perfect in all respects, is nonetheless preferable to the
existing order and consistent with human potentialities. Al-

though it may not be fully attainable, utopia serves as a target for both action and reflection, and thus offers the possibility of a revolutionary praxis. In the Marxist formulation, the utopian project is superseded by 'scientific socialism',[16] but the continuing preoccupation is with the struggle for a new society not as a subject of academic discussion but as the dynamic element in the historical becoming of humanity.[17]

It should be evident by now that underlying the utopian imagination are certain value premises or preferences which affirm both the possibility and desirability of social transformation. But not all utopias advocate the same changes or the same strategies. The variations in the goals and means they prescribe stem primarily from different perceptions of the hierarchy of basic human needs and values. Different models will emphasize different needs, depending on what they consider to be the prospects of human self-realization. While all utopias readily recognize the biological requirements of food, sex, shelter and security, they differ greatly on the economic and political arrangements needed to fulfil them. Moreover, the quest for material welfare has to be complemented by concern for such intangible needs as those of love, self-esteem, freedom, identity, creativity and community.[18] It is here that priorities normally have to be established for it may not be possible to maximize all values simultaneously. In some models stability and peace may be sacrificed for the sake of justice and equality, while in others they may be promoted at the expense of cultural diversity and individual autonomy. It is to a consideration of these utopian options and to their theoretical and practical implications that we shall now turn our attention.

Utopian prescriptions

As one would expect, most utopian programmes assume the desirability of satisfying man's basic physical needs and of eliminating those intolerable conditions of life which inevitably result from under-nourishment, disease, sub-standard housing, inadequate clothing and unemployment. Minimum welfare standards are generally recognized as a right accruing to all individuals and societies, and requiring to be safeguarded by a social order which reduces to a minimum the role of force in human affairs. Most utopias are therefore concerned, at least in the long run, with terminating the reliance which social, political and ethnic groups place on violence as they struggle for resources, influence or prestige. Desirable though it may be as a general statement of objectives, there is little that can be considered original or instructive in such an axiomatic formulation of goals. Man has little need of utopia to convince him of the value of survival. The utopian appeal has two quite different dimensions; first, the promise of a much richer sensual and cultural environment that goes beyond the minimum provision of the necessities of human life; secondly, a coherent outline of what attitudinal and institutional changes are required for this more gratifying existence to become a practical reality.

The questions to which utopia addresses itself are essentially twofold. Is there an optimal social arrangement (in the context of current historical possibilities) conducive to the satisfaction of basic welfare standards, which is at the same time compatible with the demands of self-determination and self-actualization? And, if it is possible to postulate such an arrangement, does its realization depend on a structural reorganization of society, or can it occur within the growth parameters of established society? The very magnitude of the twentieth century crisis and the structural disorder from which it springs have reinforced the natural predisposition of utopian thinking towards a revolutionary conception of change as the only means of overcoming the contradictions which make up the essence of the existing social reality. According to this perspective, it is only by destroying the foundations of the established order (more accurately characterized as disorder) that one can expect to release those forces which will authenticate the human condition and set free the victims of material necessity.

But what are the principles which are to govern the utopian project? A recurring theme in both recent and earlier writings is the stress on community, on the need to recognize and enhance the core of human sociality. Of the modern utopians, no one has articulated more eloquently the communal imperative than Paul Goodman. In *Communitas*, we are offered three different architectural blueprints based on fundamentally different values. However, it is the second plan based on 'the elimination of the difference between production and consumption' which best expresses the author's notion of community, obviously influenced by the previous contributions of Owen, Fourier, Proudhon and Kropotkin, and pointing to the creation of a decentralized economic, political and environmental system. With a view to maximizing the interrelationship between the personal and the productive environment, the worker is to be involved in every phase of the work process and to participate directly in all decision-making. The work programme, which is to be guided by moral and psychological considerations rather then by the technological requirements of efficiency, should, as far as possible, be centred in the vicinity of the home and involve the performance of both industrial and agricultural tasks. Public services and amenities are to be centrally located, thus promoting further the integration of urban and rural life and enhancing the opportunities for the interplay of meaningful work and creative leisure. Clearly, Goodman's intention is to design a community that is largely self-sufficient and yet patterned on a mode of consumption and production which is human in scale, conducive to social interaction on the basis of mutuality rather than dominance or submissiveness, and harmoniously related to the natural environment.

The desire to scale down the industrial leviathan and revive the ethos of the village or neighbourhood is inspired not so much by the romantic appeal of nature – although one should not underestimate the relevance of such an attitude in times of environmental degradation – as by the radical insight that it is only a microcosmic social order which can absorb the fallibility and villainy of human actions, and prevent the often disastrous, widespread and prolonged reverberations that rebound from decisions taken at the centre of overgrown social structures. The decentralist tendency characteristic of all communitarian models may be explained, at least in part, as a reaction to the contemporary experience of mass loneliness and collective anonymity. Equally important has been the realization that the centralized planning of the economy and the socialization of the means of production do not necessarily result in human emancipation or in the building of community.

According to Erich Fromm, a sense of community is incompatible with an approach to work which emphasizes higher wages or increased productivity at the expanse of collective or personal fulfilment.[19]

The utopian conception of community proposes therefore a form of economic and political association that is radically different from that provided by the modern state. Apart from the demand for social organizations of small size, particular stress is placed on the need for close personal relationships and an underlying sense of mutual commitment. It has been argued that the function of an organic community is to encourage rather than stifle the reciprocal awareness displayed by children at an early age as they attempt to adjust their relationships and create rules of behaviour on the basis of equality.[20] The decentralization of institutions is thus advocated not simply in order to advance the prospects of economic and political democracy, but as a means of generating the community of faith and living togetherness, as the indispensable ingredients of psychological identity and individual autonomy. For some, among whom Theodore Roszak, the utopian objective represents the very antithesis of the technocratic state; it goes beyond participatory democracy and aspires to create human communities of experience that are small, decentralized, mystical and sensual. What is in question here is not the mutualism of Proudhon, who advocates a complex network of freely chosen contractual relationships between individuals and collectivities, but a spirit of communalism that thrives on common life-styles, values and work patterns. Central to this utopian theme is the rejection of *Gesellschaft*, the mechanistic mass society which destroys community and replaces it with a superficial individualism in opposition to the principles of mutual aid, mutual respect and shared responsibility. What is posited instead is *Gemeinschaft*, the small organic community in which men are inextricably committed to live, work and seek pleasure together.

Whatever the precise form or degree of community that is envisaged, it is manifestly evident that in all these utopian models the liberation of human sensitivity and sensibility is made a primary goal of social interaction. In this sense, community becomes the hall-mark of a society that is both responsible and free. Men have rid themselves of the acquisitiveness, aggressiveness and brutality of established society and have learned to enjoy the pleasure derived from working towards their own liberation and the establishment of a natural and cultural environment favourable to such a liberated existence.[21] But, are the principles of community and freedom as easily reconcilable as some utopias would suggest? Is there not an unavoidable tension between the demands of personal freedom and self-gratification on the one hand and the requirements of the common good on the other? Many utopias are of course aware of this dilemma, although they do not always formulate it in the same terms or propose the same solution. In order to examine this issue a little more closely, it may be useful to enlarge on some utopian insights into the related concepts of freedom and liberation.

In *Eros and Civilization*, Marcuse envisages an advanced technological society which has perfected an economy of abundance, thereby eliminating the need for work as presently conceived, and inaugurating the era of total sensual and sensory self-gratification. Work, based upon a repressive performance principle, is thus replaced by the 'play impulse' which is the distinguishing feature of the non-repressive civilization.[22] For Marcuse, the realm of freedom cannot coexist with the realm of necessity; freedom is to be found outside the struggle for existence; economic security is not the content but the prerequisite of freedom. Play and display are considered fundamental principles of civilization and, as such, require the complete subordination of labour to 'the freely evolving potentialities of man and nature'.[23]

For many utopians, an essential and closely related dimension in the process of human liberation is the need to reverse the savagely repressive policies which successive civilizations have adopted towards sexual behaviour and familial relationships. Apart from ensuring the legal, political and economic equality of men and women, the proposed ethic aspires to liberate non-coercive sexual experience from all forms of repression. With disappearance of traditional sexual morality, every adult person, regardless of sex or marital status, will be better placed to develop the human relationships and the leisure pursuits which best fulfil the demands of the individual personality. Warren Wagar, expanding on Marcuse's concept of 'polymorphous perversity', envisions a culture in which Eros is no longer 'arbitrarily confined to reproduction or marriage' but a legitimate mode of self expression.[24] The liberation of Eros is thus expected to enhance the prospects of experimentation, diversity and creative play, thereby acting as a catalyst for the transition towards a higher stage of cultural development.

Crucial though it is, however, to human self-realization, sexual liberation is but one aspect of a much larger undertaking which entails the complete liberation of the non-conscious self. What is in question is the dissolution of the ego-conscious perception of external reality as something that is alien, intractable and ultimately hostile to the inner self. It is this artificial division between self and environment which lies at the root of much individual and social pathology, and which invests the alienated conscious self with a compulsive need to control and dominate. Gurth Higgin argues that by making will-power, self-reflecting rationality and task-achievement the foundation of its imposing edifice, industrial culture has tended to repress and contain non-conscious and numinous phenomena, dismissing them as mystical or supernatural nonsense and describing them as a form of illness for which appropriate physical and psychological methods of treatment have to be devised.[25] However, the stability of the ego culture is at best a mirage effect, a piece of deception which sooner or later invites rebellion in one form or another. It is only by going beyond the settled and controlled life of the ego and by gazing and venturing into the non-conscious self, that the individual can experience true liberation, where fear and delight, loss of certainty and spontaneity merge to produce a life-enhancing immediacy of experience and new symbiotic relationship between internal and external reality.

In the struggle to overcome scarcity, industrial culture has sought to maximize economic performance by relying on hierarchic arche-types of social control and so-called objective models of scientific knowledge and rational technique. The steady progress of science and technology has been understood in terms of the ever-expanding application of the scientific method to new areas of experience. However, both the scientific and the political order are facing an emerging crisis of authority, as the essential relativity of established norms of perception and social organization, so comforting to the assertive ego, is increasingly recognized.[26] For Roszak, 'objective consciousness' is not a method of perception 'uniquely in touch with the truth', but 'an arbitrary construct' whose meaning and value are historically derived.[27]

It is in order to remedy the deficiencies and imbalances set in motion by the dominance of technical or scientific culture – characterized as alienation, hierarchy and impersonality – that Roszak proclaims the splendour of the 'visionary imagination' which sees the world not as a commonplace sight or the object of scientific scrutiny, but as a magical reality transformed by the very act of perception. In this sense, magic, understood not as a repertoire of clever tricks but as a form of listening and responding to the world, is within the reach of every human being. This kind of vision enables direct communication with the forces of nature, an intimacy with the external world, experienced as a presence, however mysterious, that has an identity and a purpose of its own. For the seer as for the poet, reality is not simply what it appears to be to the naked or impersonal eye, but is impregnated with a meaning bestowed on it by a global and sensual awareness.

The implications of this mode of consciousness are many and far-reaching. In the first place, such a vision of the environment informs man that he is not a totally autonomous agent able to superimpose on nature his own schemes and designs. He needs to take account of the laws and rhythms of the life-support system on which he remains vitally dependent, and to develop a symbiotic relationship with the natural order that substitutes dignity and reciprocity for conquest and exploitation. Such a holistic vision of reality is likely to produce a more satisfying balance between the conscious and non-conscious systems, a more subtle and sensitive understanding of the creative possibilities inherent in the evolutionary process and a more intelligent appreciation of the alternatives that are open to man's future cultural evolution. A sense of purpose and direction in human history is maintained but not on the basis of a manipulative ego-conscious culture which reduces historical development to the deterministic mechanism of blind nature or to a crude and destructive struggle for existence. Rather, the creative imagination, inspired by the vision of the unity of all life, displaces the rationality of the performance principle as the most potent force in the transformation of the social and natural universe.

Another salient feature of visionary or aesthetic experience, which sharply distinguishes it from scientific or technical expertise, is its universal accessibility. It is not a specialized skill that is the preserve of a small professional elite, but a gift available to all, conferring not privilege but responsibility. Through various forms of symbolic and artistic expression, one man's vision can be shared by the rest of the community, thereby expanding the range and depth of its experience. It is this sense of sharing and participation, which holds the key to the productive and liberated person: the person who relates himself to the world trustingly not because it is entirely predictable or conforms to his conception of rational order, but because it enables him to celebrate the wonder and the beauty of existence. Such a person, while experiencing himself as a unique individual, also feels at one with his fellow-man. Personal needs become indistinguishable from social concerns, and find expression in collective art and ritual. The relationship between the individual and society remains one of tension, but tension conducive to the constant rediscovery rather than denial of the gift of life.

The utopian interest in inverting industrial consciousness and redirecting it towards the visionary and creative dimension of human experience is motivated by the need to restructure man's relationship not only with his natural but also with his cultural milieu. Ivan Illich has thus contrasted the industrial 'engineered system of social habits that fit the logiç of large-scale production' with a convivial mode of production which enable people 'to rediscover the value of liberating austerity'.[28] A 'convivial society' is distinguished by its emphasis on institutional and technological tools that can be operated by the individual in ways that are both socially productive and personally fulfilling.

The demythologization of science and the deprofessionalization of industrial culture are seen as essential steps towards the elimination of the 'malignant tool' which assigns its own logic and requirements to social arrangements and thereby reduces the range of human choice and motivation. Tools which enhance the freedom of a minority, while imposing constraints on the majority, negate the demands of justice and equality. For most modern utopians, technology, or to be more exact, technique, cannot be considered as playing a neutral role, and must therefore be consciously subordinated to human preferences in life–style and social organization.[29] Indeed, it has been argued that the effective exercise of cultural options is incompatible with a high energy policy which necessarily results in the technocratic manipulation of social relations. For Illich, only a minimum energy economy can be expected to produce high levels of equity and the necessary conditions for 'participatory democracy' and 'rational technology'.[30] Acceptance of the principle of low energy consumption would lead the poor to abandon illusory and dangerous expectations while encouraging the rich to recognize the disastrous consequences of the short-sighted pursuit of vested interest.

The advocacy of low-level technology is directed towards the creation of relatively small communities that operate on the principle of minimum environmental degradation, a functional and labour-intensive mode of production, a steady-state and self-sufficient economy, democratic and decentralist politics, cultural diversity, the integration of work and leisure, technology and culture.[31] It can be readily seen that the convivial reconstruction of society is not a mere technological exercise, but a major political revolution which goes beyond the transfer of the ownership of the means of production or the seizure of power and seeks to develop new technological models and cultural patterns, involving the restructuring of institutions and the redefinition of individual needs and collective goals.

So far, in examining the utopian concepts of community, liberation and ecological and cultural balance, we have limited our attention largely to their microcosmic implications, and have tended to ignore the problems raised by inter-community interaction. However, even if one has identified the various internal arrangements necessary to make communal life a cooperative and liberating experience, there remains the obvious but difficult question of the self-sustaining prospects of the small-scale community, especially if it is obliged to operate in a hostile environment. Unavoidably, therefore, any viable utopian perspective on the twentieth century crisis must concern itself with the theme of universal order. The most illuminating contribution to this aspect of the discussion on alternative world futures appears to have been made not so much by the advocates of structural or functional change within the international system as by the proponents of a new universal cultural synthesis. Such a cosmopolitan vision has invariably emphasized the essential unity of the human family that lies buried beneath the disparities and divisions of the present fragmented world, and portrayed the cultural unification of mankind as the only effective means of creating an organic world civilization.

The search for a new civilization does not seek to supersede but simply to assimilate into an integrated cultural movement the time-honoured ideals of social justice, personal freedom, truth and meaning, peace and well-being, which the great religious and ethical systems have consistently reaffirmed in their teachings if not always in their practice. But for Warren Wagar the very attempt to place mankind above all other loyalties (to state, church, party, community, race, class or family) will produce a 'transvaluation of all values', a radically different vision of the world – which will transform both the subjective and objective dimensions of human existence.[32] Drawing on the contributions of such cosmopolitan thinkers as Arnold Toynbee, Julian Huxley, Pierre Teilhard de Chardin, Lewis Mumford, William Ernest Hoeking and Dane Rudhyar, Wagar envisions a civilization that will give due recognition to the needs of both sociality and personality, a civilization which will achieve 'the social integration of mankind with its persons' and 'the solidarity of the cosmos with its creatures'.[33] This new cultural synthesis, combining the profound eastern sense of the unity of man and cosmos as reflected in Vedantic and Buddhist philosophy, with the western passion for freedom, self-mastery and creativity, will focus on the celebration of life. The evolving world of matter and spirit with its external appearance of harmony and conflict will be understood as one coherent universe, and all men as free moral agents informed and sustained by the common humanity which provides historical experience with its direction and internal unity.

This type of overarching cultural interpretation of the purpose and direction of human evolution has perhaps found its most powerful and sweeping expression in the thought of Teilhard de Chardin. Rejecting the purely materialist or idealist interpretation of history, he conceives of matter and spirit not as two heterogenous or antagonistic forces, coupled together by accident or force, but as the two aspects of the 'stuff of the universe'. In the world, there is no matter and no spirit. All that exists is 'spirit-matter': 'No other substance but this could produce the human molecule'.[34] From this principle it follows that every particular phenomenon has a universal extension. In every fragment of the universe lies the germ of all the possibilities that have ever been actualized at other times and in other places. The evolutionary process reflects then the transformation of the universe or, to be more precise, the spiritualization of matter. Energy, acting in accordance with the law of complexity, forms ever more complex molecules and organisms. The ascent towards increasing complexity, towards a deeper and more intense consciousness, may thus be interpreted as a struggle against dispersion or multiplicity, a struggle which gives the advantage to the improbable over the probable, to order over disorder and to life over death.

For Teilhard, evolution, which is proceeding unmistakably on the path of spiritualization, is marked by three critical thresholds: the appearance of life, the growth of consciousness and the current universalization of the earth. But his totalizing tendency is not necessarily assured of success. Should the planet become uninhabitable before mankind has reached maturity either because of the depletion or mismanagement of resources, or should man lose the desire and foresight to avoid the various traps and blind alleys that are part of the mechanism of evolution, then, the result could well be the failure of life on earth. But the enduring vision is nonetheless of an adventurous voyage towards a common destiny, 'able to activate' the newly freed energies of love, the dominant energies of human unity, the hesitant energies of research'.[35] The very intensity of the global crisis and the violence which envelops it are interpreted as 'an increase in human totalization and in human psychic change'. In other words, within the heart of disorder are to be found the seeds of an organizational and spiritual synthesis. Under the irresistible pressure of geographical, biological, political and social forces, the economic and psychic fragments of humanity are bound to fuse and coalesce into 'a new order of consciousness emerging from a new order of organic complexity: a hyper-synthesis upon itself of mankind'.[36] However, the totalization of human energies will not be depersonalizing since it will itself be intensely personal. By grouping themselves around a personality, struggling individualities would thus become more personal. Love rather than constraint would become the dominant principle, guiding men in free competition towards better groupings, making them accept the restrictions and sacrifies imposed by the total utilization of human energy, enabling 'a personality of increasing freedom [to] grow up without opposition within the totality'.[37] At a high level of utopian generality, Teilhard and other cultural synthesists are thus able to resolve the conflict between community and freedom, symbiosis and individuality.

In the foregoing discussion we have not attempted to characterize in detail any particular utopia but rather to outline some of the general themes which most frequently recur in modern utopian thinking. Admittedly these perspectives do not emanate from a single philosophical or cultural tradition nor do they suggest a conception of society that is internally consistent in every respect. Nonetheless, they point to a general and coherent consensus on the nature of human values and human potentialities. If we accept, at least as a working hypothesis, the underlying assumptions of this consensus – and they would appear to be a far more promising guide to the future than the premises of established society – then the most important issue becomes not so much the desirability as the feasibility of the utopian dream. For even if it is assumed that the utopian project accords perfectly with the possibilities inherent in human evolution, it remains to determine whether and how these possibilities can be actualized in the foreseeable future. The problem of establishing an adequate relationship between means and ends is an integral part of the calculus of politics. When utopian prescriptions are far removed from existing reality, then transitional stages and strategies have to be devised either in order to make more probable the complete realization of the stated objective at some later date, or with a view to achieving more limited but more immediate successes. However, the task is made even more complex by the fact that man has to operate in a continually changing environment requiring a high degree of adaptive behaviour. The misreading of prevailing conditions may thus result in anachronistic or maladaptive responses. To maximize the prospects of survival it is necessary to achieve both a long-term and a short-term equilibrium between the living system and its environment for, as George Gaylord Simpson has observed, the success of an enduring species is measured 'not only at each immediate point but also over its whole range in time'.[38] In this sense, the politics of survival and the politics of utopia are not two distinct options but two intricately interconnected elements of the same solution, two signposts along the same journey.

10. The politics of disorder

In our survey of some of the recently proposed paths to utopia, it was thought neither possible nor useful to construct a hypothetical society capable of satisfying all human needs, aspirations and potentialities. No definitive utopia was proposed, much less any strategy towards its fulfilment. Rather the purpose of the exercise was to contrast the almost omnipresent actuality of a stratified, hierarchical, competitive, fragmented world order with the much less advertised but far more attractive possibility of a liberated, cooperative and aesthetic form of existence. The question which immediately arises is whether the implicit antithesis between health and pathology, order and disorder, balance and imbalance, is no more than a conceptual construct which, for all its elegance and appeal, is devoid of any practical validity. Is the utopian edifice so romantic and revolutionary in its design as to preclude the possibility of a solidly based praxis of social change? Or is the visionary transformation of the existing social order perhaps a precondition for the very preservation of the human species and its progressive adaptation to the natural and man-made environment? The main thrust of the preceding chapter was to suggest that in the current phase of human evolution the prospects of survival may well depend on a purposeful, dynamic, cultural revolution rather than on a process of random, unconscious, trial-and-error biological and social variation.[1] If this is an accurate reading of the present historical juncture, then the utopian option can no longer be regarded as the fanciful and extravagant anticipation of the millenium but as a realistic and compelling policy for the not so distant future.

At this point in the discussion, it is important to return to the notion of imbalance or disorder and to systematize our analysis of contemporary trends in order to specify both the limitations and opportunities which are likely to have a direct bearing on the utopian project. We have already described in

197

different contexts the deeply entrenched international structures of dependence, large power differentials and extremes
of poverty, ignorance and backwardness which stem from the
technocratic mode of production and consumption. It would
now seem that the dehumanizing effects of the system are
beginning to sow the seeds of its own destruction. Even within
the most affluent capitalist societies, the state is proving less
and less able to act as the guarantor of a democratic polity.
The progressive control of information and the steady decline
of civil and political liberties, far from demonstrating the
stability of the state, point to the erosion of established authority, the questioning of existing values and the gradual undermining of traditional loyalties. In conditions of political
instability, repression is often the institutional response of the
prevailing social structures to the underlying economic and
cultural disorder which they are powerless to rectify. By the
same token, a sustained shift towards repression and reaction
may have progressive implications in so far as it reinforces and
multiplies the elements of collective discontent, highlights the
contradiction between the actions and self-proclaimed ideology
of the dominant elites, creates a new social consciousness and a
new impetus towards human emancipation.[2]

In the initial stages the demand for social change may not
amount to a coherent or viable programme of action; it may
not even represent a consistent set of principles or values.
Nevertheless, the very fact that the institutional fabric of society
is increasingly incapable of providing meaning and stability
for the individual, that it is 'progressively deprived of plausibility',[3] leads the individual to adopt a more detached and
critical attitude towards the established order. This break in
the existing pattern of symbolic communication may be considered as the necessary if not sufficient condition for the creation of a new social reality. It is in this context that one has to
evaluate the significance of the many forms of social protest
which arose during the 1960s in several of the advanced industrial societies within both the capitalist and communist
systems.

The importance of the increasingly widespread phenomenon of political dissent lies precisely in the challenge it
poses to the prevalent static view of society and to the tendency

of much structural theory to overestimate the importance of the seemingly objective structural principle at the expense of the subjective consciousness of society and its underlying system of values.[4] In the effort to make sense out of apparent chaos, to penetrate the logic of technical rationality and the increasingly complex division of labour, mainstream western sociology and, to a lesser extent, Marxist analysis have tended to subscribe to a structural or functionalist model of society which stresses the factors of integration and solidarity, affirms the determining socializing influence of class and status, and interprets the experience of psychological strain and stress purely in terms of social constraint.[5] According to this image of society, man is trapped in a structural machine from which there is no escape and against which no resistance is possible. Conflict is no longer a divisive or disruptive force but a functional means of balancing and maintaining social relationships as one integrated structure.[6] While not disputing the very substantial insight into contemporary industrial culture offered by this image of social reality, it nevertheless runs the great risk of completely submerging the individual within a conceptual framework which has lost all notion of freedom, choice, movement and variety.[7]

A careful examination of domestic and international society reveals in each case not stable, well-integrated structures but a heterogeneous patchwork of economic and political forces reflecting opposing interests and contradictory value-systems. The ideal and internal consistency of structural theory thus distorts the instability and discontinuity characteristic of all human relations, especially those based on power and, to a lesser extent, those based on authority. Orthodox conflict and cohesion theory as an interpretation of social reality has become less and less tenable in the face of the profound upheavals which have marked the recent history of Asia, Africa and Latin America, and of the mounting sense of insecurity and disaffection experienced in much of the western world. The structural conception is still less applicable to the international system where a tenuous organizational edifice can barely conceal the profound fragmentation which divides nations and states, political and ideological movements and transnational economic organizations.

The concentration of power over resources, labour, technology and systems of legal and cultural control in the hands of a relatively small privileged elite and the consequent pattern of stratification have acquired over the years a façade of stability. But recently even the outward appearance of order has been tarnished as a result of the struggle of ethnic, national and international movements to achieve liberation from existing structures of power and authority. Several clearly discernible trends already point to the emergence of wide fissures within the international system, to new centres of power, new conceptions of justice and liberation, new demands and new institutions which cumulatively hold forth the promise of undermining the prevalent pattern of stratification. The gradual disorganization of national and international society may gradually permit some of the less powerful or privileged strata a greater capacity for resistance, and hence a greater margin of autonomy, manoeuvrability and influence. It is already possible to identify four closely interrelated trends which are contributing to the politics of disorder: the progressive disintegration and decline of structures and societies which have been occupying a position of dominance; the increasing assertiveness of groupings or strata whose status has until now been peripheral or dependent;[8] the rise of new axes of conflict between the main established power systems; the growing ideological and institutional convergence of forces situated at the periphery. While these tendencies are still largely in their infancy and their final outcome not entirely predictable, their initial impact on different levels of social organization is already visible, as is their relevance to the general aspiration for a fundamental change of the existing world order.

Structural disintegration

In recent years the process of disintegration has been nowhere more evident than in the crisis of economic management experienced by most capitalist societies. As we have already seen, a variety of factors have combined to produce an almost blind acceptance of the economics of growth at the cost of steadily rising inflation. All conventional remedies for the disease, which has now reached endemic proportions, have lost much of their efficacy and relevance as the inflationary spiral has continued unabated in spite of recessionist conditions and high and rising unemployment. This structural imbalance, most conspicuous in the case of Britain but by no means confined to that country, has weakened the super-industrial system and reduced the number of alternatives available to it in resolving the problems of production and distribution. In the capitalist economy, the very nature of the private interests which control its most advanced sectors, and the perennial opposition between labour and management preclude the spirit of cooperation and institutional framework required to create a rational economic order. The experience of centrally planned economies, of the type which has developed in the Soviet Union, is not much more promising, for the necessary sense of genuine involvement and participation has also been stifled, in this case by an overgrown, highly centralized and inflexible bureaucracy. Consequently, in spite of all its methods of legitimation and various provisions for social welfare, the modern industrial state is finding it increasingly difficult to disguise the widening discrepancy between promise and performance, between its supposedly egalitarian ethos and the glaring inequalities in income, status and power.[9] It is this very discrepancy and its administrative and ideological ramifications which lie at the root of the emerging crisis of legitimacy.[10]

Closely related to and exacerbating the crisis of economic and political management is the ecological impact of prevailing consumption and production patterns. We have previously discussed the destabilizing consequences of continuing growth rates in energy consumption. To the extent that all the main western economies already depend in varying degrees on imported oil, the only alternative which is open to them is either growing reliance on foreign sources of energy or a reversal in the present pattern of economic growth. Alternative sources of energy will no doubt be expanded but major constraints will still operate whether in terms of the existing costs of production, the irretrievable diminution of vital resources, or the chemical, biological and thermal pollution of air, water and soil. Nor is there much likelihood that further technological advances will come to the rescue of the super-industrial society or obviate its increasing resource dependence on the

Third World. On present trends, the progress of science and technology is much more likely to create or intensify than to ameliorate the problems of economic and environmental planning.[11] The process of industrialization has already brought about the general deterioration of the environment. In addition to the serious physical problem of waste, less direct but equally dangerous side effects, including damage to agriculture and the marine food chain, have resulted from the indiscriminate recourse to pesticides and herbicides and the domestic and industrial use of heavy chemicals. Increasing exposure to radiation, disturbance of the geological equilibrium and escalating levels of thermal and noise pollution have also contributed to environmental degradation. In the wake of these developments, it is hardly surprising that a growing environmental movement should have come to the fore, ready not only to oppose vested economic and bureaucratic interests on specific ecological issues, but to question the entire set of assumptions on which is based the prevailing model of growth and energy consumption.

Reinforcing the economic and environmental predicament has been the convulsion caused by modern warfare. The frightening implications of total war in the atomic age have robbed Realpolitik of much of its apparent reasonableness. But quite apart from the public revulsion and revolt against nuclear war, serious political disorders have arisen as a result of costly and highly unsuccessful colonial or interventionist wars. The military engagements undertaken by France, Portugal and the United States in Algeria, Mozambique and Vietnam respectively created sharp ideological divisions within the metropolis and a collective crisis of conscience which eventually led large sections of society to reject the official ideology of the state and its formulation of national interests and national objectives.

In the case of the United States, the habit of deception and self-deception developed by the political and military leadership during the course of the Vietnam war provoked an unbridgeable gap – popularly known as the credibility gap – between public opinion and government policy. The graphic revelations of the Pentagon Papers merely confirmed the widespread mood of disillusionment. By the early 1970s the demoralization of the US army had reached unprecedented proportions with some 89,000 deserters 100,000 conscientious objectors and tens of thousands of drug addicts.[12] Significantly, the recourse to falsehoods and deliberate lies by American policy-makers was hardly ever aimed at the enemy but intended chiefly for public consumption. The justification of American policy assumed the character of a public relations exercise, an intricate and outwardly rational process of psychological manipulation involving the constant redefinition of objectives and designed to persuade both Congress and the public at large to accept a policy of increasing risks and diminishing returns. The bureaucratic model of decision-making, increasingly divorced from reality, sought to conform unpleasant or stubborn facts simply by ignoring or justifying them.[13] The computerized approach to problem-solving, by relying on mathematical, rational calculations, lost sight of the incalculable quality of morality and politics, thereby provoking in Indochina one of the most grotesque human tragedies of the twentieth century, and in the United States one of the most dramatic shifts in political allegiance.

The incipient crisis of legitimacy which we have been describing is not confined to capitalist societies, but has spread to most authoritarian political systems and is gradually coming to the fore in many parts of the Soviet empire, thus validating the proposition that even the most brutal power system is ultimately dependent on the widespread conviction that it is legitimate. In the Soviet Union, a rapidly expanding intellectual elite is beginning to ask searching questions about economics, politics and culture, and to reject the crude Marxist orthodoxies of the Stalinist era. The latent conflict of interests and perceptions between the scientific and cultural intelligentsia and the industrial and political bureaucracy cannot be indefinitely contained within the established parameters of ideological discourse.[14] Instances of public disaffection may still be relatively rare but their conversion into collective discontent is much more feasible than is often imagined. In conditions of political disequilibrium isolated pockets of dissent can be readily transformed into a popular movement of national dimensions as was demonstrated by developments in Czechoslovakia in 1967–8 and the rapid steps towards social democratization which were taken under Dubcek's leadership before they were brutally suppressed by the invasion of Soviet troops.[15]

Enough will have been said to suggest that even in conditions of apparent political stability there is likely to prevail considerable fluidity in the value orientation of society. Despite appearances to the contrary, variations in attitudes and a certain ideological ambivalence may permeate the entire body politic. Any society is in fact likely to comprise diverse value-systems enjoying different degrees of acceptance at different times depending on economic, political and other circumstances. Wertheim, who has most clearly outlined this dynamic model of society, argues that society is not a harmonious static structure but 'an uneasy coexistence of several divergent and competing value-systems', and that the dominance of any particular ideological framework is likely to be no more than the temporary expression of the existing power structure.[16] A point may be reached when the conflict of values which has been lying dormant for some considerable time, finally breaks out into the open and takes the form of direct opposition to the prevailing hierarchy. Such a manifest conflict of values now dominates the life of much of the Third World, where an increasingly powerful reaction against the western-inspired impulse towards modernization is encouraging the cultivation of indigenous values and resources.[17] The rejection of modernity, understood as the pervasiveness, coerciveness and anonymity of the 'technological economy' is also gaining momentum in most capitalist societies and is beginning to puncture the tranquil authoritarianism of several communist systems.

So far, in examining the trend towards structural disintegration we have laid particular stress on the crisis of legitimacy confronting the modern industrial state. There is however an important international dimension to this process which we must now consider. The increasing difficulty with which the highly industrialized metropolis is able to assert its authority over its citizenry is now paralleled by its declining capacity to wield the traditional instruments of coercion over its satellites. The nation-state in most parts of the Third World may still be highly vulnerable to internal divisions and foreign pressures, but it is gradually developing the ideology, administrative infrastructure and diplomatic leverage to ensure its viability and at least partial autonomy as an actor on the international stage. While it is true that very significant powers of retaliation are still available to the major metropolitan centres, as United States overt and covert intervention in Latin America and the Middle East amply demonstrates, the feasibility of effective military intervention is rapidly diminishing as a result of the outcome of the Indochina War and the continuing nuclear stalemate. Nor are such other options as CIA subversive activities, termination of military aid, withdrawal of foreign investments, blockage of loans by international agencies, guaranteed of success. The increasing vulnerability of metropolitan powers to internally and externally induced crises has severely deflated their ambition to act as policemen of the world. Clearly the economics of scarcity and the politics of disorder can no longer be contained within national boundaries and are gradually eroding the international network of client relationships which the major centres of world power have so consistently exploited to their own advantage.

The struggle for emancipation

As we have seen, the process of structural disintegration does not occur in a social vacuum, it inevitably reflects the shift in values which accompanies the visible discrepancy between steadily rising expectations and the system's lagging capacity to satisfy them.[18] The malfunctioning of the dominant system is likely to bring to life a contrary set of values whose strength will depend in part on their internal consistency, the universality of their appeal, the intensity of the commitment which they inspire and their contribution to collective action. The object of analysis is to identify the potentially most disruptive value-systems within a particular society, and the social strata which can most effectively take up the struggle for emancipation.

In advanced capitalist societies, the younger generation, particularly the student population, some sections of the intelligentsia and the working class, and various underprivileged minorities have constituted the focal points of dissent. Common to all of them has been the experience of frustration arising from the sense of unfulfilled individual and collective expectations. It is above all the gradual realization of the counterfeit nature of established political morality, which has aroused the anger and indignation of youth and reinforced its natural inclination to rebel against the status quo. By its spontaneous and moral impulse, youth protest is thus sharply differentiated from the self-interested power game of conventional politics.

Separate from but closely related to the political disaffection of youth is its cultural revolt, its increasing identification with a distinct sub-culture, its cultivation of life-styles in dress, speech, leisure and sexuality which are markedly antagonistic to the dominant value-system. The counter culture may in fact, be interpreted as a reaction to the 'homelessness' produced by the acceleration of bureaucratic and technological processes. It represents a struggle for liberation from the many 'discontents of modernity', a confused but authentic search for a new system of symbols which can restore meaning to the experience of pain and suffering, and reinterpret the finiteness and transience of the human condition.[19] The alienation of youth has not yet seriously affected the recruitment system on which the industrial order depends for its survival, but it has, by its rejection of affluence, status and respectability, severely impaired the psychological stability of the technocratic society.

An even more incisive and direct challenge to the established order has come from student protest. The reason why universities and colleges should have become such an important nucleus of dissent is not hard to discover.[20] It is within the intellectual environment of these institutions that the disparity between the official ideology, which affirms the principles of equality freedom and democracy, and the social reality, which often denies them, is most sharply perceived. The contradiction between magniloquent ideological principles and the actual functioning of social structures permeates, in fact, the life of universities themselves. It is not surprising, therefore, that students should have taken the initiative in asserting the need for greater autonomy and participation both within the university and the wider community.[21] An important contribution of student dissent was its ability to popularize the many academic critiques of the established order which had appeared during the 1950s and 1960s. More importantly, by going beyond the immediate issues affecting their own institutions, by endeavouring to gain some understanding of the aspirations of the industrial working class and repressed minorities, student militancy acted as a catalyst in the larger social struggle for emancipation. It is clear, however from the events in France of May 1968 as well as from the experience of other countries that none of these societies was yet ripe for revolution.[22] The potentially most powerful agents of social change were not yet psychologically or organizationally ready to seek the fundamental transformation of the socio-economic order. The universities might have planted seeds of change but a long process of maturation would be necessary before they could be brought to full fruition. On the other hand, one should not underestimate the prophetic quality of the libertarian themes and practices which emerged during the height of student contestation. For we may have witnessed not simply the rebirth of anarchism,[23] but a renewed and far-reaching confidence in the power of human action.

We have dwelt at some length on the role of youth and student dissent because it best illustrates the ideological cleavages to which advanced industrial societies are increasingly exposed. While several other social strata have also contributed to political instability, their value orientation appears to have been far more ambivalent. In spite of the recent rise in industrial militancy even in countries like Sweden and West Germany, which have enjoyed a consistently low level of labour unrest, the mass of the working class in capitalist societies has tended to accept the values of the consumer culture. On the other hand, one must not overlook the significance of worker discontent especially at the shop-floor level or the power of organized labour to frustrate government policies and accentuate the inflationary and other destabilizing trends in the capitalist economy.

More effective than working class disaffection in subverting the established pattern of cultural and political authority has been ethnic discontent, based as it is on an acute sense of deprivation and collective identity. To take the example of the black community in the United States, torn by ideological and other divisions – notably between those who believe in the efficacy of constitutional pressures through the courts and the electoral process and those who subscribe to revolutionary violence – there is no disputing the pervasive disenhancment with the dominant white value-system and the widespread readiness to affirm the peculiar identity of black experience and personality. The assertion of black interests and the demand for freedom and individuality have undoubtedly contributed to the philosophy of revolt and to a renewed determination to confront the structures of discrimination and inequality.

Of even greater significance for the future, though not yet constituting a coherent social force, is the struggle for women's liberation and the gradual emergence of a movement which stresses not only the psychological but also the political and economic dimensions of oppression. The growing recognition of the integral connection between the exploitation of women and the underlying social structure reflects a major leap in consciousness and a decisive step in the process of emancipation. The women's liberation movement, while still largely confined to the middle class, is already groping for new forms of expression and organization which may in due course give it greater political coherence and enhance its polarizing effect on society.

In focussing attention on some of the main sources of dissent, particularly as it has recently manifested itself in the industrialized western world, the intention was not to provide a historical or comprehensive account of these various protest movements but simply to underline the sharpening conflict of values and the progressive delegitimization of established authority.[24] Predictably, the struggle for emancipation has produced a much higher incidence of disobedience to the law, civil and criminal. By mirroring the conspicuous illegality and impropriety of government actions and policies, the mounting defiance of the forces of law and order is hastening and reinforcing the vulnerability of the state apparatus and its legal structures. Hostility to particular manifestations of the system is gradually giving way to the commitment to displace the system as a whole.[25] The present level of social ferment has yet to crystallize into a countervailing power base, but it has already instilled a sense of crisis deep into the consciousness of a large and expanding section of society.

While not underestimating the long-term significance of the wave of political protest which has recently swept the super-industrial state, the fact remains that it is within the predominantly peasant societies of the Third World that liberation struggles have achieved their greatest success. A series of national and social revolutions have forced the retrenchment of colonial and neo-colonial empires and thereby effected a substantial shift in the international balance of power. The fortunes of these revolutionary movements, whether directed against foreign domination or domestic oppression, have normally depended on their ability to persuade the peasantry of the need to break existing patronage ties and to transfer its allegiance to a new collective identity.[26] It was precisely this rationale which animated the Chinese revolutionary strategy of complementing guerrilla warfare with the establishment of large liberated areas. The possession of liberated territory enabled the communist leadership to provide the peasant with security, to raise his political consciousness, to commence land and other reforms, and to train armies.[27] Having secured the confidence of the peasant, the political elite was able to initiate after liberation, an effective labour-intensive agricultural policy and a radical programme of political mobilization, in spite of the fierce hostility which the underlying principle of self-reliance was to elicit first from the United States and subsequently from the Soviet Union. In this sense, the Chinese experiment may be regarded as one of the most powerful challenges to the system of international stratification.

The more recent triumph of the liberation struggles in Indo-china, opposed as they were to the most destructive military machine in the world, has also caused irreparable damage to the international structures of dominance. The commitment of more than 540,000 US troops in Vietnam, the extension of the war into Laos and Cambodia, the massive bombing of North Vietnam, the indiscriminate use of napalm and defoliants, the Vietnamization policy, all failed to secure the achievement of United States objectives. Similarly, the survival of the Cuban revolution in the face of outright American hostility, and the limited but considerable successes registered by liberation movements in Palestine, Guinea-Bissau, Mozambique. Angola, and Zimbabwe have confirmed the ascendancy of revolutionary trends in many of these underdeveloped countries.

Needless to say, the search for emancipation is not being waged exclusively by violence. An important dimension of the struggle is the growing rejection of the supposed benefits of foreign aid, foreign investment and military alliances, and the marked shift towards greater self-reliance in economic development. More and more numerous are the voices within the Third World which are demanding the right of their country to manage its own affairs, to determine its own economic and political institutions, to curb, and where necessary, eliminate the pressure of foreign governments, international agencies and multinational corporations. Even conservative governments have begun to apply restrictive quantitative and qualitative requirements on foreign investment, to insist that domestic production account for a greater share of final output, to ban limitations by the parent company on the subsidiary's distribution of local production and use of the parent's technology, and to curtail the repatriation of capital investment and profits.[28] One may be sceptical of the efficacy of these and other similar measures, but there can be no doubt of the new ideological climate which is gradually modifying existing relationships between the centre and the periphery.

Apart from the actions of governments, another element in the Third World struggle for liberation is the rising dissatisfaction of the urban and, in particular, the student population with the political status quo and with economic models of growth that are limited to the maximization of the GNP. The widespread concern for political freedom as well as economic and social progress is finding expression in a rising tide of protest and a series of political upheavals which highlight the vulnerability of even the most deeply entrenched regimes. Demonstrations and student militancy in countries like India, Sri Lanka, Thailand, Indonesia, the Philippines and South Korea symbolize the simmering resentment against the oppression, corruption and nepotism of the ruling elites. Typifying the trend towards ideological polarization is the gradual process of conscientization which has been taking place in many parts of Latin America and in which an increasingly militant form of Christianity has acted as a powerful catalyst. A series of progressively more radical declarations emanating from priests and bishops alike have condemned the local structures of oppression and exhorted all Christians to work relentlessly towards a concrete programme of liberation.[29] In committing themselves to this struggle, a large number of Christians, among whom were many priests and nuns, have been imprisoned, tortured and even killed. This rising assertiveness reflects a more sensitized consciousness of the alienating and enslaving social reality, a new conception of equity and human dignity, and a more dynamic praxis of social change.

To complete this rather simplified outline of the groping steps towards emancipation, it may be appropriate to say a final word about the Chinese experiment and the Maoist notion of permanent revolution, which have attracted so much attention in both developed and underdeveloped societies.[30] According to this concept, constant vigilance is required to prevent and, if necessary, oppose the development of bureaucratic structures which, by their very nature, contradict the principles of equality and individuality. The underlying rationale of the Cultural Revolution was, in fact, to unleash the moral and ideological impulse which would overpower the bureaucratic instinct.[31] In order to offset the preoccupation with status and self-interest, Chinese youth were to be introduced to life in the factory or in the commune as a practical demonstration of the egalitarian principle. Many have questioned the feasibility of constructing a society in which frugality and the renunciation of privilege are universally accepted as ultimate virtues, but no one can dispute the significance of an experiment in which the utopian attempt to create the selfless and self-disciplined man has been assigned the highest priority on the political agenda.

The struggle for liberation is taking different forms in different parts of the world and is being waged with varying degrees of intensity and success, but the phenomenon has assumed global proportions and its reach extends from the most sophisticated technological society to the most primitive peasant economy. The general trend towards emancipation is of course still in its infancy and represents in any case a human aspiration that is never completely fulfilled, but already it has released a store of human energy with almost unlimited potential for subverting existing social images and prevailing relationships of dominance and dependence.

New axes of conflict

Having sketched in broad outline the two global and related processes of structural disintegration and human emancipation, it remains to examine two subsidiary but complementary trends associated mainly with the emergence of new patterns of international conflict and cooperation. The bipolar division of the world whereby the United States and the Soviet Union exercised almost complete ideological, economic and military supremacy over their respective blocs has long since past. The vaunted permanence and stability of the system have proved to be illusory. A series of local and regional confrontations has shown that the Soviet–American duopoly could not prevent the rise of new centres of power or contain the advance of revolutionary forces in the Third World and elsewhere. While China has provided the focal point for the revolutionary opposition to the international status quo, other challenges have arisen both from within and outside the two alliance systems. In relatively quick succession, Britain, France, China and now India have made their separate bids to nuclear status. The great military arsenals of the two superpowers, far from evoking meek submission, have encouraged the trend towards nuclear proliferation.[32]

In the economic sphere, we have already considered at some length the rapidly evolving relationship between the United States and its Western European and Japanese allies, the fierce economic competition in the search for markets, raw materials and investment outlets, and their destabilizing effects on the world market economy. The resurgence of economic nationalism in inter-capitalist relations has considerably complicated the management of intra-alliance relationships and confirmed the view that the stability of the 1950s and early 1960s was no more than the façade of an unequal relationship now in rapid decline.[33]

Another major axis of international conflict was to arise from the Sino–Soviet dispute, which grew in the 1960s in direct pro-

portion to the Soviet–American rapprochement.[34] China sought
to contrast the Soviet betrayal of the revolutionary cause with
its own commitment to a liberation strategy based on the principles of revolutionary zeal and the necessity of armed struggle.
Peking's quarrel with Moscow, conducted chiefly in terms of
Marxist–Leninist orthodoxy, became a competition for the
leadership of the international communist movement. But
underlying and reinforcing the ideological schism was the
border conflict which resulted in serious clashes in 1969 and
the massive build-up of Soviet and Chinese troops along the
border areas. In the diplomatic arena, the conflict has now
reached global proportions with both countries trying to consolidate their respective positions and thwart each other's
designs. The Soviet Union is attempting to contain the expansion of Chinese influence in Asia, while China is seeking to
accentuate the polycentric tendencies which have developed
within the Soviet empire and particularly in Eastern Europe.
The Sino–Soviet dispute is thus helping to lay bare the profound divisions in international politics which were merely
concealed or distorted by nearly two decades of ideological
bipolarity.

The dissolution of bipolar politics has not meant the end of
the Soviet–American adversary relationship but an increasingly
heterogenous international system in which the traditional
hostility between the two superpowers, while more muted than
before, persists nevertheless and is compounded by new and at
least equally powerful economic and strategic antagonisms.
An additional source of tension in international relations has
derived from the spectacular growth of multinational corporations and their increasing capacity to pursue transnational
objectives and strategies in direct opposition to the objectives
of both home and host states.[35] The mounting immunity of
multinational enterprise to effective territorial control, should
it continue unchecked, is likely to undermine further the efficacy and credibility of the sovereign state. The emerging
conflict between national and transnational actors is beginning
to combine with traditional great-power rivalries to produce an
increasingly fragmented and polarized international system
whose net effect is to reduce the effectiveness of existing structures of power and authority.

Cooperation at the periphery

Parallelling and reflecting the process of international fragmentation and polarization and the constraints which it imposes on metropolitan domination is the expanding leverage
and scope for collective action available to nations and movements in the periphery. As already intimated, Third World
countries have developed in recent years, in spite of continuing
rifts and divisions, a greater sense of common identity and a
more acute awareness of their bargaining power. This psychological and behavioural change has been nowhere more apparent than at the United Nations, notably in the General
Assembly, where First World powers have suffered a succession
of diplomatic defeats. The quasi-official status accorded in
1974 to the Palestinian Liberation Organization, as a result
of the invitation to its leader, Yasser Arafat, to address the
Assembly, the decision to restrict Israeli participation in the
debate on Palestine, the exclusion of the South African delegation from the entire proceedings of the Assembly, the adoption of the 'Charter of Economic Rights and Duties of States',
the reaffirmation of the call to establish the Indian Ocean as a
'zone of peace', are symbolic measures largely devoid of immediate practical impact, but sufficiently indicative of the
growing cohesiveness and assertiveness of the Third World to
have caused the American administration to launch a series of
unprecedented verbal assaults denouncing Third World diplomacy inside and outside the United Nations.

More immediate and concrete results have followed the
concerted action of OPEC countries in effecting within the
space of a few months a fourfold increase in the price of oil. The
dramatic rise in OPEC oil revenues and the consequent deterioration in the OECD trade balance reflected an unprecedented
transfer of wealth which would further destablize an already
vulnerable international monetary system. The drastically
altered relationship between oil consumers and oil producers
appeared to call into question the entire framework of international finance, trade and investment.

While recognizing the unique economics of oil and the
peculiar political situation created by Arab solidarity in the
Middle East conflict, it is nonetheless a fact that the OPEC ex-

perience has provided a powerful psychological impetus to other Third World initiatives.[36] Underdeveloped nations are beginning to explore seriously the economic opportunities as distinct from the diplomatic manoeuvrability accruing from political independence. The increasingly heterogeneous international system is enabling them, perhaps for the first time, to play off capitalist states one against the other, to balance the communist world against the capitalist world, and to trade off one type of economic benefit for another. Apart from the OPEC example, the last few years has seen a noticeable increase in collective bargaining through such institutions as the Andean Pact, the United Nations Conference on Trade and Development, the special UN Session on Resources and Development and the Conference on the Law of the Sea. An alliance of the major producers of copper, tin, bauxite, iron ore is gradually becoming an organizational reality that western consumers cannot ignore. Apart from the growing capacity to charge – or threaten to charge – higher prices for these commodities, underdeveloped nations are insisting on processing these commodities themselves. A concerted resources diplomacy is likely to provide Third World countries with two additional leverages. In those cases where there is a limited number of producers (e.g. as in copper, where 80 per cent of the world's supply is controlled by Chile, Peru, Zaire and Zambia), and where finance is available to build a stockpile of the particular commodity (already there are indications that OPEC funds may be used to finance producer associations in other raw materials), they may be able to engage in discriminatory action against one or more of the consuming countries. They may decide, with a much greater prospect of success than the recent oil embargo against the United States and the Netherlands, to cut supplies of one or more key commodities to one great power in favour of its competitors. Similarly, where export earnings are high, decisions could be made with regard to investment in international money markets which produce marked shifts from one currency to another, with serious destabilizing consequences for both the national and international economies. The trend towards regional and global collective action will undoubtedly prove a slow and arduous process, but its potential to modify the existing framework of economic relationships between industrialized and underdeveloped economies cannot be disputed.

The value of collective bargaining is now also becoming apparent in the Third World's relationship with multinational corporations. To be effective such devices as the forcible nationalization of foreign interests, the unilateral acquisition of majority ownership in foreign enterprises and the withholding of supply of key raw materials have to be applied collectively. Here again the OPEC experience has been particularly significant. Following the acceptance by the oil corporations in February 1971 of a general rise in the posted price of oil, additional demands for further price rises and greater participation in the production process became an integral part of OPEC strategy. Soon after the outbreak of the Yom Kippur War in October 1973, the OPEC countries assumed complete control over production and export levels and sharply increased their share of the financial revenue. Since then the trend towards nationalization has continued to gather momentum, and most producer governments have successfully negotiated a 60 per cent share of oil production. Moreover, OPEC's increasing control over the oil pricing system has had the effect of forcing the major companies to increase their profit margins on refining and marketing operations in order to retain their overall integrated margins.

In stressing the political leverage and economic advantage that Third World governments can expect to derive from collective decision-making, it is not being argued that these benefits will be necessarily or automatically passed on to their respective populations. A more symmetrical bargaining relationship between the metropolis and the satellite, which does not, at the same time, eliminate the underlying convergence of interests between the respective elites, cannot be considered a sufficient condition for the removal of the structures of underdevelopment. On the other hand, to the extent that such a modification in the pattern of international stratification contributes to the politics of disorder, it is likely to weaken the power of the metropolis and add to the fluidity of ideological and political attitudes within the satellite. In this sense, the trend towards greater Third World solidarity, irrespective of its immediate domestic implications, may be regarded as an intermediate but important stage in the process of emancipation.

Mirroring the collective response of Third World countries to the pattern of international stratification are the efforts of diverse groups and movements operating within the national boundaries of advanced industrial societies to pool resources and extend lines of cooperation. Increasing contact between activists drawn from various dissenting elements is meeting an acute need for mutual support and contributing to a much more lucid analysis of established authority structures and hence to a much more sophisticated action strategy. While not renouncing their separate identities, organizations committed to such diverse goals as peace, racial equality, workers' control, women's liberation, consumer protection or ecological balance, are beginning to appreciate the close interconnection of their respective endeavours, all of which stand in direct opposition to the prevailing principles of hierarchy, competition and domination. The sharing and coordination of the limited resources available to these movements is a trend that is still in its embryonic stage but is likely to accelerate with the passage of time. Equally significant are the current attempts to create a network of transnational linkages, again for the purpose of reinforcing the political struggles that are being waged at the national level but with the added objective of promoting a social consciousness which recognizes the need for international perspectives and initiatives.[37] In so far as this type of transnational solidarity thrives chiefly on the dissemination of ideas and the crystallization of common attitudes, it is spared the need for elaborate bureaucratic institutions which invariably obstruct the principle of emancipation. The worldwide growth of the anti-war movement and of opposition to American actions in Indochina provides perhaps the clearest demonstration yet of the efficacy of this form of collective protest. Although lacking the same intense fervour, a similar wave of dissent appears to be rising in many parts of the industrialized world in response to the continued impoverishment of the natural environment. The progressive universalization of these antithetic values represents one of the most subversive forces tending to undermine the ideology of the existing world order.

This general and much simplified review of the politics of disorder has attempted to highlight four trends which significantly impinge on contemporary structures of power and authority. A series of political, economic and ecological crises which overflow the boundaries and the competence of the nation-state have given rise to a process of structural disintegration in both national and international society. Diverse social and political movements committed to changing life-styles and new concepts of equity and world order are contributing to a disparate but worldwide struggle for emancipation. The emergence of new centres and new sources of power is accentuating the tendency towards a more fragmented, heterogeneous and polarized international system. Equally disruptive of the status quo is the new pattern of alignments which is providing underprivileged nations and social strata with a much enhanced capacity for collective action. To argue that these trends have already produced a revolutionary situation would be an extreme overstatement of the case. On the other hand, the continuing evolution of these trends promises to release nations and men from their cultural captivity and to give birth to a new set of values, interests and loyalties which may eventually permit the construction of new bridges both within and between societies.

11. The politics of survival

In juxtaposing the utopian vision with the politics of disorder the intention was not to suggest that utopia is at hand or that the established structures of power and authority, nationally and internationally, are all facing imminent collapse. Rather the aim was to identify those trends which point towards institutional breakdown, and to indicate the role which utopian insights may play, not in averting the impending crisis, but in providing the basis for a response to it which may enhance the chances of survival and steer human values and institutions in new and more promising directions.

The utopian conception of a communal yet autonomous form of existence, with its emphasis on the aesthetic and cosmic dimension of human experience, may not be capable of immediate or complete realization, but it can nonetheless animate the struggles for emancipation that are currently being waged by numerous national, subnational and transnational movements. In other words, the present historical possibilities implicit in the politics of disorder can be exploited to achieve a new value consensus which corresponds far more closely with utopian aspirations and redefines man's long-term needs in relation to the total evolutionary process. By learning to balance his values against the requirements of the other components of the 'biotic pyramid', man is able to contribute to the growth of life in all its richness, complexity and diversity. By integrating the fragmented, alienated and tainted pieces of his image of the world into a vision of wholeness, he is more likely to forsake the notion of the struggle for existence and the consequent attempt to eliminate all competitive forms of life, including fellow-individuals and societies. The self-centred faith in 'the survival of the fittest' is thus replaced by the more ethical and universal commitment to the survival of life itself.

The ecological perspective clearly indicates that man cannot achieve abundance at the expense of his natural environment. The technological utopia in which every human whim and fancy finds complete and instant satisfaction is outside the realm of feasibility.[1] Far from disappearing as a result of industrial growth, scarcity remains the dominant characteristic of contemporary society. By affirming and institutionalizing the concept of infinite wants, consumer affluence has hindered the fulfilment of psychological needs and moral values and exacerbated the perennial problem of scarcity. In its physical manifestation, the historical phenomenon of scarcity is simply the product of three interacting factors: population, resources and technology. Given the limitations of the globe's carrying capacity, exponential growth rates in population and technology must ultimately act as a drain on the earth's finite resources, with a resulting decline in the real value of the per capita share of the world's goods.[2] It is conceivable that continuing technological innovation may provide new and inexhaustible sources of energy, but such a possibility is unlikely to materialize in the foreseeable future. In any case, the economics of scarcity is not merely a function of the acquisition of energy, but also of its dissipation. It is the result of both depletion and pollution.

Beyond a certain level, the maximization of population and energy consumption is incompatible with any ethical or rational calculus aimed at achieving an optimum of value or the greatest good for the greatest number. If some technological enthusiasts have already proclaimed the end of scarcity it is because they have confused universal and absolute abundance with the relative affluence of the minority of the world's population achieved, in great measure, at the expense of the poverty of a much larger fraction of humanity, and at the cost of environmental degradation whose far-reaching effects on the survival prospects of the human species have yet to be fully calculated. Nor can it be argued that the technocratic culture has yet eliminated, or is likely to eliminate in the future, the routine and stultifying aspect of toil except for a privileged minority. The blissful state in which man does not have to exert himself in order to take care of his material needs remains a technological fantasy.

If one accepts then the twin propositions that scarcity is yet to be overcome and that all notions of effortless and unlimited abundance are contradicted by the finite dimensions of the earth's ecosystem, the question arises as to whether the human condition can ever rise above the struggle against necessity. It must be understood, however, that this is a supremely ethical and political question capable only of a political answer, in which technology must play a subordinate role. If scarcity is to be replaced by even minimal sufficiency then man will need to revise his economic goals, his mode of consumption and production, and the existing allocation of political and economic power. Indeed, it is the very primacy of the economic dimension of existence which will have to be challenged if the individual is to find a way of affirming his being which does not depend on competition and success expressed in monetary terms.[3] What is called for is not some form of social engineering, however complex or sophisticated its technical operation, but a general reappraisal of individual and collective ideals. The excessive emphasis which industrial culture attaches to productivity has necessitated the conspicuous neglect of other fundamental social values and sacrificed optimal human development for the sake of maximal production.[4]

The stunting of man's ethical instincts has been nowhere more evident than in his uncaring and unimaginative attitude towards the future. The inability of the individual to identify with the larger interest of the human community extends then to the temporal as well as the spatial dimension of human experience. The obsessive preoccupation with the present has entailed almost complete disregard for the lessons of the past and the refusal to accept any sense of obligation towards posterity. Inevitably, however, any civilization, which loses sight of its image of the future and abdicates all responsibility for the consequences of its actions, undermines its capacity to deal with the present and soon disintegrates.[5] If decisions are repeatedly made simply with a view to securing immediate advantage, they will of necessity minimize the social and political options available to succeeding generations. But the addictive habit of discounting the future, of attributing priority to short-term parochial interests, especially apparent in the modern state's economic and defence policies, merely serves to hasten the arrival of the future and to compound the difficulties it poses for the present. It is of the very essence of rapid technological change that it shortens the time lag between actions and their consequences, thereby telescoping prospective time into present time and making it impossible for man to escape from the effects of his myopic vision. In the face of actual scarcity and potential destruction, the politics of survival requires a sharper ethical perspective and a wider-ranging framework of decision-making able to reconcile the conflicting demands of immediate and long-term objectives.

Throughout our analysis, we have taken the view that technology cannot of itself resolve the crisis of scarcity or ensure physical, let alone spiritual, stability. Indeed, the scientific and technological explosion which has accompanied the growth of the industrial state, far from eliminating the manifestations of bondage in society, has tended to accentuate relationships of dominance and dependence. As C. S. Lewis has incisively observed, the power that man has achieved over nature has turned out to be a power exercised by some men over other men with technology as its instrument.[6] Inventions and discoveries in such fields as medicine, communications and transport may have revolutionized man's relationship with the natural order, but they have at the same time made him the victim of these new forms of power. What is in question is not the misuse of power, widespread though it is, but the disparity in power which enables a small minority of bureaucrats, planners and engineers to establish their technocratic rule over millions of men, and one dominant age to achieve mastery over generations yet unborn. It is not that this new race of conditioners is composed of evil men but that they have undermined their own humanity and that of their subjects by their very decision to shape humanity. In this sense, both the conditioners and the conditioned have been reduced to artifacts. Far from subduing reality to the wishes of men, the technical process of conditioning risks producing 'the abolition of man'.

At this point, a word of clarification may be necessary, for we may have created the erroneous impression that technology lies at the root of the modern human predicament. The problem of domination and dehumanization that we have been describing cannot be attributed to technology as such but only to

the specific role assigned to it by the ideology of industrialization. Technology has not caused the problem and cannot
therefore be expected to resolve it. If technology is to function
as an instrument of liberation then it must be integrated into a
new ideological framework and made responsive to a new conception of ethical, political and social change. Any alternative
to the advanced technology characteristic of industrialized
societies must begin by challenging the existing economic organization of society.

We have already analysed at some length both the human
and material costs of economic growth. A growing body of
scholarly literature now exists which enables us to draw up a
more objective but less flattering balance sheet of GNP growth
than has been possible until recently. Simultaneously, there
has arisen mounting public awareness of the disequilibrium
between social needs and economic management, between
ecological balance and production objectives, between psychological stability and the growth mentality, between human
values and planning techniques. These various imbalances
and the inequities to which they give rise, compounded by the
instability and totalitarian tendencies of industrial organization, point to the serious anomalies which have gradually
developed within the confines of the growth paradigm. To
remedy these imbalances it is no longer enough to effect minor
adjustments or modifications to the prevailing economic
model. What is required is a radical break with the underlying
assumptions of GNP growth and their replacement by a more
balanced conception of political economy, which recognizes
the finiteness of the ecosystem and translates it into a steady-
state economy. Needless to say, the shift from the economics
and politics of growth to a system based on homeostasis and
distributive justice will entail large-scale structural changes
and widespread disruption of existing beliefs, habits and
expectations. In any case, the process of decay has already set
in and is causing a growing proportion of the population to
experience feelings of anxiety and insecurity. The resulting
sense of emergency is beginning to provide the necessary
stimulus for a reorientation of values and a much greater readiness to reach decisions, formulate strategies and engage in
practical action in line with a new symbolic image of society.

The steady-state society

It is worth noting that the dogma of maximal economic growth is in fact of relatively recent origin, and that the goal of the limitless rise of production as an end in itself was foreign to much nineteenth-century writing in political economy. For John Stuart Mill, a stationary condition of capital and population was in no way inconsistent with moral and cultural progress. On the contrary, precisely because he considered even the limited increase of wealth and population as detracting from the richness of life, and because such increase could not be maintained indefinitely, he postulated the 'stationary' society as the only realistic option open to posterity.[7] The governing principle of such a society is the need to keep consumption to a minimum, that is, to consume only what is absolutely necessary to maintain a desired psychic or physical state of existence.

Kenneth Boulding, for whom the stock concept is fundamental, argues that being well-fed is more important than eating, and that even intangible services are valuable only in so far as they restore a given stock of depleted psychic capital. In sharp contrast to the 'cowboy economy', which he associates with an exploitative mentality and maximum throughput as measured in terms of GNP, he envisages a 'space-man economy' in which the essential measure of success is not production or consumption, but 'the nature, extent, quality and complexity of the total capital stock', in which is included the biological and psychological condition of the human race.[8] The steady-state society is, therefore, one which has achieved a durable balance between the demands of its population and the resources of its environment. Such a balance presupposes an optimal but stationary population and the equalization of physical production and consumption rates at the lowest feasible level. All physical parameters are thus kept constant while human wants are made the key variable, and technology the dependent variable, its principal function being to achieve the required balance between constant physical wealth and ethical requirements. In this context, E. F. Shumacher has advanced the concept of 'Buddhist economics' defined as the study of how to attain given ends with the minimum means, or how to achieve the highest degree of human satisfaction with maximum frugality and non-violence.[9]

It is important to note that the equilibrium which is being advocated here does not imply a state of stagnation. On the contrary, it is envisaged that the stationary level of physical activity will free the individual from preoccupation with material accumulation and redirect his energies into cultural, artistic and ethical pursuits that enhance the purpose and meaning of social relations. What is proposed in a stable society, a dynamic equilibrium, which recognizes both the physical necessity of the steady-state economy and the unlimited possibilities for intellectual and moral growth.

From the above discussion it follows that the steady-state model cannot operate in the context of the private control of production. It is not simply that the capitalist system is inefficient in an economic sense and inequitable in an ethical sense, but that it lacks the institutional and psychological constraints necessary to maintain a constant population, a constant stock of physical wealth and a stable system of distribution. It is for this reason that most advocates of zero economic growth accept, though from quite different premises, the Marxist notion of the social character of productive activity and the need for the social ownership and democratic control of the means of production. It is perhaps ironic that socialist economics, once thought to hold the key to continued economic growth, should now be seen as the necessary foundation on which to build the steady-state economy.[10] A most forthright case for coercion has been presented by Garett Hardin who, by way of illustration, points to the tragedy of freedom in the commons, whereby the effects of over-grazing, produced by the apparently rational decision of each individual herdsman to increase his herd, finally bring ruin to all.[11] However, the author is careful to insist that by coercion he does not intend the 'arbitrary decisions of distant and irresponsible bureaucrats' but 'mutual coercion, mutually agreed upon by the majority of the people affected'.

Among the more specific controls proposed by the exponents of the steady-state model, of particular interest is the notion of depletion quotas, a system which would enable governments to auction off periodically to groups and individuals the legal right to deplete to the amount of the quota for each of the basic resources. These quotas could be sub-

sequently transferred by sale or gift, but, by controlling their
supply and through the natural operation of the price mechanism, the government would be able to reduce total resource
consumption and maintain aggregate throughput whether it
be in the form of inputs (resource depletion) or ultimate outputs (pollution) to an absolute minimum.[12] Another suggestion
which has recently gained widespread currency is the notion of
a guaranteed income as an incentive for reduced production
and the development of new methods of livelihood where the
crucial yardstick would no longer be the prevalent narrow conception of economic efficiency.[13]

In determining the parameters of the new steady-state
economy, it will eventually be necessary to devise a method of
accounting which is both accurate and comprehensive, which
can specify the level at which stocks of wealth and people are to
be maintained constant. Equally important will be the need to
indicate the optimal level of maintenance throughput for a
given stock of physical wealth and the optimal time span during
which wealth and population are to remain constant. Where
precise answers to these questions are not feasible, it should
nevertheless be possible to indicate the general direction to be
followed and the rate at which a transition from the growth
economy to the steady state is to be effected. While aiming for
a clearer definition of the structure of the steady-state, we can
already discern in broad outline the main characteristics of the
appropriate technology and social institutions. A stable ecological equilibrium will almost certainly dictate smaller energy
inputs; the use of reversible materials and energy sources; production techniques that stress durability and serviceability;
more labour-intensive methods and lower degrees of specialization. Other requirements may include the replacement of the
nuclear family by the commune as the basic economic unit, the
reversal of the trend towards urbanization, a much more decentralized system of decision-making, a far greater element of
local self-reliance, much greater emphasis on local exchanges
than on international trade, and new criteria for the regulation
of technological innovation based on human need and the
prevention of undesirable social and ecological side-effects.

The conceptual framework that we have been outlining is
still in its embryonic stage and many of its practical implica-

tions still await careful examination. Enough will have been said nevertheless to suggest that a series of major dilemmas revolving around the perennial question of freedom will need to be resolved before the steady state can become a viable and acceptable proposition. In the first place, we are confronted with the problem of transition, for the maximization of production is unlikely to give way to the stationary economy merely as a result of some form of technical or social engineering. Given that the rejection of the growth paradigm will require a cultural revolution of very considerable proportions, we are obliged to ask whether such a mutation can occur through the democratic processes of persuasion and education or whether it is conditional on an arbitrary programme of coercion and violence.

The problem is complicated by the fact that such a cultural mutation, to be effective, must not only create a new majority outlook but also contain those minority tendencies determined to subvert the newly formed consensus. Nor can it be reasonably expected that the predicament will necessarily fade away once the foundations for the steady-state economy have been established. How, for example, will the maintenance of a constant state be reconciled with the perfectly justifiable cultural demand for variety, whether in food, dress, housing, recreation, social contact or education. Even if one accepts the view that extravagant diversity is neither useful nor legitimate, it still remains to draw the line between wasteful variety and repressive uniformity. Expressed in somewhat different terms, the difficulty is that of combining social control with personal freedom, macro-stability with micro-variability. It is doubtful whether the concept of mutually agreed coercion can completely resolve the quandary implicit in the marriage of these two potentially conflicting values. After all, self-imposed constraints are likely to operate only in a climate of mutual trust and social responsibility. But have men yet developed the moral resources needed to maintain such a climate? Or is the collective selfishness and irresponsibility manifested in human history such as to make unavailable the sacrifice of freedom and the Hobbesian solution to the tragedy of a shrinking and fragmented planet? On the other hand, while not discounting the evidence of the past, we also have to bear in mind that man's current predicament constitutes a challenge without precedent, and that the crisis of survival may elicit responses that are equally unprecedented in the breadth and depth of their vision. Such at least is the possibility that no serious analysis can afford to ignore.

Distribution and exchange

In so far as the growth-oriented economy militates against equity as well as against ecological balance, the steady state may prove to be an important instrument of distributive justice. It is difficult to conceive how the steady-state could survive at all unless it made the redistribution of economic and political power one of its central objectives. To the extent that the entire globe will ultimately need to adapt to a steady-state, the process of redistribution must occur both within and across national boundaries. The desired equilibrium between the human economy and the environmental system can be achieved only with the establishment of certain upper and lower limits on the individual and collective ownership or control of resources, and on the wealth and income that accrue from such ownership or control. Such a distributist policy would face the common but not insuperable difficulty of defining acceptable margins of inequality. It would have in any case the merit of reducing, if not altogether removing, both the incentive and the opportunity for the progressive concentration of power and wealth.

Such economic controls have become necessary because of the failure of the market mechanism and the unpredictability of the so-called 'invisible hand'. The assumption that the long-term common interest is best served by the efforts of each individual, organization or society to maximize its own position in the short-term is no longer tenable. The existing institutional machinery has manifestly failed, both nationally and internationally, to ensure that competition, and private rights do not conflict with the public interest. Indeed, as we have already explained, the present international maldistribution of wealth is directly related to the prevailing system of exchange, a network of asymmetric relationships which has consistently favoured the advanced industrial world at the expense of underdeveloped economies. The international system of unequal exchange has been most dramatically evident in the trading patterns established in colonial times and subsequently reinforced in the post-independence period. Far from operating as an engine of growth, international trade and the web of financial and commercial transactions have tended to accentuate the dependence of underdeveloped economies on the export of primary commodities and, hence, on the pattern of demand and the structure of production prevailing in the developed economies. Nor is it only Third World countries which have become increasingly vulnerable to the vagaries of the international marketplace. Theoretically, the world economy represents a loosely structured framework which coordinates the economic activities of a large number of autonomous collectivities, each similarly engaged in the rational pursuit of its interests. In practice, this form of interaction, euphemistically described as 'interdependence', has proved to be neither rational nor equitable.[14] The various national and transnational actors are not equal in terms of their trading power, financial leverage or stage of technological development. With the passage of time, the initial advantage enjoyed by the more powerful is multiplied and gradually institutionalized, often with the aid of physical force, into permanent inequality. Whatever the apparent rationality of individual decisions, globally the system has been singularly incapable of ensuring the rational allocation of goods and services.

If one accepts the inherent irrationality and inequality of the international marketplace, as it has tended to operate since the Industrial Revolution, two responses immediately suggest themselves for consideration. The first is to seek a greater degree of equality or symmetry in the benefits flowing to the various parties from the worldwide system of exchange. To this end a much higher level of national and international regulation is required if effective constraints are to be imposed on the activities of the more powerful economic actors, whether they be national governments or multinational corporations. Some of these controls may have to be applied unilaterally by the sovereign state or multilaterally by regional and international organizations. For much of the Third World, the state will undoubtedly continue, at least in the medium term, to provide an important source of leverage in relation to foreign economic interests. Equally important will be the collective pressures to be applied by the underdeveloped countries for the introduction of a new economic code of behaviour, as is already evident by the stand they have adopted at a series of international meetings recently called to consider the critical issues of population, food production, resources, trade and the law of the sea. By cooperating in areas in which they face similar problems, especially in their export trade, and by exploiting divisions among metropolitan centres, the Third World may be able to construct a more symmetric and independent relationship vis-à-vis the rest of the world economy. Ultimately, however, this approach is bound to have serious limitations for, though it may attenuate the wide disparities in economic power between industrial and peasant economies, it is unlikely to bridge them. The disadvantaged sectors of the international economy may be able to register some successes by conducting a more assertive resources policy and by exploiting the growing number of balancing techniques now available to them, but of themselves these measures cannot bring about the profound structural changes needed to transform the prevailing system of unequal exchange.

A second more radical option, in no way incompatible with and perhaps complementary to the first, is to curtail the growth of trade and sharply reduce the anarchic expansion of economic transactions, many of which serve no useful or rational purpose other than the accumulation of capital and profit. Very frequently, an underdeveloped country would significantly benefit, at least in the long run, from a policy of dissociation enabling it to reduce its external economic ties and thereby develop a greater measure of self-reliance and autonomy. Greater use of local human and material resources would prevent the serious dislocation that often follows the absorption of foreign technologies, foreign capital and foreign standards of consumption, and permit an extensive programme of technical and social innovation adapted to local conditions and conducive to a closer and more cooperative relationship between the rural masses and the political leadership.

One of the most negative yet neglected consequences of asymmetrical international transactions is the widening cultural gap which they have usually interposed in underdeveloped countries between urban elites and the peasantry, since it is only the former, a minute fraction of the population, which is absorbed into the transnational network and offered the rewards of participation. In so far as development, as distinct from GNP growth, is understood to depend on the elimination of these social and economic tensions, a viable development strategy as exemplified by the Chinese and Tanzanian models, would make sparing use of capital-intensive production techniques, reduce the division between the city and the countryside, and between manual and mental labour, lessen the control exercised by foreign economic interests, terminate military alliances and remove all foreign troops and military bases. Needless to say such a policy may have to be implemented gradually and with caution in order to minimize the possibility of internal and external subversion, and the severe dislocation which inevitably accompanies the radical reorganization of society. However, all poor countries, regardless of their special circumstances and the particular strategies which these dictate, face the same fundamental choice of either asserting their independence and mobilizing the energies and enthusiasm of their respective populations around an indigenous and coherent programme of development, or of gravitating the locus of their decision-making towards the private and public interests of metropolitan powers, thus perpetuating the global pattern of stratification and inequality.

It must not be thought, however, that the Third World is alone in experiencing the injurious effects of worldwide interpenetration. There can be little doubt that imported inflation had contributed substantially to the spiral of rising prices and costs of production which periodically affected most western economies. Such limited success as OECD countries recently had in containing the high rate of inflation occurred mainly in the context of stagnation or negative growth. But as governments proceeded to reflate their interconnected economies, all the indications were that the mutually reinforcing character of their policies would again activate the inflationary engine. Similarly, by introducing an additional element of instability, the floating exchange system had made national economies increasingly vulnerable to external monetary fluctuations. The danger of steadily rising commercial and financial interdependence lies in the simple fact that the level and scope of these exchanges now far exceed the capacity of the world economy to rationalize and regulate them. It is precisely this consideration which underlines the urgent need for industrial societies to cultivate a greater margin of national independence and self-sufficiency. However, in the attempt to relieve the pressure from trans-national institutions, many of which are on the verge of collapse, such a reversal of policy, if it is to succeed, will need to avoid a return to the divisive nationalisms of the past, and to abandon the ecologically untenable concept of infinite wants and the equally untenable objective of unlimited economic growth.

Combining the demands of universalism and communalism

Our analysis of the present condition of disorder in human affairs and of the many imbalances in which it is reflected has already alluded to the desirability of a new universal order, not as a static or closed system but as a continuous and dynamic process capable of eliciting the support and participation of the vast majority of nations. The various dangers threatening the physical and social fabric of the planet all point to the need for a world order design which would absorb and regulate the diversities and divisions of the present fractionated inter-national system. The dual phenomenon of economic strati-fication and political fragmentation and its culmination in the nuclear threat system clearly indicate the explosive potential of the competitive approach to human survival, which measures success in terms of the primacy and sufficiency of violence. Obviously, we require a new conception of political authority which supersedes the claims of nationalism and state sovereignty, not by imposing on a global scale a highly centralized, arbitrary and homogeneous social system, but by inculcating a universal tolerance for diversity in culture and political ideology, and by extending the scope of cooperative economic relationships.[15]

While many may accept the validity of a planetary strategy for survival, there is no denying the arduousness of the task of persuading and enabling individuals, communities and nations to take collective responsibility for such a strategy. By far the greatest obstacle to this enterprise derives from the profound sense of helplessness or despair which permeates public attitudes. Aware of the present perilous course of world affairs, yet sceptical of the ideological alternatives or of the vision and integrity of political leaders, many prefer to turn a blind eye to the dangers that surround them and devote themselves to private and immediate pursuits that never require more than marginal adjustments to existing social reality. By the same token, a global perspective is already in evidence in the transnational movement which is unifying the diverse struggles for emancipation and generating new concepts and symbols of international solidarity, although these have yet to be translated into a coherent vision of world order, and in many cases have yet to proceed beyond mere verbalization.

A much higher level of participation in transnational organization committed to specific political and educational tasks is likely to prove an important first step in acclimatizing people to the need for a new system of world authority. Whatever its theoretical and practical limitations – and they are considerable – the functionalist conception of world order, by linking authority with specific functions and tasks, does at least underline the psychological and institutional conditions which must precede an effective transfer of authority.[6] In other words, the creation of a new viable world order cannot be imposed from above, but must proceed on the basis of consensual analysis and widespread collaboration involving all the ideological, ethnic and interest groups which have a legitimate stake in the future structure of world society.

Sooner or later any world order design must come to terms with the institutional requirements of such a concept.[17] Some have envisaged the creation of one or more authoritative and centralized political institutions commanding universal consensus, resources and prestige, which, in sharp contrast to the performance of the United Nations and the International Court of Justice, would empower them to impose their will on all member states, and especially on the sensitive issues of security and economic relations. Others have sought to supplement this skeletal framework of world government with a series of specialized agencies devoted to special functions of international coordination in such fields as health, labour standards, food and agriculture, culture and science. In the main, these may be regarded as a continuation or logical development of existing UN agencies, such as the International Labour Organization, the World Health Organization, the Food and Agricultural Organization, or the International Monetary Fund, although considerable controversy has arisen on the question of whether or not these institutions should be politicized to the extent of engaging in direct political confrontation with the governments of individual member states. As a third source of useful institutionalization, students of world order have proposed, again on the basis of existing prototypes, a variety of regional and sub-regional organizations performing certain cooperative functions, particularly in the critical issues of trade and defence.[18] Undoubtedly, the structuralist, functionalist and regionalist approaches to world order could all be expected to make, singly or collectively, some positive contribution to the regulation of international political and economic life, and to the ecological requirements of physical survival.[19] What is much less clear, however, is whether the merits of such an organizational framework would not be largely offset by its defects, especially when it is remembered that all these institutional arrangements would draw their being and inspiration from the existing system of sovereign states, thereby inheriting many of its flaws and superimposing on it an even more centralized and remote bureaucracy than the national bureaucracies which it is supposedly replacing or supplementing.

It is, in fact, difficult to understand how the modern industrial state, which is one of the principal contributing factors to the crisis, can at the same time be regarded as the keystone of a new and stable equilibrium. The great danger of any centralist concept of world order, however formal or informal the proposed institutional machinery, is its apparent incompatibility with the commitment to a libertarian, decentralized and democratic order for domestic society. International organization is unlikely to lead to a better ordered planet unless it promotes maximum cultural diversity and exercises a less rather than a more structured control over the actions and decisions of individual human communities. This assessment is in keeping with our previously stated conclusion that the fulfilment of human needs is likely to be maximized in the small, organic and largely self-reliant community in which personal identity, mutual responsibility and ecological balance are given political priority.

How then is the need for international regulation to be reconciled with the requirements of autonomy and community? The first and perhaps most important step in the resolution of this dilemma consists in discerning the dialectical nature of the forces currently operating within the international system. Paralleling the manifest trend towards economic and administrative integration is the equally visible movement towards political and cultural decentralization. Our analysis of these conflicting forces has indicated, at least implicitly, the desirability of a two-pronged strategy which aims at the development of a universal culture while at the same time hastening the demise of the modern industrial state.

The first element of this strategy involves the mobilization of the intellectual and psychological resources of religion, philosophy, science, ethics and art to advance the realization that all men are part of a single human family, members of a universal civilization in the making. Such a cultural mutation will no doubt have to be expressed in common values, goals, symbols and institutions. However, the purpose of this historical synthesis will be largely negated if it should succumb to the inducements of bureaucratic centralization, technical rationality and economic growth. While some form of international regulation is certainly necessary, its parameters ought to be very clearly specified and integrated into a much richer and more complex process of decision-making centred primarily on autonomous political and economic entities that are much closer in size and organization to the small town than to the large industrial state. It is these self-reliant communities, functioning within a steady-state equilibrium, which will provide the basis for building larger social relationships and hence the foundation for a new world order.

Intercommunal interaction will be promoted to the extent that it serves common interests and needs and contributes to cultural diversity. From such interaction may arise local, regional and international institutions, which must, however, remain answerable to the communities which gave them birth or which are subsequently affected by their actions and decisions. This form of mutually beneficial interchange would constantly need to resist the trend towards centralization of authority and power.[20] Global organisations established to consider issues of universal concern should ideally restrict themselves to the collection and dissemination of information, the projection of models of future collective action, and certain carefully defined responsibilities in environmental protection and wealth redistribution. This rather tentative conception of a viable world community is offered not as the perfect blueprint of human interaction but merely as one of several possible alternative world futures consistent with the balanced development of man's social and physical environment.

Constructing a viable peace strategy

In the foregoing discussion we have attempted to outline the general direction that human society must follow if it is to achieve a tolerable relationship with its natural environment, an adequate system of distributive justice, and a civilization which satisfies the need for both autonomy and regulation. This proposed programme of structural transformation, aimed essentially at the eradication of social pathology, may be thought to have only marginal relevance to the issue of peace and war. But on careful reflection, it will be seen that peace is itself dependent on the possibility of radical social change, on the elimination of the various imbalances which typify contemporary social reality. A dynamic and holistic conception of peace must be based on the negation of both physical and structural violence. Peace may be considered the direct opposite of violence provided that the latter is understood as any activity which violates the humanity of man, which frustrates or undermines the prospects of human self-realization. We may therefore define peace as the development-oriented process of conflict resolution and violence as the pathological process of conflict creation.

This broader definition of violence enables us to do away with the frequent one-sidedness of past notions of conflict. It highlights the fact that hostilities may arise out of objective circumstances which may or may not correspond with subjective perceptions. For example, no detached observer can dispute the reality of the antagonism which divides the exploiter from the exploited, the slave-owner from the slave, although the disparity in power between the two parties may temporarily obscure the true nature of their conflict. Consequently, a valid peace strategy must seek to remove the veil of mystification which so often surrounds the phenomenon of structural violence, and address itself to both symmetric and asymmetric conflicts. In the case of the cold war, which has pitted one alliance system against another, it can be legitimately argued that one of the main functions of the more or less symmetric strategic confrontation between the two superpowers has been to disguise, distort and magnify the asymmetric economic relationship between advanced industrial societies and the Third World. Deriving from this conception is the need to break loose from the fiction that the only significant actors in the international political system are sovereign states, all of which are in some sense made equal by the mere fact of sovereignty. In actual fact, economic and technological developments have combined with the ideology of sovereignty to produce highly centralized economic and military machines which constitute the apex of power in a system of global stratification. The present reality, not to speak of the desired world order of the future, negates the billiard-ball theory of international relations which considers states as self-contained and autonomous political units.[21]

Given the instability of state boundaries, it follows that peace cannot be manufactured through a process of political engineering on the part of the governing elites of the major powers. If peace is to be more than a pious aspiration, it can no longer be considered the exclusive or even principal responsibility of the diplomat or soldier, who is often no more than the agent of a powerful strategic–industrial complex. We have already seen how armaments programmes, collective security agreements, balance of power arrangements, have repeatedly failed to give enduring substance to the legal boundaries between states. By combining these and other similar techniques with the advantages of geographical distance and other physical barriers, it was hoped that the principle of statehood would help maintain the peace by keeping apart potentially conflicting parties. Such a dissociative strategy may have had some validity in the phase of human history when the maximum speed of locomotion was between ten and twenty kilometers an hour. Since the advent of the steam engine, the wireless and the aeroplane, many of the assumptions underlying the strategy have become largely obsolete. It is now hardly credible that states should still be trying to create effective defence perimeters by relying on such technological devices as intercontinental ballistic missiles, satellite communication systems and nuclear warheads which, by their very nature, render state boundaries totally vulnerable.

The increasingly anachronistic character of defence policies should not be taken, however, as a general refutation of the dissociative approach to peace-making but as an indication that, to be viable, dissociation must be applied in completely different contexts and by quite different methods. Dissociative strategies will be most appropriate in asymmetric conflicts, where a phase of dissociation or decoupling may be necessary to ensure that the weaker party regains its autonomy and a measure of equality. In the kind of exploitative relationship which has existed between the overdeveloped West and the underdeveloped Afro-Asian and Latin American world, the indispensable first step towards a more harmonious and stable relationship has been a heightened consciousness by the exploited nation of the colonial or neo-colonial nature of its external links. Once its perceptions correspond more closely with its objective interests, the disadvantaged nation is better placed to formulate a series of demands designed to establish a more balanced relationship with the dominant power. If the demands are not met, then the dependent party may exercise the option of curtailing or terminating the process of asymmetric interaction. A period of dissociation may provide the conflict with a greater degree of symmetry at which point, the conflicting parties, perceiving their position to be one of greater equality, may be more inclined to proceed to the associative phase of peace-making and to consider lines of cooperation based on mutual benefit and respect of one another's autonomy. It would seem that the evolution of Sino–Soviet relations has passed through the stage of psychological (ideological) and institutional (economic) dissociation but has yet to enter the stage of associative peace-building.

Before examining one of the more fruitful avenues to international association, it may be relevant to comment briefly on the possible peace-making role of third parties whether as peace-making or mediating agents. Recent experience from the deployment of UN peace-keeping forces in Cyprus and the Middle East provides an important caution. Such operations are unlikely to succeed unless the policing force is used sparingly and only for a short duration. The control of violence through the use of neutral force will fail unless the parties to the dispute are ready to engage in a sustained analysis of the causes of the conflict, a reappraisal of costs and benefits, and, if necessary, a redefinition of goals. Although mediatory efforts tend to encounter the same difficulties, there is generally a greater probability of conflict resolution especially with the less conventional type of mediation which addresses itself to manifestations of both physical and social violence, focusses on the structural conditions of conflict, draws attention to the relevance of such values as participation, equality and autonomy, and concerns itself with divisions within as well as between parties.[22] It would by naive, however, to believe that mediation can provide a lasting solution to the many intractable conflicts which characterize the international system. Apart from the obvious obstacles which inhibit the injection of a sustained mediatory input into most conflict situations, there is no guarantee that any reassessment undertaken by the parties at the negotiating table will be accepted by their respective constituencies. Mediation suffers from the disadvantage of being a secretive operation which, by its very nature, prevents the direct involvement of large sections of the population, and thus runs the danger, unintended though it may be, of resolving one dispute only to produce new and perhaps more formidable conflicts between the conflict-managers and the conflict-managed.

The main thrust of the argument is that associative arrangements, whether or not they include third parties, will not make a lasting contribution to peace unless they are inclusive in inspiration and permit maximum participation, for it is not so much the formal provisions of a settlement as its universal legitimacy which ultimately determines its effectiveness as a peace-building mechanism. The ability of international organization to resolve or alleviate the tensions and crises that punctuate the global strategic and diplomatic system will significantly depend on the degree of participation which it fosters in international decision-making.

It is estimated that by the year 2000 international governmental organizations (IGOs) will grow from the present 200 to 850, and international non-governmental organizations (INGOs) from 2000 to 9600.[23] However, the effects of this phenomenal increase in the institutionalization of international relations are likely to be ambivalent. Against the positive potential implicit in the growth of transnational association, must be set the negative consequences that will inevitably arise from the parallel concentration of international wealth through the agency of the multinational corporation. These corporations are likely to pose a mounting threat to peace not simply as a result of the profound and widespread antagonism which their control of the world's resources inevitably arouses, but because they are even less accountable than the state to the populations whose lives they influence and often control. A judicious combination of the dissociative and associative peace strategies will be required to resist the increasing power of multinational enterprise to unleash both social and physical violence. International organizations will contribute to this task in so far as they provide their members with an opportunity to share in the policy-making process, and with frames of reference and role experiences which reinforce the vision of a unified but decentralized order.[24]

As individuals come to belong to diverse transnational associations, they will be increasingly exposed to a variety of cultural and ideological cross-pressures tending to restrain and modify national loyalties. The development of a strong anti-war movement in the United States and in other parts of the western world has already resulted in significant sections of the population rejecting national policies and national stereotypes of the enemy. To the extent that international organizations create new and independent channels of communication they are likely to reduce the level of national bias in the perception of international reality. Ultimately, however, their success as peace-building institutions will be governed by their capacity to focus attention on the structural causes rather than the symptoms of conflict. The specific functions of such organizations as the World Federation of Trade Unions, the International Olympic Committee, the International Commission of Jurists, War Resisters International, Amnesty International, the World Council of Churches, Friends of the Earth, may differ considerably but they can all play an invaluable role in widening the agenda of domestic and international politics and in alerting citizen of this planet to the urgency of creating a new organic world civilization.

12. Transitional strategies and cultural change

In spite of the emergence of a large socialist sector in the world economy, the almost universal trend towards political decolonization, and the ever present role of force in international relations, western capitalism was regarded until recently by both supporters and detractors alike as a stable and flourishing political and economic system. We now know this to have been a rather hasty and optimistic conclusion, which failed to take sufficient account of the psychological, cultural, political and economic dimensions of human disorder and of the underlying imbalances (or in Marxist terms 'contradictions') in contemporary social organization. These imbalances – notably the pyramidal concentration of power, wealth and authority and the consequent structures of underdevelopment, the bureaucratic and technical objectification and subjective needs, the escalation of domestic and international violence, and the widespread degradation of the environment – have become progressively more acute with the acceleration of industrialization and the expansion of productivity under conditions of technical rationality.

In the course of our analysis we have found it necessary to juxtapose the dominant reality manifested in these trends with a utopian image of society in order to provide a standpoint from which to evaluate the present reality and a conceptual basis on which to construct alternative models of social organization. The validity of the utopian project derives from its capacity to translate, more faithfully than the existing order, certain enduring but unfulfilled human aspirations, which explain and justify the periodic revolt against the status quo. While advanced industrial society has thus far succeeded to a considerable degree in containing qualitative change, the continued operation of several disintegrative tendencies is likely to make such containment increasingly difficult and may eventually produce a social explosion of unparalleled proportions. The present conditions of disorder and the future possibility of institutional breakdown have thus made survival the overriding political issue of the last quarter of the twentieth century. On the basis of this normative premise, we have sought to formulate a conception of world order more in keeping with the utopian vision and with the requirements of long-term survival.

Our study has contrasted two world orders, one actual and the other potential, and two sets of forces, one tending to reinforce and the other to undermine present reality. What has now to be determined is the degree to which discernible change can be consciously steered along the path we have proposed. Is it within man's power to devise a response to the crisis that minimizes the prospects of ultimate catastrophe while at the same time maximizing the positive functions of disintegration? Is it possible to formulate a strategy for social change which validates the expectation that the demise of the old order (disorder) will not bring in its wake intolerable levels of human suffering and material destruction? An affirmative answer to this question is necessarily premised on the view that the future is not predestined, that men are not helpless, that the outlook for tomorrow is determined by today's decisions, that human society can regain control over the seemingly random sequence of events, that transitional strategies can be found to ease man's passage into a safer and more convivial environment.

Strategies for change

One of the most serious obstacles to the formulation and implementation of such strategies stems from the ideological bias which colours some of the most prevalent attitudes to the political process. Foremost among these is the strong and widespread inclination to accept technocratic management as the only valid solution to the crisis of survival in spite of the devastating impact that bureaucratic rationality has already had on the social order. It is, of course, perfectly conceivable that the majority may be willing to submit, especially in times of growing tension and uncertainty, to the rule of technocratic caretakers, and that such rule may succeed in imposing otherwise unpalatable remedies, thereby eliminating the more acute symptoms of the crisis. However, such social engineering is more likely to aggravate than to cure the disease, to escalate the degree of coercion, and to transform society into a highly ordered but vulnerable machine from which man's deepest values and instincts will have largely disappeared.

While it may be a relatively simple matter to demonstrate the negative proposition that the bureaucratic management of survival is inconsistent with the principles of a communitarian world order, it is a much more difficult enterprise to provide an affirmative definition of what actually constitutes a viable revolutionary praxis. Needless to say, such a praxis will assume different form and substance in different societies, given that significant variations are likely to exist with respect to the stage of economic development, the distribution of power and wealth, political and legal institutions, cultural traditions, the degree of ideological conflict. For the purpose of this discussion we shall focus our attention primarily on the prospects for radical social change within the advanced industrial nations of the western world.

What then are the practical options available to those within the West who, aware of the contradictions inherent in the capitalist system and of the dangers which they imply, share a profound commitment to the restructuring of domestic and international society? One line of action might be to adopt a reformist strategy directed in the first instance to the reversal of those symptoms pointing towards an uncontrollable explosion. In this context, the danger of nuclear warfare and ecological disaster has already prompted a variety of initiatives and proposals designed to reduce the degree of risk indicated by current trends. A wide range of arms control measures and peace-keeping arrangements have been canvassed as a means of mitigating the possible repercussions of the war system.[1] Similarly, a series of institutional and technical measures (e.g. the use of economic incentives by way of taxes or subsidies or various forms of government regulation) have been advocated in response to the growing number of environmental threats.[2] No doubt all these responses have a certain utility and many of them may be considered important first steps in retrieving the rapidly deteriorating imbalance in social interaction. But the danger of such measures, even assuming timely introduction and effective implementation, is that they may prove to be no more than palliatives which leave intact the technocratic mentality, the values and perceptions on which are based existing economic and political institutions.

We have referred to some of the proposed changes to the international security system and to environmental policy not in order to berate the value of these reforms but simply with a view to underlining their obvious limitations. While they may have an immediately beneficial impact in terms of crisis-management and may even usefully contribute to political education, they are unlikely to provide a lasting remedy for the fundamental imbalances which pose the greatest threat to long-term survival and which underlie the expanding phenomenon of social pathology. Any strategy which does not grapple with the militarization and bureaucratization of the modern state or with the larger ethical and ecological issues of existential balance cannot be expected to induce the painful collective choices needed for the preservation of life and the realization of other basic human values.

In sharp contrast to the reformist philosophy just described is the anarchist alternative based on romantic and nihilist notions of confrontation and committed to the thoroughgoing, and where necessary violent, destruction of the prevailing structures of power, wealth and authority.[3] A particularly instructive, although somewhat ambiguous application of such a strategy was evidenced in the spontaneous student uprising and the subsequent wave of industrial strikes, occupations and demonstrations, which took France by storm in May 1968.[4] Although few would dispute the significance of this brief but intense mood of revolt and the profound challenge it posed to the established system, the fact remains that, when it came to an ultimate trial of strength with the forces of 'law and order',' the revolutionary movement, unable to secure the wide or sustained support needed to carry the struggle to its logical conclusion, collapsed into isolated outbursts of rage and recrimination.[5] The conclusions to be drawn from the events have obvious relevance for the study of contemporary French society, but they also illuminate the nature of modern capitalism and the difficulties confronting the development of an effective revolutionary praxis.

According to the classical Marxist conception, capitalist society objectively consists of only two classes: a small minority of capitalists who own the means of production and the vast majority of propertyless people who are obliged to sell their labour in order to exist and are therefore dependent on the vagaries of the market and the fluctuations in the process of capital accumulation. Notwithstanding its many inner differentiations, the working class is said to be clearly separate from the ruling class whose decisions are directed to the special needs of capital, that is, to the perpetuation of the propertied class. While accepting the validity of this fundamental polarity, two important qualifications would seem critical to an understanding of the dynamics of industrially advanced capitalism. On the one hand, status differentiations, which do not refer merely to difference in education, social standing or income (purchasing power) but also to gradations of political power, constitute an important divisive factor within the working class and hence a major obstacle to the formation of a united front against the ruling class. On the other hand, while the decisions of the ruling class determine the general conditions of society, such decisions do not operate in a vacuum but are invariably constrained by the bargaining power of organized labour as well as by the unpredictable course of market events and technological developments. The reluctance of the amorphous mass of wage-receiving occupations and professions to recognize its class position may serve to reinforce the legitimacy of the ruling ideology, but there remain nevertheless clear limits to the power of the decision-making class.

Although the ruling elite derives its power from the control it exercises over the productive process and the ideological and coercive resources of society, ultimate power must reside with the mass of the people since they constitute the essential source of productive labour and political legitimacy. It is not without significance that, despite the relative decline in its numerical strength, the industrial proletariat remains a keystone in the social edifice. Indeed its power to control society has grown with the technical organization of the productive process and the increasing dependence of urbanized living on the uninterrupted flow of production.[6] A somewhat similar situation has arisen in the military arena, where the capacity of governments to maintain far-flung empires has sharply diminished partly as a result of the rising opposition to national conscription and the unpredictability of the system of voluntary recruitment. Clearly, those who are presently excluded from the higher echelons of decision-making have it within their power, simply by refusing to work, pay taxes or fight, to destroy society or, at least, shake it to its very foundations.

But the revolutionary potential of the working class to overcome the material forces of coercion remains only a possibility, however real, which may or may not be actualized. The powerful conformist, atomizing and manipulative pressures operating within capitalist society obviously militate against its transformation. By the very nature of its control over the market economy and the dominant political institutions, the capitalist ethos has achieved a near monopoly over the public imagination and a capacity for extensive manipulation of the vision, the language, the needs of society. It is precisely this subtle mechanism of institutionalized myth-making which has impeded the awakening of critical consciousness whereby men can become aware of their role as subjects of the revolutionary process.

But quite apart from this powerful ideological lever, the ruling class in advanced capitalism has at its disposal a very substantial power of blackmail. For, any attempt to disrupt the industrial system, assuming that such a strategy could gain the necessary support, would not only damage the vested interest of the capitalist class but cause the breakdown of the highly complex technological machine on which advanced industrial communities depend for their existence.[7] It is undoubtedly the fear of such widespread and irreparable chaos which tempers the militancy of the working class and arouses the deep suspicion of the affluent society towards any strategy of industrial sabotage. Moreover, even if such a strategy should succeed in dispossessing the capitalist class without producing an irreversible breakdown, there would remain the problem of creating a new order capable of satisfying the community's welfare. One possibility might be for the conditions of the present industrial system to be restored essentially unaltered, though under new and supposedly more efficient management, in which case little more would have been accomplished than a transient period of acute hardship and instability. In this context, it is perhaps worth considering the fetishized, one-dimensional culture and quite moribund revolutionary process characteristic of present day Soviet society. A more promising alternative would be for human and material resources to be channelled into the development of new forms of social organization, new patterns of production, distribution and consumption. Regrettably, there exists at present no coherent or detailed programme for such a fundamental restructuring of society, nor is there any social or political movement in sight capable of bringing such a programme to a successful conclusion. There is certainly no visible mass movement ready to break through the veil of social mystification and the unquestioned cultural values of the dominant order.

In the socio-industrial conditions of highly sophisticated technocratic systems, neither the reformist strategy nor the violent destruction of the industrial order provides a satisfactory basis for revolutionary praxis. A gradualist policy underestimates the capacity of vested interests to obstruct qualitative change through subtle mechanisms of cultural and political control and to assimilate the expression of dissatisfaction through the politics of welfare and cooption; and fails to translate specific changes in the existing institutional order into the general conditions for a radical rearrangement of society. As for the simple advocacy of the violent seizure of power, whether by the industrial proletariat or by any other section of society, it overlooks not only the obvious lack of popular support for such a course of action and the extreme and widespread dislocation which would result from it, but the almost total absence of a concrete project for cultural liberation. The failure of the French revolutionary forces in May 1968 stemmed directly from the truncated praxis of intellectuals and workers whose vision was so abstract or so conditioned by the dominant culture as to degenerate into generalized rhetoric on the one hand or into a clamouring for the redistribution of the system's rewards on the other.

Cultural revolution

No one would dispute the necessity for a material lever with which to overturn the defence of existing society. But where is such a lever to be found? Clearly, the answer lies in the growing irrationality of the capitalist system itself, its imbalances and internal contraditions. It is this underlying disorder which poses the most explosive and rapidly accelerating challenge to the status quo, and which indicates that in the foreseeable future the revolutionary struggle will have to be conducted primarily in the ideological and cultural spheres. It is not at all surprising, therefore, that students, intellectuals and other propertyless members of the middle classes rather than the industrial working class should have played the leading role in contemporary political dissent, since they constitute the element in society which can most readily interpret the existential implications of technocratic management, and most clearly perceive the contradiction between the ideological lip service paid to freedom and the repressive reality of everyday life.

All the available evidence confirms the view that the various imbalances and antagonisms generated by advanced capitalism will intensify in the years ahead. Its solution of the problem of material scarcity is proving to be a partial, temporary and expensive enterprise. The heavy psychological costs exacted by the unparalleled rapidity of technological and social change are combining with the environmental risks of unrestricted industrial growth and the widening disparities between the developed and underdeveloped world to produce a wave of rising disillusionment with capitalist abundance. However, these are the early signs of uneasiness and disorientation which may gradually turn to desperation as the 'new industrial state' becomes less and less immune to the storms currently traversing the world economy, and as conventional solutions prove less and less effective in correcting the imbalances underlying the structure of national economies. The increasing difficulty in satisfying the affluent society's ingrained expectations of high and rising living standards will no doubt accentuate existing inequalities and exacerbate both intra-societal conflict and inter-capitalist rivalries as classes and nations fiercely compete to maintain their share of a stagnant and possibly declining world product. It is significant that both the liberal and Marxist critique of modern capitalist society, which had until recently concentrated almost exclusively on the concepts of alienation, manipulation and bureaucratization, should now be expanding its horizons to incorporate the issues of economic inequality, industrial conflict and the general crisis of economic mangement.

The central question, then, to which revolutionary praxis must address itself is how to take advantage of these disintegrative tendencies in order to hasten the demise of the capitalist order while at the same time preventing the unavoidable upheaval from turning into an irrevocable catastrophe. In the first place, it cannot be stressed enough that for such a vast and ambitious undertaking to have any real prospect of success it will need to engage the energies of a large revolutionary movement and prevent the differentiated praxis of its constitutent parts from degenerating into so many unconnected expressions of self-contained but ultimately self-defeating spontaneity. The second urgent requirement is that the revolutionary project should take a cultural form, focussing most of its attention on the liberation of social consciousness rather than on the seizure of state power.[8] Although existing social relations and dominant institutions tend to impede the process of liberation, they are at the same time the source of considerable confusion, anguish and frustration and hence a contributing factor to the transformation of the cognitive and normative image of objective reality. The very tension between the actual and the potential world of experience, between present alienation and prospective emancipation can act as a catalyst for the process of critical discovery, whereby the divided and un-authentic victims of ideological repression begin to participate in the pedagogy of their own liberation.

It may be argued that, under current conditions, the possibility of realizing such a cultural project is somewhat remote. But early signs pointing to such a development are already in evidence and they will almost certainly multiply with the deepening awareness of impending crisis. Once the crash has arrived, then one may reasonably expect a dramatic loss of confidence in established institutions and existing procedures of crisis management, with a corresponding decline in their capacity to define societal values. Although our analysis has suggested several plausible scenarios, the crash may be triggered off by any number of unforeseen incidents. Whatever the fortuitous coincidence of events, its net effect will be to lay bare the growing distance between man and the structures and techniques he had created, and the widening institutional gap between stated objectives and actual performance. The sudden and widespread realization of the system's fundamental contradictions will transform the public imagination and with it the very foundation of authority and legitimacy.

But it is hardly accurate to speak of crisis in the future tense since it is already with us. The private construction of fall-out shelters, acquisition of firearms, creation of paramilitary forces, and hoarding of gold and food supplies are only some of the more visible manifestations of growing fear and anxiety. While doomed to failure these highly individualistic endeavours to ensure survival in the event of disaster or breakdown are nonetheless indicative of the need to analyse the causes of the approaching crisis, and, on the basis of such insight, to develop a praxis which anticipates the dissolution of prevailing structures and prepares for the sudden rise to prominence of previously submerged social groups. Expressed somewhat differently, the task of the cultural revolution is to foresee and interpret the trend towards disintegration and to make its analysis readily accessible to the community at large, thereby converting the crisis into a moment of decision, a transitional stage in the creation of a new order.

However, such a liberating response to the crisis cannot be spontaneously improvised; it requires a prolonged period of maturation, during which a concerted attempt is made to redefine both objective and subjective reality and to develop a new and viable conception of man in society. Under conditions of technocratic capitalism, a lengthy process of cultural fermentation is essential to the success of the revolutionary project. A cultural revolution, which has perhaps already begun, is needed to neutralize the process of coercive socialization and to provide alternatives to institutional programmes predicted on predictable and controlled behaviour. Any cultural challenge to the institutional order must take into consideration both the cognitive and normative dimensions of legitimation. Authority structures are legitimated not only by the ethics of their prescriptions but also by the knowledge which defines both 'right' and 'wrong' actions. Such knowledge, usually transmitted by tradition, is obviously a legitimating instrument, since it explains to the individual why things

are as they are and consequently predisposes him to the acceptance of the status quo. A cultural revolution must therefore
revise both the knowledge and the values of the collectivity and
provide it with a fresh interpretation of its history and sociology.

If it is not to operate in a vacuum, this process of symbolic
redefinition has to be sustained and objectivated by a social
base serving as the laboratory of transformation. According to
Berger and Luckman, the construction of such a base depends
on the establishment of bonds of strong affective identification
which replicate 'childhood experiences of emotional dependency on significant others'. It is these 'significant others'
who 'mediate the new world to the individual' and endow the
revolutionary project with a continuing sense of its plausibility.[9]

The significance of small radical communities lies precisely
in the social base they provide for the new definition of reality
and the recognition and support they extend to the new revolutionary vision. It is the collectivity which enables the individual
to maintain his deviant conception of reality, and endows it with
subjective plausibility in his consciousness. Crucial, therefore, to
the success of this type of cultural action is the formation and
growth of those communities which are likely to constitute the
principal agents of cultural change and eventually become the
legitimators of the new order.

Obviously, the emergence of a radical mass movement composed of these diverse communities or groups would require
a very considerable degree of solidarity founded on the sharing
of deep human experiences rather than on common adherence
to rhetoric or to a series of abstract ideological propositions.
In this regard, the small face-to-face group, whose members
share the same conceptions of the new man and actively strive
to realize it in their interpersonal relations, can coexist with
and reinforce the more strictly political form of association,
provided that the underlying rationale of all activity is the
transformation of the alienated personality from a passive,
technically manipulated object into an active, liberated and
creative subject.

But the revolutionary project cannot confine itself to the
reinterpretation and repudiation of social reality. It must set
out to legitimate the entire conceptual and institutional
apparatus that will be used in the process of rediscovery and

recreation. For this, if for no other reason, the proclamation of the new reality must have its roots in a close and dialogical relationship with the people, encouraging the emergence of a popular consciousness, which explodes the cultural silence imposed on the majority, sharpens the perception of contradictions and yields new dynamism in all dimensions of social life.

Without the active and extensive participation of the people, cultural action will be deprived of its revolutionary significance, of its capacity to undermine the functioning of existing institutions, foster new centres of decision-making, and foreshadow the remaking of society. The process of 'conscientization' dictates, by its very nature, profound respect for the people who cannot be manipulated into situations of struggle while they are not yet fully conscious of the need for the objectives that are at stake. It is only when the mass of society has acquired a clear perception of existing reality and discarded the cultural myths on which it is based that it will be inclined to take the necessary risks to create a new social order. But for this to be a viable cultural project, it will need to be animated by ideas that are specific and relevant to the oppressive reality which it is seeking to overthrow. The force of these ideas will depend on the extent to which they reflect the concrete aspirations of various social classes or strata in relation to economic justice, peace, the quality of life or the more intangible search for autonomy and authenticity.

One would therefore expect the cultural revolution, at least in its inception, to be concerned principally with such partial struggles as workers' control, civil rights, student participation, environmental protection, or educational reform. However, by directing attention to the more vulnerable aspects of the system, the ideas underlying these limited initiatives can act as an important catalyst in mobilizing and channelling human energy towards the larger social struggle. Local community action, whether by way of restructuring existing institutions or initiating independent programmes, has already proved a valuable instrument enabling groups and individuals to take increasing control of the decisions which directly affect their lives. The leverage afforded by these localized struggles can serve to discredit the status quo while at the same time crystallizing the new sense of urgency which derives from the redefinition of objective reality. Nor is there any need, in this stage of cultural preparation, for the various protest movements to be institutionally unified. The greater the diversity of groups and perspectives that can be encompassed by the revolutionary project, the higher the probability that the implicit commitment to radical change will be accepted by the rest of society. At this point, it becomes important for dissent to go beyond the politics of mere negation and withdrawal. It is only by deciding to act out the alternative culture in the public arena, by attempting to live out the future now, by complementing the propaganda of the word with the drama of action, that the revolutionary movement can reveal for all to see the decadence of the old order and the promise of the new.[10] Once the counter-institutions, whether it be free universities, underground churches, free presses, community schools, worker directed enterprises, or neighbourhood-controlled welfare services, have demonstrated their efficacy and legitimacy through a continuous process of innovation and experimentation based on service and direct participation, the established institutions are likely to collapse with little or no coercion required to achieve the final transfer of power and authority.

Revolutionary non-violence

At this point we are confronted once again with the inescapable issue of coercion and violence. For, it is not a totally unwarranted assumption to expect the prevailing structures to allow, either nationally or internationally, these counter-institutions to emerge without first placing every possible obstacle in their path. And does not such opposition almost inevitably rely on the overt and covert use of force or threat of force? The readiness of established institutions to preserve power and privilege by resorting to physical and other more subtle forms of coercion is often cited in defence of revolutionary violence which, it is argued, is not only justified but indispensable if the victims of repressive violence are to have any effective means of protection. Revolutionary violence is not an end in itself but simply the instrument required to neutralize and eliminate relationships based on exploitation and inequality.[11] A non-violent challenge to oppression merely serves to perpetuate the rule of the oppressor and hasten the destruction of the oppressed. Far from reflecting higher standards of ethical conduct, the advocacy of non-violence is little more than an immoral recommendation for continuing tyranny and suppression. Nor, it is claimed, need violence militate against the construction of a new order provided that those who resort to it have a clear understanding of its objectives and of the specific circumstances which necessitated it. Violent struggle, far from diminishing the humanity of those who engage in it, can help to sensitize them to the nature and purpose of the revolutionary project.

While recognizing the cogency of many of these arguments and the obvious dedication and self-sacrifice of many exponents of violent revolution, the weight of the evidence suggests that terrorism, especially when applied in the urbanized conditions of advanced industrial society, is a counter-productive instrument of revolutionary politics. The tactical recourse to violence, which is in itself a veiled admission of the failure of political and educational action, will normally tend to strengthen the established order. To the extent that acts of violence threaten the physical and psychological security of ordinary people, they are likely to reduce the degree of popular support for the revolutionary project and provide the dominant institutions with a ready-made pretext for the adoption of more repressive policies and the accelerated erosion of civil liberties. Moreover, a violent strategy, particularly in an urban setting, can mobilize the energies of only a few, leaving the majority of those that favour revolutionary change as spectators rather than agents of the struggle. By minimizing the possibility of direct involvement, such a strategy whether wittingly or unwittingly, reinforces the silence of the majority and perpetuates its profound sense of impotence. It fails, in other words, to expose the myths and ideologies of the prevailing order, and deflects people from grasping 'with their minds the truth of their reality'.

The strategic and tactical limitations of revolutionary violence are likely to be even more pronounced in the course of a prolonged conflict where self-confidence becomes harder to sustain and initial defeat may easily lead to a drastic loss of morale. Apart from its probable intimidatory effect on many potential supporters of radical change, the violence of the struggle may provoke such alarm within the ranks of the ruling elite as to unleash a wave of irrational violence resulting in inestimable human and material destruction. The technological factor is now such that an escalating armed struggle could turn to genocide or ecocide even without the use of nuclear weapons. The devastation wrought by the American military machine on the Vietnamese nation has already demonstrated the lengths to which desperate men will go when vested interests are under attack. Momentous though it was, the Vietnamese challenge was nevertheless aimed at a distant and strategically marginal corner of the empire. How much more devastating and irrational, therefore, is the response likely to be when force is directed against the very nerve centre of the imperial structure. There may be some validity to the argument that industrial culture, especially in its capitalist manifestation, is deeply attracted to the mechanical, to that which is non-alive, and that this necrophilic attraction may ultimately lead to self-destruction.[12] The fulfilment of such a death wish, however, would provide little cause for revolutionary celebration if, together with the disintegration of capitalism, it should also mean the extinction of all hope of human development.

But perhaps the most dangerous flaw in any revolutionary strategy predicated on the efficacy of violence is not so much the miscalculation of the resultant costs, the inappropriateness of the tactics, or even the probability that violent militancy will end in defeat, as the tendency to identify success with armed victory, that is, to mistake the seizure of power for the revolution. A strategy based on the use of physical violence and aspiring to take command of the state apparatus necessarily requires the creation of a highly centralized organization whose very success is bound to negate the purpose of the cultural project and foreclose the options of the revolutionary movement by committing it to the continued operation of the bureaucratic machine it has inherited.[13]

If, within the conditions currently prevailing within advanced capitalist society, the potential of violent action is not commensurate with the demands of the revolutionary project, is there any reason to believe that non-violent action holds the key to a more productive praxis? Non-violence does not of course imply passivity. On the contrary, its most celebrated exponents have all emphasized an assertive commitment to social change.[14] Non-violent action is both a strategy for structural and cultural transformation and a technique of struggle. It makes use of power, but instead of opposing the adversary's apparatus of violence with comparable force, it relies exclusively on political and moral weapons. By developing and refining various forms of protest (e.g. fasts, parades, marches, vigils, religious services, street theatre), non-cooperation (e.g. strikes, tax refusal, civil disobedience, draft resistance), and intervention (e.g. occupation of buildings, parallel government), non-violence threatens the opponent's power position. One of the great advantages of a non-violent strategy is that it deprives the dominant institutions of the justification for violent retaliation. But apart from reducing the likelihood of repression, a non-violent movement foments dissension within the ranks of the enemy by making it considerably more difficult for him to respond decisively to the challenge to his authority. Indeed, by refusing to be intimidated by the coercive power of the establishment, non-violence undermines the opponent's respect for and dependence on the gun. Accustomed to protect his vested interests behind a shield of violence he is disconcerted and devitalized when others unilaterally forsake such means of defence.

The merit of non-violence lies not only in its debilitating effect on established structures but also in the self-confidence which it instils in the revolutionary movement. By its very accessibility to the bulk of the population, political non-cooperation can provide the basis for an on-going and broadly-based struggle, in which people learn to rebel against their former submissiveness and to cultivate their newly acquired sense of freedom. Moreover, such a liberating experience, precisely because it does not depend on the physical disintegration of the enemy, although it keeps disrupting the order to which he is so closely attached, can lead him in certain circumstances towards a fundamental reappraisal of both subjective and objective reality. In this admittedly theoretical sense, which is not, however, altogether devoid of practical implications, the non-violent revolutionary movement presents both oppressor and oppressed with an opportunity for liberation.

It remains to say a word about the costs of non-violent action for they are not insignificant. Unarmed people have been known to be imprisoned, beaten, tortured, shot and killed in their hundreds and thousands. People are of course instinctively, and quite understandably, distressed to see their side suffer more than the opponent, a situation which they often interpret as a sign of defeat. But on closer consideration, it becomes clear that victory bears little relationship to the degree of punishment that is inflicted on the enemy. The point of revolutionary praxis is not to punish the adversary but to deflect him from his goal, to negate his purpose. The object of revolution is not vengeance but change. The effectiveness of the non-violent movement may be gauged not by estimating its losses and gains as against those of the enemy, but by comparing both the suffering it incurs and the structural and ideological changes it initiates with the situation which would obtain if it turned to violence. On this point the historical record seems rather clear: struggle of any kind tends to provoke a violent response, but a violent struggle will normally provoke a more brutal response and with it a much greater number of casualties.

The same principles which validate a non-violent revolutionary praxis in the national or domestic context are also applicable to international or intersocietal relations.[15] Here again a host of widely held assumptions need to be questioned. As we have already observed, the capacity for military defence appears to have been largely undermined, if not completely destroyed, by the very nature of modern technology. But is the concept of defence necessarily predicated on the use of physical force? How valid is the assumption that the capacity to defend is synonymous with military power and military occupation the necessary and sufficient condition for political control? Given that military preparedness is proving less and less able to fulfill the security objective, is it not possible to conceive of a non-military form of defence? If military technology has drastically reduced the possibility of effective geographical defence, is it not possible that societies may substantially enhance the capacity to defend themselves by using the resources of their civilian populations, by developing a resistance movement which would make it virtually impossible for the enemy to establish and maintain political control in spite of vastly superior military power?

Crucial to the concept of civilian defence is the notion that the entire citizenry and all political institutions can and must share in the struggle against the enemy. Such widespread participation provides a striking and democratic affirmation of the society's determination to defend its freedom and other values, while at the same time giving rise to a mass movement committed to a policy of non-cooperation until the collapse or withdrawal of the invader. In this case, victory is achieved by the direct and pedagogic efforts of the whole population rather than by the destructive actions of a relatively small professional elite. The added advantage of civilian defence is the restraining impact it is likely to have on the invader's freedom of action. For non-violent resistance may not only weaken the resolve of the opponent but also create serious divisions within his ranks and subject him to a series of international pressures, including economic sanctions, which may severely hamper his attempts to maintain military occupation.

Although several examples of unprepared resistance in occupied countries, such as Colonial India, Norway during World War II and Czechoslovakia in 1968, have already confirmed the effectiveness of non-violent action, nevertheless civilian defence is unlikely to become a practical and realistic alternative to military defence until it has first become the subject of intensive study and public debate. However, once governmental institutions, local communities, occupational groups, schools, universities, the churches, the media have all participated in such an educational programme and come to accept the philosophy of non-violence, it may then be possible for individuals and groups to receive the specialized training needed to equip them with the necessary self-discipline, the thorough understanding of the requirements of non-cooperation and familiarity with the civilian defence strategies adopted by their society. Even in the event of failure, which is by no means inconceivable though far less probable than would be the case with military retaliation, civilian resistance would, at the very least, prevent a nuclear holocaust thus ensuring survival and sustaining the hope for eventual freedom. In any case, the non-violent struggle and the accompanying suffering would not be in vain for, even if the tyranny of the invader cannot be immediately removed, the country and its institutions may retain a measure of autonomy and hence a basis for future independence.

The main thrust of the above discussion has not been to

establish an absolute moral difference between violent and non-violent methods of resistance, or to suggest that physical violence, much less the destruction of property, is a morally impossible instrument of social change. Rather the intention has been to stress the strategic and tactical advantages of non-violent action and its relevance to revolutionary praxis in a period of cultural preparation; a period in which the structural causes of alienation, hunger, inequality, repression and war will increasingly impinge on the consciousness of society; a period in which a new conception of society will gradually emerge and with it a life-affirming strategy imbued with a sense of urgency, ready to challenge the present structures of society and prevailing modes of thinking and acting.

The cultural revolution is the historical moment when reflection and practice, interacting with each other, break through the material and ideological veil of society to discover the hitherto hidden potentiality of men and things, of society and nature. Although unmistakably oriented towards the future, the progressive establishment of counter-institutions enables the cultural revolution to be experienced by its participants as a living reality in the here and now. Indeed, it is the dramatic contrast between the confusion and uncertainty of the existing order and the clarity and simplicity of the revolutionary message which awakens the human sensitivity and creative imagination that often lie buried beneath the massive weight of industrial culture. But even as it presents society with a stark choice between life and death, between justice and oppression, the cultural revolution is careful not to make an idol of the revolutionary creed. While seeking to turn society inside out, to abolish the centric structures which corrupt and dehumanize, it takes care not to create new hatreds and new resentments, new gods that men must worship. If it is to be true to its purpose, revolutionary praxis must always proclaim the sometimes unpalatable truth that the revolution was made for man and not man for the revolution.

In the preceding chapters we have surveyed many of modern man's reasons for despair as he gropes for survival in the last quarter of the twentieth century. The undertaking is indeed a vast one. It demands a major renewal of life-styles, a radical restructuring of society, a broadening of horizons to encompass the entire human race. Some may wish to argue that he cannot embrace this task with any hope. And yet, for all the dangers that lie ahead and all the signs of impending crisis, hope remains the most human of all emotions, a universal state of mind illuminating the reality which exists and that which is to come, a vision projected into the future, capable of transforming the present. Hope is, in fact, an integral part of man's present commitment in history. A true praxis of liberation proceeds on the assumption that the present is already pregnant with the future. It penetrates the present reality in all its dimensions, discerns the movement of history without illusions. It sees the world as it is, alienated, vulnerable, dangerous. It realizes that greed and the struggle for power have to be taken seriously, that vested economic, military and political interests largely determine the shape of the modern world. But it also knows that these strivings are not all powerful, that their dominion is built on fatalistic lines that are not in accord with the true nature of man's evolutionary development. They are an artificial construction which denies the open-ended dynamism of history.

To hope, however, does not mean to know the future or to foresee the outcome of the struggle that has yet to unfold. To be able to see through every twist and turn of the future course of events would imply a wholly transparent and ultimately aetherial world. Hope is not prediction but openness to the movement of history, denunciation of the existing order, repudiation of an intolerable state of affairs, the 'great refusal', but also annunciation of what is not yet, anticipation of a new order, affirmation of man's triumph over death.

Notes

Chapter 2. Underlying causes of disorder

1. Lewis Mumford, *The Myth of the Machine*, New York, Harcourt, Brace & World, 1966.
2. See Theodore Roszak, *The Making of a Counter-culture*, London, Faber & Faber, 1971, chapter 1.
3. Jacques Ellul, *The Technological Society*, translated by John Wilkinson, New York, A. A. Knopf, 1964, p. 138.
4. Erich Fromm, *The Revolution of Hope: Toward a Humanized Technology*, New York, Harper & Row, 1968, pp. 33–4.
5. For an interesting historical survey of the concept of economic growth see H. V. Hodson, *The Diseconomics of Growth*, London, Pan/Ballantyne, 1972, chapter 24.
6. See R. N. Tawney, *The Acquisitive Society*, New York, Harcourt, Brace & Co., 1920; and Erich Fromm, *The Sane Society*, London, Routledge & Kegan Paul, 1963.
7. Herbert Marcuse, *Negations: Essays in Critical Theory*, Harmondsworth, Penguin Books, 1972, pp. 223–4.
8. Herbert Marcuse, *One Dimensional Man*, London, Abacus, 1972, chapter 6.
9. Aldous Huxley, *Brave New World*, Harmondsworth, Penguin Books, 1955, pp. 11–12.
10. This term has been employed by Henri Lefebvre to suggest the bureaucratic rationality of advanced capitalism and its consumer-oriented economy in, *Everyday Life in the Modern World*, (trans. by Sacha Rabinovitch), London, Allen Lane, The Penguin Press, 1971.
11. T. Roszak, *The Making of a Counter-culture*, p. 19.
12. T. Roszak, *Where the Wasteland Ends*, London, Faber & Faber, 1974, p. 46.
13. For a stimulating discussion of the compatibility of totalitarianism and rationality in the Soviet context, see Zbigniew K. Brzezinski, *Ideology and Power in Soviet Politics*, New York, Frederick A. Praeger, 1962.
14. H. Marcuse, 'Freedom and Freud's Theory of Instincts' in Five Lectures: *Psychoanalysis, Politics and Utopia*, Boston, Beacon Press, 1970, p. 15.
15. The very development and appeal of existentialist philosophy points to the increasing anguish of alienated man. Although expressed in different idioms and viewed from different perspectives, the concept of alienation seems to unify the work of such diverse writers as Kierkegaard, Nietzsche, Jaspers, Heidegger, Tillich and Sartre. See *Existentialism: From Dostoevsky to Sartre* edited by Walter Kaufmann, New York, New American Library, 1956.

16. For a systematic analysis of the concept of alienation and its role in Marx's critique of society, see Istvan Meszaros, *Marx's Theory of Alienation*, (3rd ed.), London, Merlin Press, 1972.

17. E. Fromm, *The Sane Society*, p. 126.

18. Zbigniew Brzezinski, *Between Two Ages: America's Role in the Technetronic Age*, New York, Viking, 1970.

19. Herman Kahn, *On Escalation, Metaphors and Scenarios*, London, Pall Mall Press, 1965.

20. Alvin Toffler, *Future Shock*, London, Pan Books, 1970.

21. For a sensitive and illuminating appreciation of the sociological meaning of abstract art see Joseph-Emile Muller, *L'Art moderne*, Paris, Livre de Poche, 1963.

22. Bruce Brown, *Marx, Freud and the Critique of Everyday Life*, New York, Monthly Review Press, 1973, p. 165.

23. Raymond Aron, *Progress and Disillusion: The Dialectics of Modern Society*, London, Pall Mall Press, 1968.

24. John Kenneth Galbraith, *The New Industrial State*, (2nd ed.), Harmondsworth, Penguin Books, 1974.

25. H. L. Nieburg, *In the Name of Science*, Chicago, Quadrangle Books, 1966.

26. Sidney Lewis, *The Military–Industrial Complex*, Philadelphia, Philadelphia University Press, 1970.

27. See James Weinstein, *The Corporate Ideal and the Liberal State*, Boston, Beacon Press, 1968.

28. See Andrew Schonfield, *Modern Capitalism*, London, Oxford University Press, 1969, especially part 2, chapters 13–14 and part 4.

29. See E. J. Mishan, *The Costs of Economic Growth*, Harmondsworth, Penguin Books, 1969.

30. Kenneth R. Schneider, *Destiny of Change*, New York, Holt, Rinehart & Winston Inc., 1968.

31. Some have argued that income inequality is functionally necessary to the capitalist mode of production. See Thomas E. Weisskopf, 'Capitalism and Inequality' in R. C. Edward *et al.*, *The Capitalist System*, Englewood Cliffs, NJ, Prentice Hall Inc., 1972.

32. Edward C. Budd (ed.), *Inequality and Poverty*, New York, W. W. Norton & Co. Inc., 1967, Table 1, p. xiii.

33. Martin Carney (ed.), *Schooling in a Corporate Society*, New York, David McKay Co., 1972; John Holt, *Freedom and Beyond*, Harmondsworth, Penguin Books, 1972.

34. See Everett Reimer, *School is Dead*, Harmondsworth, Penguin Books, 1971, chapter 6.

35. Paul Baran and Paul Sweezy, *Monopoly Capital*, Harmondsworth, Penguin Books, 1968, p. 349.

36. The most dramatic illustration of this process was provided by the hundreds of thousands executed and the millions incarcerated in labour camps for daring to defy or obstruct the Stalinist programme of industrialization.

37. J. K. Galbraith, *The New Industrial State*, chapter 30; see also Ian L. McHarg, 'Values Process and Form' in, *The Ecological Conscience: Values*

for Survival, edited by Robert Disch, Englewood Cliffs, NJ, Prentice Hall Inc., 1970.

38. J. K. Galbraith, *The Affluent Society*, Harmondsworth, Penguin Books, 1962.

39. See William J. Baumol, 'Macroeconomics and Unbalanced Growth: The Anatomy of Urban Crisis', *American Economic Review*, June 1967, pp. 415–26.

40. Walter Weisskopf, 'Economic Growth Versus Existential Balance', *Ethics*, Vol. 75, no. 2, January 1965.

41. J. K. Galbraith, *The New Industrial State*, Chapter 19; E. J. Mishan, *The Costs of Economic Growth*, chapter 10.

42. See Ivan Illich, *Tools for Conviviality*, London, Calder & Boyars, 1973, p. 51ff.

43. See Ivan Illich, 'The Futility of Schooling' in, *Celebration of Awareness*, Harmondsworth, Penguin Books, 1973.

44. Cf. Gunnar Myrdal, *The Challenge of World Poverty*, London, Allen Lane, The Penguin Press, 1970, chapter 7.

45. For a discussion of this phenomenon in the Southeast Asian context see J. Camilleri and M. Teichmann, *Security and Survival*, Melbourne, Heinemann, 1973, chapter 7.

46. One of the most influential theorists of dependence has been Andre Gunder Frank, author of *Capitalism and Underdevelopment in Latin America*, Harmondsworth, Penguin Books, 1971 and *Latin America: Underdevelopment or Revolution*, New York, Monthly Review Press, 1970. See also H. Magdoff, *The Age of Imperialism*, New York, Monthly Review Press, 1969 and P. Jalée, *The Pillage of the Third World*, New York, Monthly Review Press, 1968.

47. See Pierre Jalée, *The Third World in World Economy*, New York, Monthly Review Press, 1969, especially chapter 6, and Robert Stauffer, *In Defence of Disorder* (mimeo, 1972).

48. See Richard Barnet, *Intervention and Revolution*, London, Paladin, 1968, Michael T. Klare, *War Without End: American Planning for the Next Vietnams*, New York, Vintage Books, 1971.

49. Cf. Stockholm International Peace Research Institute, *The Arms Trade with the Third World*, Harmondsworth, Penguin Books, 1975.

50. The phenomenon of military imperialism has been readily acknowledged by writers of quite different persuasion: G. Liska, *Imperial America*, Baltimore, Johns Hopkins Press, 1967; Felix Greene, *The Enemy: Notes on Imperialism and Revolution*, London, Jonathan Cape, 1970. See also L. P. Bloomfield *et. al.*, *The Control of Local Conflict*, prepared for the US Arms Control and Disarmament Agency, Vols. 1 and 2, Washington DC, US Government Printing Office, 1967.

51. The concept of stratification is developed by G. Lagos, *International Stratification and Underdeveloped Countries*, Chapel Hill, University of North Carolina Press, 1963; J. P. Nettl and R. Robertson, *International Systems and the Modernization of Societies*, London, Faber & Faber, 1968; and R. Jenkins, *Exploitation*, London, Paladin, 1971.

52. The fragmentation of the international system is a recurring theme in

the literature on international relations. For a highly systematic treatment see R. Aron, *Peace and War*, Garden City, NY, Doubleday & Co. Inc., 1966.

53. For one of the most penetrating analyses of the impact of the nuclear weapon on the search for security see J. Herz, *International Politics in the Atomic Age*, New York, Columbia University Press, 1962, chapter 8.

54. The dialectic between regulation and disturbance provides the basis for one of the more illuminating analyses of the contemporary international system in, Richard Rosecrance, *Action and Reaction in World Politics: International Systems in Perspective*, Boston, Little, Brown & Co., 1963.

55. See Paul and Anne Ehrlich, *Population, Resources, Environment*, San Fransisco, W. H. Freeman & Co., 1970; Ian McHarg, *Design with Nature*, Garden City, NY, Natural History Press, 1969; Barry Commoner, *The Closing Circle: Nature, Man and Technology*, New York, Bantam Books, 1971; Barbara Ward and Rene Dubos, *Only one Earth: The Care and Maintenance of a Small Planet*, Harmondsworth, Penguin Books, 1972.

56. The dangers arising from the failure to integrate ecological values into the scientific, technological, economic and political process have recently inspired several useful anthologies: William L. Thomas, Jr *et al.* (eds.), *Man's Role in Changing the Face of the Earth*, Chicago, University of Chicago Press, 1956; Paul Shepard and Daniel McKingley (eds), *The Subversive Science, Essays Toward an Ecology of Man*, Boston, Houghton Mifflin & Co., 1969; Andrew P. Vayda (ed.), *Environment and Cultural Behaviour*, Garden City, NY, The Natural History Press, 1959; Robert Disch (ed.), *The Ecological Conscience*, Englewood Cliffs, NJ, Prentice Hall Inc., 1970; Harold W. Helfrich (ed.), *The Environmental Crisis*, New Haven, Conn., Yale University Press, 1970; Paul R. Ehrlich, John P. Holdren, Richard W. Holm (eds), *Man and the Ecosphere: Readings from Scientific American*, San Francisco, W. H. Freeman & Co., 1971.

57. Cf. George M. Woodwell, 'Toxic Substances and Ecological Cycles' in, *Man and the Ecosphere: Readings from Scientific American*, pp. 128–35.

58. Edward S. Deevy, Jr, 'The Human Population' in, *Men and the Ecosphere: Readings from Scientific American*, p. 49.

59. *The Limits to Growth*, A Report for the Club of Rome's Project on the Predicament of Mankind by Donnella H. Meadows, Dennis L. Meadows, Jorgen Randers, William W. Behrens, London, Earth Island Ltd, 1972, p. 56.

60. For a devastating attack on the fashionable and middle-class ideology shared by much of the environmental movement, see Johan Galtung, 'The Limits to Growth and Class Politics', *Journal of Peace Research*, 1973.

61. See Clarence J. Glacken, 'Man Against Nature: An Outmoded Concept' in, Harold W. Helfrich, Jr (ed.), *The Environment Crisis*; Alan Watts, 'The World is Your Body' in, Robert Disch (ed.), *The Ecological Conscience*.

Chapter 3. The decadence of industrial culture

1. Cf. Ellen Meiksins Wood, *Mind and Politics*, Berkeley, University of California Press, 1972, p. 174.
2. Henry Jacoby, *The Bureaucratization of the World*, (trans. from the German by Eveline L. Kanes), Berkeley, University of California Press, Press, 1974, p. 167.
3. This concept derives largely, though not exclusively, from the neo-Marxist cultural critique of late industrial society, to which theorists such as Lukacs, Adorno, Horkheimer, Marcuse, Habermas, Lefebvre, Fromm, have all made important contributions. This interpretation, often associated with the Frankfurt School, has provided a new foundation for critical theory and a new conceptualization of the mode of domination, emphasising the notions of cultural dependence, psychological manipulation and political powerlessness. For a theoretical and historical analysis of this tradition see Paul Breines (ed.), *Critical Interruptions*, New York, Herder & Herder, 1970; Martin Jay, *The Dialectical Imagination*, Boston, Little Brown & Co., 1973; D. Koward and K. Klare (eds.), *The Hidden Dimension*. For an incisive fusion of recent and traditional European critical social thought, see Trent Shroyer, *The Critique of Domination*, Boston, Beacon Press, 1975 (especially chapter 6).
4. Erich Fromm, *The Sane Society*, p. 153.
5. R. D. Laing, *The Politics of Experience and the Bird of Paradise*, Harmondsworth, Penguin Books, 1967, p.80.
6. Lewis Mumford, *The Conduct of Life*, New York, Harcourt, Brace & Co., 1951, p. 14. See also Vance Packard, *The Hidden Persuaders*, New York, D. McKay Co., 1957.
7. The concept of the 'mass society' is developed in some detail by C. Wright Mills in, *The Power Elite*, London, Oxford University Press, 1956. The growing distance between the individual and the state is also analysed by William Kornhauser in, *The Politics of Mass Society*, New York, Free Press, 1959, although there is little to support his faith in pluralism as an antidote to the totalitarian tendency of the mass society. Even less tenable is the thesis of those technological enthusiasts who argue that modern industrial civilization has significantly enhanced the power of interest groups which mediate between the state and the individual and extend the range of ethical and political choices available to him. See Peter F. Drucker, *Landmarks of Tomorrow*, New York, Harper & Row, 1959; Marshall McLuhan, *Understanding Media*, New York, McGraw-Hill, 1965; Victor C. Ferkiss, *Technological Man*, New York, New American Library, 1970.
8. See William H. Whyte, Jr, *The Organization Man*, New York, Simon & Schuster, 1956.
9. Karl Mannheim, 'The Problem of Democratization as a General Cultural Phenomenon', in *Essays on the Sociology of Culture*, London, Routledge & Kegan Paul, 1956, p. 202.
10. See Vance Packard, *The Pyramid Climbers*, New York, McGraw-Hill, 1962.

11. T. W. Adorno, 'Cultural Criticism and Society', in *Prisms*, (translated by Samuel and Shierry Weber), London, Spearman, 1967, p. 21.

12. For a discussion of the destructive impact of the industrial state on the associative order see Robert Nisbet, *Tradition and Revolt*, New York, Vintage Books, 1970.

13. Robert Michels, *Political Parties: A Sociological Study of the Oligarchical Tendencies of Modern Democracy*, (translated by Eden and Cedar Paul), New York, Dover Publications, 1959 (first published in 1915).

14. Herbert Marcuse, *One Dimensional Man*, p. 11.

15. Thorstein Veblen, 'Why is Economics not an Evolutionary Science?' in *The Place of Science in Modern Civilization and other Essays*, New York, B. W. Huebsch, 1919, p. 13.

16. See Daniel Bell, *The End of Ideology*, New York, Collier Books, 1962.

17. For a formulation of the 'veiled' quality of the class system in advanced capitalist societies see Norman Birnbaum, *The Crisis of Industrial Society*, London, Oxford University Press, 1969.

18. Cf. Konrad Lorenz, *Civilized Man's Eight Deadly Sins*, London, Methuen & Co. Ltd, 1974, chapter 5.

19. Ivan Illich, *Tools for Conviviality*, p. 54.

20. M. Harrington, *The Accidental Century*, Harmondsworth, Penguin Books, 1967, p. 182.

21. David Riesman, *The Lonely Crowd*, New Haven, Conn., Yale University Press, 1967, p. 121.

22. T. S. Eliot, *The Cocktail Party*, London, Faber & Faber, 1958, Act Two, pp. 133, 134. Reprinted by permission of Faber & Faber Ltd and Harcourt Brace Jovanovich, Inc. (New York).

23. See R. D. Laing, *The Divided Self*, Harmondsworth, Penguin Books, 1965, chapter 5.

24. Jeffrey K. Hadden, 'The Private Generation' in Kenneth L. Jones (eds.), *Age of Aquarius*, Pacific Palisades, California, Goodyear Publishing Co. Inc., 1971.

25. *Ibid*, p. 236.

26. *Ibid*, p. 237.

27. Jürgen Habermas, *Toward a Rational Society*, (translated by Jeremy J. Shapiro), London, Heinemann, 1971, p. 112.

28. Cf. C. B. MacPherson, *The Political Theory of Possessive Individualism*, London, Oxford University Press, 1962.

29. Karl Marx, *Critique of Hegel's 'Philosophy of Right'* edited by J. O'Malley (translated by A. Jolin and J. O'Malley), Cambridge, Cambridge University Press, 1970, pp. 77–8.

30. J. Ellul, *The Technological Society*, pp. 363–75.

31. Herman Kahn and Anthony J. Wiener, *The Year 2000: A Framework for Speculation on the Next Thirty-Three Years*, New York, Macmillan, 1967.

32. Alvin Toffler, *Future Shock*, p. 213.

33. Henri Lefebvre, *Everyday Life of the Modern World*, p. 146.

34. R. D. Laing, *The Politics of Experience*, p. 55.

35. Herbert Marcuse, *Eros and Civilization*, London, Abacus, 1972, p. 42.

36. Sigmund Freud, *Civilization and its Discontents*, (translated by Joan

Riviere), revised and newly edited by James Strachey, London, Hogarth
Press, 1973. For a useful comparative analysis of Marx's and Freud's
conception of social pathology see Erich Fromm, *Beyond the Chains of
Illusion*, New York, Simon & Schuster, 1972.

37. Herbert Marcuse, 'Progress and Freud's Theory of Instincts', in *Five
Lectures.*
38. Cf. Lewis Mumford, *Technics and Civilization*, New York, Harcourt, Brace
& Co., 1934.
39. For an examination of the changes required for the liberation of society
in the form and socializing function of the family see Agnes Heller and
Mihaly Vajda, 'Family Structure and Communism', *Telos*, No. 7,
January 1971.
40. Cf. Isaac Deutscher, *Stalin*, Harmondsworth, Penguin Books, 1966,
p. 362.
41. Theodore Roszak, *The Making of a Counter Culture*, p. 15.
42. See Edward M. Brecher and the Editors of Consumer Reports, *Licit and
Illicit Drugs*, Boston, Little Brown & Co., 1972.
43. Jacques Ellul, *The Technological Society*, p. 320.
44. Karl Marx, *Critique of Hegel's Philosophy of Right*, p. 47.
45. J. Habermas, *Toward a Rational Society*, p. 107.
46. Cf. George Steiner, *In Bluebeard's Castle*, London, Faber & Faber, 1971,
pp. 40–1.
47. Herbert Marcuse, *One Dimensional Man*, p. 57.
48. *Ibid.* p. 62.
49. *Ibid.* pp. 62–3.
50. George Steiner, *In Bluebeard's Castle*, p. 46.
51. See Herbert Marcuse, 'Aggressiveness in Advaned Industrial Society'
in *Negations.*
52. Noam Chomsky, *For Reasons of State*, London, Fontana, 1973, p. 90.
53. C. W. Mills, *The Sociological Imagination*, Harmondsworth, Penguin
Books, 1970, p. 27.
54. Of particular interest in the evaluation of scientific enquiry is Abraham
Maslow's, *The Psychology of Science*, New York, Harper & Row, 1966.
See also Theodore Roszak, *The Making of a Counter Culture* (especially
chapter entitled 'The Myth of Objective Consciousness').
55. For a closely argued critique of modern liberal political theory and its
implications for the role of man in society see Ellen Meiskins Wood,
Mind and Politics (especially chapter 4).

Chapter 4. World economy in disarray

1. For one of the most readable but also most penetrating examinations
of the world economic crisis, see Geoffrey Barraclough, 'The Great
World Crisis 1', *New York Review of Books*, Vol. 21, Nos. 21–2, January
23, 1975, and 'Wealth and Power: The Politics of Oil and Food', *New
York Review of Books*, August 7, 1975.
2. A. A. Berle, Jr, 'What GNP Doesn't Tell Us', *Saturday Review*, August 31,
1968.
3. See H. V. Hodson, *The Diseconomics of Growth*, especially chapters 4 and
7.

4. Kenneth E. Boulding, 'Is Scarcity Dead?' in, *Is Economics Relevant?*, edited by R. L. Heilbroner and A. M. Ford, Pacific Palisades, California, Goodyear Publishing Co. Inc., 1971, p. 184.

5. Cf. Robert L. Heilbroner, *The Worldly Philosophers*, New York, Simon & Schuster, 1972, pp. 292–3.

6. See *Main Economic Indicators*, July 1974, Paris, OECD, 1974, pp. 144–7.

7. See James O'Connor, *The Fiscal Crisis of the State*, New York, St Martin's Press, 1973.

8. A similar situation had arisen elsewhere. In France 20 per cent of French companies accounted for 90 per cent of total business, while a handful of Italian, Dutch and Belgian firms dominated their respective economies.

9. R. Heilbroner, *The Worldly Philosophers*, p. 298.

10. Charles Levinson, *Capital, Inflation and the Multinationals*, London, George Allen & Unwin Ltd, 1971, p. 152.

11. Tad Szulc, *The Energy Crisis*, New York, Franklin Watts, Inc., 1974, p. 101.

12. Cf. Michael Reich, 'Military Spending and the U.S. Economy' in, S. Rosen (ed.), *Testing the Theory of the Military-Industrial Compled*, Lexington, Mass., Lexington Books, 1973.

13. See Murray L. Weidenbaum, 'Our Vietnamized Economy', *Saturday Review*, May 24, 1969; Charles E. Nathanson, 'The Militarization of the American Economy' in David Horowitz (ed.), *Corporations and the Cold War*, New York, Monthly Review Press, 1970.

14. See George Thayer, *The War Business, The International Trade in Armaments*, New York, Simon & Schuster, 1969; SIPRI, *The Arms Trade with the Third World*, part 2.

15. Paul Sweezy and Harry Magdoff, 'Economic Stagnation and the Stagnation of Economics', *Monthly Review*, April 1971.

16. For an analysis of the stimulus to capital investment provided by the military budget and its inflationary consequences, see Victor Perlo, *The Unstable Economy*, New York, International Publishers, 1973, pp. 92–3, 156–72.

17. Immanuel Wallerstein, 'Trends in World Capitalism', *Monthly Review*, May 1974, Vol. 25, No. 12, p. 16.

18. For a very stimulating discussion of the paradoxical convergence of these two trends (internationalization and fragmentation), see Nicos Poulantzas, 'L'Internationalization des rapports, capitalistes et l'état-nation', *Les Temps Modernes*, 29ᵉ année, No. 319, Février 1973, pp. 1456–500. See also Robert Rowthorn, 'L'Internationalisation du capital et pouvoir national d'état', *Les Temps Modernes,* 29ᵉ année, No. 328, Décembre 1973, pp. 965–97.

19. Helmut Schmidt, 'Struggle for the World Product', *Foreign Affairs*, April 1974, Vol. 52, No. 3, p. 442.

20. See *International Financial Statistics*, Vol. 27, No. 9, September 1974, p. 36; *Direction of Trade*, July 1974, p. 102.

21. See Ernest Mandel, *Europe vs. America: Contradictions of Imperialism*, New York, Monthly Review Press, 1972; Jean-Jacques Servan-Schreiber, *The American Challenge*, Harmondsworth, Penguin Books, 1969.

22. United Nations, Department of Economic and Social Affairs, *Multinational Corporations in World Development*, New York, 1973, p. 127.

23. Michael Tanzer, *The Energy Crisis: World Struggle for Power and Wealth*, New York, Monthly Review Press, 1975, p. 135.

24. See Eric Wyndham White, 'The Evolution of the General Agreement on Tariffs and Trade' in, F. B. Jensen and I. Walter (eds.), *Readings in International Economic Relations*, New York, Roland Press Co., 1966.

25. Paul M. Sweezy and Harry Magdoff, *The Dynamics of U.S. Capitalism* New York, Monthly Review, 1972, p. 176.

26. Cf. Harold van B. Cleveland and W. H. Bruce Brittain, 'A World Depression?', *Foreign Affairs*, Vol. 53, No. 2, January 1975.

27. See Christopher J. Morse, 'The Evolving Monetary System', *Finance and Development*, Vol. 11, No. 3, September 1974, p. 14.

28. See Richard N. Gardner, *The World Food and Energy Crises*, Rensselaerville, NY, Institute on Man and Science, 1974, p. 27; Edward J. Mitchell (ed.), *Dialogue on World Oil*, Washington, DC, American Enterprise Institute, 1975, p. 85; *OECD Economic Outlook*, July 15, 1974, pp. 33–4.

29. See Gerard Pollack, 'The Economic Consequences of the Energy Crisis', *Foreign Affairs*, Vol. 52, No. 3, April 1974, p. 453.

30. *OECD Economic Outlook*, July 1974, p. 95.

31. *Financial Times*, January 24, 1975.

32. Richard N. Cooper, 'The Invasion of the Petrodollar', *Saturday Review*, January 25, 1975, p. 13.

33. Hollis B. Chenery, 'Restructuring the World Economy', *Foreign Affairs*, Vol. 53, No. 2, January 1975, p. 257.

34. *IMF Survey, Annual Reports Issue*, August 26, 1975.

35. *International Financial Statistics*, IMF, Vol. 28, No. 5, May 1975.

36. *OECD Economic Outlook*, July 1975, p. 56.

37. Geoffrey Barraclough, 'The Great World Crisis 1', p. 22.

38. *A Time to Choose: America's Energy Future* by the Energy Policy Project of the Ford Foundation, with a foreword by McGeorge Bundy, New York, Ballinger, 1974.

39. Tad Szulc, *The Energy Crisis*, pp. 40–5.

40. C. Fred Bergsten, *Toward A New International Economic Order: Selected Papers of C. Fred Bergsten 1972–1974*, Lexington, Mass., Lexington Books, 1975 (especially part 1).

Chapter 5. Underdevelopment and structural dependence

1. The 'Third World' is nevertheless a useful term to designate all those countries which were subjected to the process of colonization whether by territorial conquest or economic domination. See Peter Worsley, *The Third World*, London, Weidenfeld & Nicolson, 1967.

2. *Trends in Developing Countries*, World Bank, 1973, Table 1.4. For an equally discouraging forecast of future inequality on the basis of current trends, see Bruce M. Russett, 'Rich and Poor in 2000 AD: The Great Gulf', *Virginia Quarterly Review*, Spring 1968, pp. 182–98.

3. Elaborations of this paradigm were provided by Gabriel Almond

and James Coleman (eds.), *The Politics of the Developing Areas*, Princeton, NJ, Princeton University Press, 1960; Harry Eckstein and David Apter (eds.), *Comparative Politics*, New York, The Free Press of Glencoe, 1963; G. Almond and G. Powell, Jr, *Comparative Politics: A Developmental Approach*, Boston, Little, Brown & Co., 1966. Much of the theoretical foundation for this approach is to be found in Talcott Parsons, *Structure and Process in Modern Societies*, New York, The Free Press of Glencoe, 1960, and Bert F. Hoselitz, *Sociological Factors in Economic Development*, New York, the Free Press of Glencoe, 1960.

4. An explicitly economic version of this model was developed by Walt Whitman Rostow. *The Stages of Economic Growth: A Non-Communist Manifesto*, Cambridge, Cambridge University Press, 1960.

5. For a discussion of these theoretical pitfalls see Norman T. Uphoff and Warren F. Ilchman (eds.), *The Political Economy of Development*, Berkeley, University of California Press, 1972 (especially part 1); Gunnar Myrdal, *The Challenge of World Poverty*, (especially part 1); Charles Moskos and Wendel Bell, 'Emerging Nations and Ideologies of American Social Scientists', *The American Sociologist*, May 1967; Andre Gunder Frank, *Latin America: Underdevelopment or Revolution*, (especially part 2).

6. For some very instructive case studies, see J. S. Furnivall, *Netherlands India: A Study of Plural Economy*, Cambridge, Cambridge University Press, 1939; Surendra J. Patel, *Essays on Economic Transition*, New York, Asian Publishing House, 1965; Stanley J. and Barbara H. Stein, *The Colonial Heritage of Latin America: Essays on Economic Dependence in Perspective*, New York, Oxford University Press, 1970.

7. Cf. Clifford Geertz, *Agricultural Involution: The Process of Ecological Change in Indonesia*, Berkeley, University of California Press, 1963.

8. Cf. Stephen Resnick, 'The Second Path to Capitalism: A Model of International Development', *Journal of Contemporary Asia*, Vol. 3, No. 2, 1973.

9. Contrary to Gunder Frank's thesis, the evidence indicates that the widespread incorporation of the colonial economy into the capitalist system did not automatically or completely eliminate the feudal mode of production. See Ernesto Laclau, 'Feudalism and Capitalism in Latin America', *New Left Review*, No. 67, May–June 1971.

10. The apt reminder that national systems are not immune to external influences infuses many of the contributions in James Rosenau (ed.), *Linkage Politics*, New York, the Free Press, 1969. See also G. M. Lagos, *International Stratification and Underdeveloped Countries*, and J. P. Nettl and R. Robertson, *International Systems and the Modernization of Societies*.

11. Among these, possibly the most influential has been Andre Gunder Frank (author of *Latin America: Underdevelopment or Revolution, Capitalism and Underdevelopment in Latin America*, and *Lumpen-Bourgeoisie and Lumpen-Development: Dependence, Close and Politics in Latin America*, translated by Marian Davis Berdecio, New York, Monthly Review Press, 1972), considerably influenced by Paul Baran, who may be regarded as one of the most significant contemporary innovators in

the Marxist theory of imperialism. His works include *The Political Economy of Growth, Monopoly Capital* (with Paul Sweezy), and *The Longer View*, New York, Monthly Review Press, 1969. Among the more important Latin American 'dependistas', particularly deserving of attention are: Fernando Henrique Cardoso and Enzo Falletto, *Dependencia y Desarollo en América Latina*, Mexico, Siglo Veintiuno Editores, 1969; Celso Furtado, *Obstacles to Development in Latin America*, New York, Anchor Books, 1970; Theotonio dos Santos, 'The Structure of Dependence', *American Economic Review*, Vol. 60, May 1970. Other valuable contributions include: H. Magdoff, *The Age of Imperialism*, New York, Monthly Review Press, 1969; Pierre Jalée, *Imperialism in the Seventies*, New York, The Joseph Okpaku Press, 1972; Samir Amin, *Accumulation on a World Scale: A Critique of the Theory of Underdevelopment* (2 vols.), New York, Monthly Review Press, 1974; Johan Galtung, 'A Structural Theory of Imperialism', *Journal of Peace Research*, Vol. 8, No. 2, 1971.

12. Theotonio dos Santos, *El nuevo caracter de la dependencia*, Santiago, Cuadernos de Estudios Socio-Económicos (10), Centro de Estudios Socio-Económicos, Universidad de Chile, 1968, p. 6.

13. Osvaldo Sunkel, 'Big Business and "Dependencia"', *Foreign Affairs*, Vol. 50, April 1972, p. 519.

14. For a very useful bibliographical review of dependence literature see Ronald H. Chilcote, 'A Critical Synthesis of the Dependency Literature', *Latin American Perspectives*, Vol. 1, No. 1, Spring 1974.

15. Raúl Prebisch, whose analysis was to exert considerable influence over the thinking of the United Nations Economic Commission for Latin America (ECLA), was perhaps the first to formulate the dependence concept in relation to international trade. See *The Economic Development of Latin America and its Principal Problems*, New York, United Nations, 1950. For a much more elaborate analysis of the division of labour in international trade and its relationship to the disparity in wage structure between developed and underdeveloped economies, see Arghiri Emmanuel, *Unequal Exchange: A Study of the Imperialism of Trade*, New York, Monthly Review Press, 1972.

16. See P. Jalée, *The Third World in World Economy*, Table V-12.

17. *Ibid*, Tables II–6, 7, 10, 11.

18. ECLA, *Economic Survey of Latin America*, New York, United Nations, 1968, p. 58.

19. These are calculated from the relevant tables in *Direction of Trade, 1969–73*, jointly published by the International Monetary Fund and the International Bank for Reconstruction and Development.

20. See P. Jalée, *The Third World in World Economy*, p. 72.

21. Paul Bairoch, *Diagnostic de l'évolution du tiers-monde*, Paris, Gauthier-Villars Editeur, 1967, p. 162.

22. Between the second and last quarter of 1974 price of rubber fell by more than 25 per cent and that of zinc by more than 50 per cent. See IMF, *International Financial Statistics*, Vol. 28, No. 7, July 1975, pp. 30–1.

23. Bension Varon and Kenji Takeuchi, 'Developing Countries and Non-Fuel Minerals', *Foreign Affairs*, Vol. 52, No. 3, April 1974, p. 502.

24. Pierre Jalée, *The Third World in World Economy*, pp. 55–8.
25. *Trends in Developing Countries*, 1973, Table 5.1.
26. For an elaboration of the concept of 'independent industrialization' see Bob Sutcliffe, 'Imperialism and Industrialization in the Third World' in, *Studies in the Theory of Imperialism*, edited by Roger Owen and Bob Sutcliffe, London, Longman, 1972. For an opposing view, arguing that substantial progress in capitalist industrialization within the Third World has already occurred, see Bil Warren, 'Imperialism and Capitalist Industrialization' *New Left Review*, No. 8, September–October 1973.
27. For a fuller account of this analysis see ECLA, *Development Problems in Latin America: An Analysis by the United Nations Commission for Latin America*, with a foreword by C. Quintana, Austin, Texas, 1970.
28. *World Hunger: Causes and Remedies*, a report by the Transnational Institute, Washington, DC, 1974, pp. 5–6.
29. *Ibid*, p. 9.
30. *Ibid*, Table 2.
31. Lyle P. Schertz, 'World Food: Prices and the Poor', *Foreign Affairs*, vol. 52, No. 3, April 1974, p. 514.
32. *World Hunger: Causes and Remedies*, p. 33.
33. See Chabert, M. Marloie, P. Spitz, and B. Vallois, *Pénurie naturelle ou pénurie sociale?* (mimeo), Paris, Institut National de la Recherche Agronomique, 1973; also Lester Brown and Erick Eckholm *By Bread Alone*, New York, Praeger, 1974.
34. Thomas E. Weisskopf, 'Capitalism and Underdevelopment in the Modern World' in, R. C. Edwards *et al.*, *The Capitalist System*, p. 445.
35. See Montek S. Ahluwalia, 'Income Inequality: Some Dimensions of the Problem' in, Hollis Chenery *et al.*, *Redistribution with Growth*, London, Oxford University Press, 1974.
36. Cf. Rodolfo Stavenhagen, 'Marginality, Participation and Agrarian Structure in Latin America', *Bulletin of the International Institute for Labor Studies*, No. 7, 1970.
37. Cf. H. W. Singer, 'Dualism Revisited: A New Approach to the Problems of the Dual Society in Developing Countries', *Journal of Development Studies*, Vol. 7, 1970.
38. Rodolfo Stavenhagen, 'The Future of Latin America: Between Underdevelopment and Revolution', *Latin American Perspectives*, Vol. 1, No. 1, Spring 1974.
39. For a penetrating analysis of the community of interests between the multinational corporation and the economic elites of underdeveloped societies, and the accompanying exclusion of the masses from the benefits of accumulation, in the light of the Brazilian experience, see Celso Furtado, 'The Brazilian Model', *Social and Economic Studies*, Vol. 22, 1973.
40. Cf. Robert Stauffer, *In Defence of Disorder* (mimeo), 1972.
41. A. I. Schiller, 'Madison Avenue Imperialism', *Trans-Action*, March–April 1973, p. 53.
42. Albert Memmi, *The Colonizer and the Colonized*, with an introduction by Jean-Paul Sartre, London, Souvenir Press, 1974 (originally published

in French in 1957); Frantz Fanon, *Black Skin, White Masks*, New York, Grove Press, 1967. See also Juan Corradi, 'Cultural Dependence and the Sociology of Knowledge: The Latin American Case', *International Journal of Contemporary Sociology*, Vol. 8, January 1971.

43. Ivan Illich, 'Planned Poverty: The End Result of Technical Assistance' in, *Celebration of Awareness*, Harmondsworth, Penguin Books, 1973.

44. See Michael Klare, *War Without End*, especially chapter 9.

45. Cf. Dale L. Johnson, 'Dependence and the International System' in James D. Cockcroft *et al.*, *Dependence and Underdevelopment*, Garden City, NY, Anchor Books, 1972.

46. See C. R. Hensman, *Rich Against Poor: The Reality of Aid*, Harmondsworth, Penguin Books, 1975, especially chapters 7–8.

47. Pierre Jalée, *The Pillage of the Third World*, p. 97.

48. This body was set up in 1960 under the aegis of the OECD, comprising all the developed capitalist economies.

49. *Trends in Developing Countries*, 1973, Table 4.1.

50. *Development Cooperation 1968 Review (OECD)*, Table 7 and *1973 Review*, Table 7.

51. *Development Cooperation 1973 Review (OECD)*, Table 7.

52. *Ibid*.

53. *Ibid*. Table 4.5.

54. Cf. E. L. Wheelwright, *Radical Political Economy : Collected Essays*, Sydney, ANZ Book Co., 1974, pp. 327–31.

55. Harry Magdoff, *The Age of Imperialism*, p. 198.

56. ECLA, *Economic Survey of Latin America*, 1970, p. 288.

57. Ronald Müller, 'More on Multinationals ... Poverty is the Product', *Foreign Policy*, No. 14, 1973–4, pp. 71–103.

58. For an interesting case study of the impact of such external pressures, see Robert B. Stauffer, 'The Political Economy of a Coup: Transnational Linkages and Philippine Political Response', *Journal of Peace Research*, Vol. 11, No. 3, 1974.

59. Michael Kidron illuminates this process in his analysis of the impact of foreign investment on the Indian economy, *Foreign Investments in India*, Oxford University Press, 1965.

60. See Cheryl Payer's powerful attack on the IMF, *The Debt Trap: The International Monetary Fund and the Third World*, New York, Monthly Review Press, 1974.

61. For a case study analysis of the role of international institutions in promoting this particular model of development, see T. Hayter, *Aid as Imperialism*, Harmondsworth, Penguin Books, 1971.

62. Andrew Learmonth, 'The Demographic Regions of the Indian Subcontinent' in, *The Population Explosion: An Interdisciplinary Approach*, Open University Press, 1971.

63. Barbara Ward, 'The Poor World's Cities', *The Economist*, December 6, 1969.

64. Colin Clark, *Population Growth and Land Use*, London, Macmillan, 1967.

65. Roger Revelle, 'Food and Population', *Scientific American*, September 1974.

Chapter 6. Economic transnationalism

1. See F. A. Mackenzie, *The American Invaders*, London, Grant Richards, 1902. It is worth noting that in the initial stages the invasion took mainly the form of imported rather than locally produced goods.
2. These statistics are drawn mainly from the US Department of Commerce, *Survey of Current Business* (annual articles).
3. See Thomas E. Weisskopf, 'United States Foreign Private Investment: An Empirical Survey' in, *The Capitalist System*, p. 430.
4. See John Diebold, 'Multinational Corporations . . . Why be Scared of Them?', *Foreign Policy*, Fall 1973, p. 80.
5. J. A. Bain, 'Changes in Concentration in Manufacturing Industries in the United States, 1954–66. Trends and Relationships to the Levels of 1954 Concentration', *Review of Economics and Statistics*, November 1970.
6. Cf. Anthony Sampson, *The Sovereign State: The Secret History of ITT*, London Coronet Books, 1974, p. 146.
7. See 'The Merger Movement: A Study in Power' in Paul Sweezy and Harry Magdoff, *The Dynamics of US Capitalism*.
8. See R. B. Sutcliffe, Introduction to *The Political Economy of Growth* by Paul Baran, p. 73; also Christopher Tugendhat, *The Multinationals*, Harmondsworth, Penguin Books, 1973.
9. Paul A. Baran and Paul M. Sweezy, *Monopoly Capital*, p. 51.
10. For an analysis of the superior profit-making potential of the global corporation, see James O'Connor, *The Corporations and the State*, New York, Harper & Row, 1974, pp. 179–96.
11. Cf. C. F. Bergsten, *Toward a New International Economic Order*, chapter 32.
12. *The Multinational Corporation and the World Economy*, report by the Senate Committee on Finance, 93 Cong., 1 Session, 1973, p. 11.
13. *Multinational Corporations in World Development*, published by the Department of Economic and Social Affairs, United Nations, New York, 1973, p. 162.
14. C. F. Bergsten, *Toward an International Economic Order*, chapter 17. For an indication of increasing concern at the role of foreign investment on specific sectors of the American economy, see John C. Culver, 'Foreign Investment in the United States', *Foreign Policy*, No. 16, Fall 1974.
15. See John H. Dunning, *The Role of American Investment in the British Economy*, Political and Economic Planning Broadsheet 507, London, February 1969, p. 119.
16. Jean-Jacques Servan-Schreiber, *The American Challenge* (translated by R. Steel), New York, Athenaeum, 1968.
17. Charles Levinson, *Capital, Inflation and the Multinationals*, Table IV.4 (the table does not include communist countries or international merchant banks).
18. Ralph C. Deans, 'Multinational Companies', *Editorial Research Reports*, Vol. 11, No. 1.
19. P. F. Drucker, 'The New Capitalism', *Dialogue*, Vol. 4, No. 3, 1971, pp. 3–16.

20. 'A Rougher Road for Multinationals', *Business Week*, December 19, 1970, p. 58.

21. For a most revealing analysis of this process see Anthony Sampson's description of 'the Geneen machine' which underpins ITT's corporate structure in *The Sovereign State* (especially chapters 4–5).

22. Raymond Vernon, *Sovereignty at Bay: The Multinational Spread of US Enterprises*, Harmondsworth, Penguin Books, 1973, p. 141.

23. James O'Connor, *The Corporations and the State*, pp. 184–5.

24. Cf. Lawrence B. Krause, 'The International Economic System and the Multinational Corporation' in, *Annals of the American Academy of Political and Social Sciences*, Vol. 403, September 1972, p. 100.

25. Cf. Anthony Sampson, *The Sovereign State*, p. 111; *Multinational Corporations in World Development*, pp. 60–4.

26. For an illuminating discussion of the loss of government control over economic policy-making, see *Foreign Ownership and the Structure of the Canadian Industry*, Report of the Task Force on the Structure of Canadian Industry, Privy Council Office, Ottawa, 1968.

27. Cf. Osvaldo Sunkel, 'Intégration capitaliste transnationale et désintégration nationale en Amérique Latine', *Politique Etrangère*, No. 6, 1970.

28. See C. Fred Bergsten, 'Coming Investment Wars', *Foreign Affairs*, Vol. 53, No. 1, October 1974, pp. 135–52.

29. See Andrew Schonfield, 'Business in the Twenty-First Century', *Daedelus*, Winter 1969, pp. 191–207.

30. See David H. Blake, 'Trade Unions and the Challenge of the Multinational Corporation', *Annals of the American Academy of Political and Social Sciences*, Vol. 403, September 1972; I. A. Litvak and C. J. Maule, 'The Union Response to International Corporations', *Industrial Relations*, Vol. 2, No. 1, February 1972.

31. For a probing though somewhat exaggerated account of the linkages between American foreign policy and the most powerful corporate and financial interests within the United States, see G. William Domhoff, 'Who Made American Foreign Policy, 1945–1963?' in, *Corporations and the Cold War* edited by David Horowitz, New York, Monthly Review Press, 1970.

32. David Horowitz, 'Introduction' in, *Corporations and the Cold War*, pp. 14–5.

33. Cf. Stephen Hymer, 'The Efficiency (Contradictions) of Multinational Corporations', *American Economic Review*, May 1970.

34. For some typical examples of this perspective, see Daniel Jay Baum, 'The Global Corporation: An American Challenge to the Nation-State?', *Iowa Law Review*, No. 55, December 1969, pp. 410–37; George W. Ball, 'Cosmocorp: The Importance of Being Stateless', *Columbia Journal of World Business*, No. 2, November–December 1967, pp. 25–30; Roy L. Ash, 'A New Anatomy of World Business', *Vital Speeches of the Day*, No. 36, December 15, 1969, pp. 154–7.

35. Cf. Enno Hobbing, 'The World Corporation as Catalytic Agent', *Columbia Journal of World Business*, Vol. 6, No. 4, August 1971, p. 51.

36. See Neil H. Jacoby, 'The Multinational Corporation', *Center Magazine*, Vol. 3, 1970, pp. 37–55.

37. Anthony Sampson, *The Sovereign State*, p. 266.

38. See Irving Louis Horowitz, 'Capitalism, Communism and Multinationalism' in, *The New Sovereigns*, pp. 120–38.

39. See Patrick Gutman et Francis Arkwright, 'Multinationalisation et pays de l'Est', *Politique Etrangère*, No. 4–5, 1974, pp. 517–38.

40. James R. Kurth, 'The Multinational Corporation, U.S. Foreign Policy, and the Less Developed Countries' in, *The New Sovereigns*, p. 143.

41. C. P. Kindleberger, *American Business Abroad: Six Lectures on Direct Investment*, New Haven, Conn., Yale University Press, 1969, p. 192. See also S. E. Rolfe, *The International Corporation*, Istanbul, International Chamber of Commerce, 1969, p. 30.

42. For an examination of 'enclave investment' see H. S. Singer, 'The Distribution of Gains Between Investing and Borrowing Countries', *American Economic Review*, Vol. 60, No. 2, May 1950, pp. 473–85; Charles E. Rollins, 'Mineral Development and Economic Growth', *Social Research*, Vol. 23, No. 3, Autumn 1956, pp. 253–80.

43. See Edith T. Penrose, *The Large International Firm in Developing Countries: The International Petroleum Industry*, London George Allen & Unwin, 1968.

44. See Peter F. Drucker, 'Multinationals and Developing Countries: Myths and Realities', *Foreign Affairs*, Vol. 53, No. 1, October 1974, pp. 126–8.

45. See James P. Grant, *Multinational Corporations and the Developing Countries: The Emerging Job Crisis and Its Implications*, Washington, DC, Overseas Development Council, 1972.

46. Ronald Müller, 'Poverty is the Product', *Foreign Policy*, No. 13, Winter 1973–4, p. 80.

47. *Ibid*, pp. 93–4.

48. For a discussion of corporate pricing policies and their effects on underdeveloped economies, see J. O'Connor, 'International Corporations and Economic Underdevelopment', *Science and Society*, No. 34, 1970, pp. 42–60.

49. See Ronald Müller, 'The Multinational Corporation and the Underdevelopment of the Third World' in, C. K. Wilber (ed.), *The Political Economy of Development and Underdevelopment*, New York, Random House, Inc., 1973.

50. Peter B. Evans, 'National Autonomy and Economic Development' in, R. O. Keohane and Joseph S. Nye, Jr, *Transnational Relations and World Politics*, Cambridge, Mass., Harvard University Press, 1972, p. 333.

Chapter 7.   The energy crisis

1. *World Energy Requirements in the Year 2000*, A/Conf. 49/P/420, Fourth UN International Conference on the Peaceful Uses of Atomic Energy, United Nations, July 1971.

2. *Energy and U.S. Foreign Policy*, A Report to the Energy Policy Project

of the Ford Foundation, Cambridge, Mass., Ballinger, 1975, p. 143.

3. John Holdren, 'Energy Resources' in, *Environment: Resources Pollution and Society* edited by William W. Murdoch (2nd edition), Sunderland, Mass., Sinauer Associates Inc., 1975, p. 127.

4. *Ibid*, p. 125.

5. Cited in Bharat Wariavwalla, 'The Energy Crisis, the Developing World and Strategy' in *Adelphi Papers*, No. 115, p. 32.

6. Jahangir Amuzegar, 'The Oil Story: Facts, Fiction and Fair Play', *Foreign Affairs*, Vol. 51, No. 4, July 1973, pp. 676–89.

7. *Ibid*, p. 672.

8. See A. J. Surrey and J. Bromley, 'Energy Resources in, A. S. D. Cole *et al.* (eds.), *Thinking About the Future: A Critique of the Limits to Growth*, London, Chatto & Windus for Sussex University Press, 1973.

9. OECD, *Oil; The Present Situation and Future Prospects*, Paris, 1973, p. 42.

10. *Energy and U.S. Foreign Policy*, p. 144.

11. *U.S. Energy Outlook, An Initial Appraisal, 1971–1985*. An Interim Report of the National Petroleum Council, Vol. 2, Table III, p. xxvii.

12. US Information Service, *Fact Sheet Excerpts: The President's Energy Programme*, January 15, 1975.

13. 'Focus on Energy', *Asia Research Bulletin*, Vol. 4, No. 1, June 30, 1974.

14. OECD, *Energy Prospects to 1985*, Vol. 1, Paris, 1975.

15. For a discussion of the difficulties surrounding the investment of the OPEC surplus in western countries see Robert Mabro and Elizabeth Monroe, 'Arab Wealth From Oil: Problems of its Investment', *International Affairs*, January 1974, pp. 15–27.

16. See *Kissinger Address in Chicago on Energy Crisis*, United States Information Service, November 14, 1974.

17. For a very useful discussion of the European response to the oil crisis, see Louis Turner, 'The Politics of the Energy Crisis', *International Affairs*, July 1974, pp. 404–15.

18. The implications of a policy of greater US energy self-sufficiency for the world energy market are discussed in Edward R. Fried, 'World Market Trends and Bargaining Leverage' in, *Energy and U.S. Foreign Policy*, pp. 231–75.

19. *President Ford's State of Union Message*, January 15, 1975, United States Information Service.

20. It is significant that, in all three scenarios ('Historical Growth', 'Technical Fix', 'Zero Energy Growth') of possible energy futures until the year 2000, constructed by the Energy Policy Project of the Ford Foundation, the United States remains dependent for its energy requirements on the import of several million barrels of oil per day. See *A Time to Choose: America's Energy Future*, p. 110.

21. See Bharat Wariavwalla, 'The Energy Crisis, the Developing World and Strategy', p. 34; also 'OPEC Aid to Developing Countries Rising', *IMF Survey*, November 18, 1974, pp. 360–2.

22. Cf. John P. Lewis, 'Oil, Other Scarcities and the Poor Countries', *World Politics*, Vol. 28, No. 1, October 1974, pp. 63–86.

23. Cf. R. Tucker, 'Oil: The Issue of American Intervention', *Commentary*, January 1975, pp. 21–31.

24. Cf. Walter J. Levy, 'World Oil Cooperation on International Chaos', *Foreign Affairs*, Vol. 52, No. 4, July 1974, p. 694. See also Edith Penrose, 'The Oil "Crisis": Dilemmas of Policy', *The Round Table*, No. 254, April 1974, pp. 135–46.

25. Norman Medvin, *The Energy Cartel: Who Runs the American Oil Industry*, New York, Vintage Books, 1974, pp. 26–7.

26. See H. R. Warman, 'The Future of Oil', *The Geographical Journal*, Vol. 138, September 1972, p. 293. Although Warman's estimates have been attacked as unduly conservative (see Peter R. Odell, 'The Future of Oil: A Rejoinder', *The Geographical Journal*, Vol. 139, June 1973, pp. 436–54), they appear validated by the declining rate of discovery. See R. D. H. Simpson, 'Further Remarks on the Future of Oil', *The Geographical Journal*, Vol. 139, June 1973, pp. 455–9.

27. The significance of some of these reserves may have been over-estimated. See James E. Akins, 'The Oil Crisis: This Time the Wolf is Here', *Foreign Affairs*, Vol. 51, No. 3, April 1973, p. 406.

28. M. King Hubbert, 'The Energy Resources of the Earth' in, *Scientific Technology and Social Change: Readings from Scientific American* edited by Gene I. Rochlin, San Francisco, W. H. Freeman & Co., 1974, pp. 266–7.

29. See M. King Hubbert, 'Energy Resources' in, *Resources and Man*, US National Academy of Sciences and National Research Council, San Francisco, W. H. Freeman & Co., 1969.

30. See *Solar Energy Research in Australia* published by the Australian Academy of Science, Canberra, 1974.

31. William C. Gough and Bernard J. Eastlund, 'The Prospects of Fusion Power' in, *Scientific Technology and Social Change*, pp. 304–18.

32. Preston Cloud, 'Mineral Resources in Fact and Fancy' in, H. E. Daly (ed.), *Toward a Steady-State Economy*, San Francisco, W. H. Freeman & Co., 1973, pp. 59–60.

33. M. King Hubbert, 'The Energy Resources of the Earth', p. 270.

34. See Glenn T. Seaborg and Justin L. Bloom, 'Fast Breeder Reactors' in, *Scientific Technology and Social Change*, pp. 295–303.

35. For a concise discussion of the environmental impact of energy use, see John Holdren, 'Energy Resources', pp. 141–2; Garrett de Bell, 'Energy' in, *Economic Growth vs. the Environment* edited by Warren A. Johnson and John Hardesty, Belmont, California, Wadsworth Publishing Co., 1971, pp. 30–5.

36. See John R. Clark, 'Thermal Pollution and Aquatic Life' in, *Scientific Technology and Social Change*, pp. 301–10.

37. See *Inadvertent Climate Modification*, Report of the Study Man's Impact on Climate, Cambridge, Mass., MIT Press, 1971.

38. See Earl Cook, 'Ionizing Radiation' in, *Environment: Resources, Pollution and Society*, pp. 308–20; Thomas C. Hollocher, 'Storage and Disposal of High Level Wastes' in D. F. Ford *et al.*, *The Nuclear Fuel Cycle*, Cambridge, Mass, Union of Concerned Scientists, 1973.

39. See Ian A. Forbes *et al.*, 'Nuclear Reactor Safety: An Evaluation of New Evidence', *Nuclear News*, September 1971, pp. 32–40.

40. See Bhupendra Jasani (ed.), *Nuclear Proliferation Problems*, Stockholm,

SIPRI, 1974; William Epstein, 'The Proliferation of Nuclear Weapons', *Scientific American*, Vol. 232, No. 4, April 1975; Frank Barnaby, 'Preventing the Spread of Nuclear Weapons', *New Scientist*, May 1, 1975.

41.   Cf. Mason Willrich and Theodore B. Taylor, *Nuclear Theft : Risks and Safeguards*, Cambridge, Mass., Ballinger Publishing Co., 1973; L. Douglas DeNike, 'Radioactive Malevolence', *Bulletin of the Atomic Scientists*, Vol. 30, No. 2, February 1974.

42.   D. H. Meadows *et al.*, *The Limits to Growth*; Jay W. Forrester, *World Dynamics*, Cambridge, Mass., Wright-Allen Press, 1971.

43.   Nicholas Georgescu-Roegen, 'The Entropy Law and the Economic Problem' in, *Toward a Steady-State Economy*, p. 39.

44.   Herman E. Daly, 'Electric Power, Employment, and Economic Growth: A Case Study in Growthmania' in, *Toward a Steady-State Economy*, pp. 252–77.

Chapter 8. The security crisis

1.   Many writers have at various times sought to apply concepts drawn from the theory of biological evolution to an analysis of war, arguing that the latter fulfils an adaptive function in human social behaviour. For a comprehensive examination of some of the major exponents of Social Darwinism see R. Hofstadter, *Social Darwinism in American Thought*, New York, George Braziller Inc., 1959. See also Lester Ward, *Pure Sociology*, New York, The Macmillan Co., 1903; Herbert Spencer *The Principles of Sociology* (3 vols.), New York, D. Appleton & Co., 1876–1897; William Graham Summer, *Social Darwinism*, Englewood Cliffs, NJ, Prentice Hall Inc., 1963. For a more recent contribution see R. Bigelow, *The Dawn Warriors*, Boston, Atlantic–Little, Brown, 1969. The notion of the maladaptiveness of war is developed in D. N. Daniels, M. F. Gilula and F. M. Ochberg (eds.), *Violence and the Struggle for Existence*, Boston, Little, Brown & Co. 1970.

2.   Richard N. Rosecrance develops this concept in terms of 'environmental capacity' and applies it to the European scramble for colonies in the late nineteenth century in, *Action and Reaction in World Politics : International System in Perspective*, Boston, Little, Brown & Co., 1963, pp. 149–68, 254–7, 274–5.

3.   See Nazli Choucri and Robert C. North, 'Dynamics of International Conflict: Some Policy Implications of Populations, Resources, and Technology' in, Raymond Tanter and Richard H. Ullman (eds.), *Theory and Policy in International Relations*, Princeton, NJ, Princeton University Press, 1972.

4.   For a social–psychological analysis of the cognitive and evaluative sources of ethnocentric behaviour see Robert A. LeVine, 'Socialization, Social Structure, and Intersocietal Images' in, *International Behaviour* edited by Herbert C. Kelman, New York, Holt, Rinehart & Winston, 1965.

5.   There is a very large and growing literature seeking to explain the nature and consequences of American military interventionism since

World War II. Among the more useful contributions one would include: Richard J. Barnet, *Intervention Revolution*, New York, World Publishing Co., 1968; Theodore Draper, *The Abuse of Power*, New York, Viking Press, 1967; Pierre Gallois, 'U.S. Foreign Policy: A Study of Military Strength and Diplomatic Weakness', *Orbis*, Vol. 9, Summer 1965, pp. 338–57; Gabriel Kolko, *The Roots of American Foreign Policy*, Boston, Beacon Press, 1969; Carl Oglesby and Richard Shaull, *Containment and Change*, New York, Macmillan, 1967; Herbert K. Tillema, *Appeal to Force*, New York, Thomas Y. Crowell Co., 1973; William Taubman (ed.), *Globalism and its Critics*, Lexington, Mass., D. C. Heath & Co., 1973.

6. For an analysis of the costs of the Vietnam War see *Strategic Survey 1972*, London, International Institute for Strategic Studies, 1973, pp. 48–52.

7. For details of the Yom Kippur War see *Strategic Survey 1973*, London, International Institute for Strategic Studies, 1974, pp. 13–55.

8. John H. Herz, *International Politics in the Atomic Age*, New York, Columbia University Press, 1962, chapter 6.

9. See John W. Spanier, *Games Nations Play*, London, Nelson, 1972, pp. 114–15.

10. US Department of State, Bureau of Public Affairs, *News Release*, August 1, 1972.

11. *The Military Balance 1974–1975*, London, International Institute for Strategic Studies, 1974, p. 78.

12. See Herman Kahn, *Thinking About the Unthinkable*, New York, Horizon, 1962.

13. For a critical analysis of this argument see the introduction by Anatol Rapoport to the Pelican edition of Carl Von Clausewitz, *On War*, Harmondsworth. Penguin Books, 1968.

14. Cf. R. S. McNamara, *The Essence of Security*, New York, Harper & Row, 1968.

15. For an examination of the rationale and implications of the counter-force strategy as enunciated by the US Secretary of Defence, James Schlesinger, see Barry Carter, 'Flexible Strategic Options, No Need for New Strategy', *Survival*, Vol. 17, No. 1, January–February 1975, pp. 25–31.

16. For a detailed and imaginative analysis of the nuclear contribution to the use of violence see Thomas C. Schelling, *Arms and Influence*, New Haven, Conn., Yale University Press, 1966, (especially chapter 1).

17. See Richard J. Barnet, 'The American Approaches to Disarmament' in, *Arms and Arms Control* edited by Ernest W. Lefever, New York, Praeger, 1962.

18. See Hedley Bull, *Control of the Arms Race* (2nd edition), New York, Praeger, 1965; also David V. Edwards, *Arms Control in International Politics*, New York, Holt, Rinehart & Winston Inc., 1969.

19. The modern version of the concept was given its earliest and most sophisticated formulation by C. Wright Mills in his classic, *The Power Elite*. Important recent contributions have included: Richard Barnet, *The Economy of Death*, New York, Atheneum, 1969; Fred J. Cook. *The Warfare State*, New York, Macmillan, 1962; J. K. Galbraith, *The New*

Industrial State; Ralph E. Lapp, *The Weapons Culture*, New York, Norton, 1968; Sidney Lens, *The Military–Industrial Complex*, Boston, Pilgrim Press, 1970; Seymour Melman, *Pentagon Capitalism*, New York, McGraw-Hill, 1970; Clark R. Mollenhoff, *The Pentagon: Politics, Profits and Plunder*, New York, G. P. Putnam's Sons, 1967; Herbert I. Schiller and Joseph D. Phillips (eds.), *Superstate: Readings in Military–Industrial Complex*, Urbana, University of Illinois Press, 1970; Steven Rosen (ed.), *Testing the Theory of the Military–Industrial Complex*, Lexington, Mass., D.C. Heath & Co., 1973; John M. Swomley, Jr, *The Military Establishment*, Boston, Beacon Press, 1964; Adam Yarmolinsky, *The Military Establishment*, New York, Harper & Row, 1971. See also Kenneth Boulding, 'The Role of the War Industry in International Conflict', *Journal of Social Issues*, Vol. 23, No. 1, January 1967; Robert F. Ferell, 'The Merchants of Death, Then and Now', *Journal of International Affairs*, Vol. 26, No. 1, 1972; Marc Pilisuk and Thomas Hayden, 'Is There a Military Industrial Complex which Prevents Peace?', *Journal of Social Issues*, Vol. 21, No. 3, July 1965.

20. See 'Pressures from "Military–Industrial Complex": focus on New Secretary of Defense', *Congressional Quarterly Weekly Report*, Vol. 26, May 24, 1968, p. 1159.

21. Ralph E. Lapp, *The Weapons Culture*, pp. 186–7.

22. Cf. Victor Perlo, 'Arms Profiteering: It's Not a Myth', *New Republic*, January 7, 1970, p. 24.

23. C. A. Vernon V. Aspaturian, 'The Soviet Military–Industrial Complex: Does It Exist?' in S. Rosen (ed.), *Testing the Theory of the Military–Industrial Complex*, p. 125.

24. For a wide-ranging discussion of the assumptions and objectives of 'collective security' and alliance systems see J. W. Burton, *International Relations: A General Theory*, Cambridge, Cambridge University Press, 1965; Inis L. Claude, *Power and International Relations*, New York, Random House, 1962; J. Garnett (ed.), *Theories of Peace and Security: A Reader in Contemporary Strategic Thought*, London, Macmillan, 1970; A. Martin, *Collective Security: A Progress Report*, Paris, UNESCO, 1952; Otto Pick and Julian Critchley, *Collective Security*, London, Macmillan, 1974; K. J. Twichett (ed.), *International Security: Reflections on Survival and Stability*, Oxford, Oxford University Press, 1971.

25. In December 1974, after more than twenty years of fruitless endeavour by legal and political experts, the United Nations General Assembly finally adopted without a vote a definition of aggression, which nevertheless left room for considerable ambiguity and the UN Security Council with wide powers of interpretation. See *Le Monde* (weekly edition), December 26, 1974–January 1, 1975.

26. For a general overview of the United Nations peace-keeping function, see Norman A. Padelford and Leland M. Goodrich (eds.), *The United Nations in the Balance*, New York, Frederick A. Praeger, 1965; David A. Kay (ed.), *The United Nations Political System*, New York, John Wiley & Sons, 1967.

27. Cf. Roland N. Stromberg, *Collective Security and American Foreign Policy*, New York, Frederick A. Praeger, 1963.

28. See G. Clark and L. B. Sohn, *World Peace through World Law* (rev. ed.), Cambridge, Mass., Harvard University Press, 1966; Elizabeth Mann Borgese, *Constitution for the World*, Santa Barbara, Calif., Center for the Study of Democratic Institutions, 1965; S. M. McDougal, 'Perspectives for an International Law of Human Dignity', *Proceedings of the American Society of International Law*, Vol. 53, 1959.

29. For a very perceptive analysis of the desirability of world government and the consequent centralization of power, see Inis L. Claude, Jr, *Power and International Relations*, especially pp. 206–78.

30. See H. D. Lasswell, 'The Prospects of Cooperation in a Bipolar World', *University of Chicago Law Review*, Vol. 15, 1948; Edward McWhinney, 'Soviet and Western International Law and the Cold War in the Era of Bipolarity', in *The Strategy of World Order (Vol. 2), International Law*, edited by Richard Falk and Saul Mendlovitz, New York, World Law Fund, 1966.

31. This argument is developed at some length by Roger Fisher, 'Bringing Law to Bear on Governments in, *The Strategy of World Order* (Vol. 2).

32. For a review of the different meanings and conceptions of the balance of power see Ernest B. Haas, 'The Balance of Power: Prescription, Concept or Propaganda?', *World Politics*, Vol. 5, No. 4, 1953; and M. Wight, 'The Balance of Power', in Herbert Butterfield and Martin Wight (eds.), *Diplomatic Investigations*, London, Allen & Unwin, 1966.

33. The most thorough exposition of the balance of power model as a major key to the understanding of international politics is to be found in Hans Morgenthau, *Politics Among Nations*, (4th ed.), New York, Alfred A. Knopf, 1967.

34. Kaplan in his model of the balance of power system, suggests that the ideal number is at least five. See Morton Kaplan, *System and Process in International Politics*, New York, John Wiley and Sons, 1957.

35. See Glenn H. Snyder, 'The Balance of Power and the Balance of Terror' in Paul Seabury (ed.), *Balance of Power*, San Francisco, Chandler Publishing Co., 1965; Kenneth Waltz, 'The Stability of a Bipolar World' in, *Daedalus*, Summer 1964, pp. 881–909.

36. For a useful analysis of the underlying balance of power assumptions in the Nixon–Kissinger formulation of US Foreign Policy see A. Hartley, *American Foreign Policy in the Nixon Era*, (Adelphi Papers, no. 110), London, International Institute for Strategic Studies, 1974. The restoration of the balance of power in the contemporary international system is examined by H. Bull, 'The New Balance of Power in Asia and the Pacific', *Foreign Affairs*, Vol. 49, No. 4, July 1971 and S. Hoffman, 'Weighing the Balance of Power', *Foreign Affairs*, Vol. 50, No. 4, July 1972.

Chapter 9. The claims of morality and utopia

1. Cf. Erich Fromm, *The Sane Society*, pp. 273–4.

2. By the very act of consciousness man is able to transcend his objective situation, leave behind the dimension of actuality and enter the realm of potentiality. For a discussion of the possibility of choice and the

necessity of decision based on guiding values, see Walter Weiskopf, 'Existence and Values' in, *New Knowledge in Human Values* edited by Abraham H. Maslow, Chicago, Gateway, 1970.

3. See Mulford Q. Sibley, 'Apology for Utopia: I', *The Journal of Politics*, February, 1940, pp. 57–74; 'Apology for Utopia: II', *The Journal of Politics*, May, 1940, pp. 165–88 and Martin Buber, *Paths in Utopia*, Boston, Beacon Press, 1958.

4. Important contributions to the utopian conception of small-scale communities include: Thomas More, *Utopia* (edited by Edward Arber), London, A. Murray, 1969; Robert Owen, *A New View of Society and Report to the County of Lanark* (edited with an introduction by V. A. C. Gattrell), Harmondsworth, Penguin Books, 1970; *Harmonian Man: Selected Writings of Charles Fourier* (edited by Mark Posker), Garden City, NY, Anchor Books, 1971; *Selected Writings of Pierre Joseph Proudhon* (edited with an introduction by Stewart Edwards), London, Macmillan, 1970; Peter Kropotkin, *Revolutionary Pamphlets* edited by Roger N. Baldwin, New York, Dover Publications, 1970. More global conceptions of world order are to be found in C. I. Castel de Saint Pierre, *Abrégé du Projet de Paix Perpétuelle* (translated by Hale Bellot), London, Grotius Society Publication, 1927; Jean-Jacques Rousseau, *A Lasting Peace Through the Federation of Europe* (translated by C. E. Vaughan), London, Constable & Co., 1917; Jeremy Bentham, *Plan for a Universal and Perpetual Peace*, London, Grotius Society Publication, 1927.

5. Recent utopian contributions include: B. F. Skinner, *Walden Two*, New York, Macmillan, 1948; Paul Goodman, *Utopian Essays and Practical Proposals*, New York, Random House, 1962; Paul and Percival Goodman, *Communitas*, New York, Vintage Books, 1960; Aldous Huxley, *Island*, New York, Bantam, 1963; Theodore Roszak, *The Making of a Counter Culture*, London, Faber and Faber, 1970; Robert Paul Wolff, In *Defense of Anarchism*, New York, Harper & Row, 1970; Murray Bookchin, *Post-Scarcity Anarchism*, Berkeley, California, Ramparts Press, 1971; Warren Wagar, *The City of Man*, Baltimore, Penguin Books, 1967, and *Building the City of Man*, San Francisco, W. H. Freeman & Co., 1971; Pierre Teilhard de Chardin, *The Future of Man*, New York, Harper & Row, 1964.

6. Pope Paul VI, *Apostolic Letter to Cardinal Maurice Roy on the Occasion of the Eightieth Anniversary of the Encyclical 'Rerum Norarum'*, Vatican, May 14, 1971.

7. Cf. Gustavo Gutierrez, *A Theology of Liberation*, New York, Orbis Books, 1973, p. 160.

8. Martin Buber, *Paths in Utopia*, p. 7.

9. See Sidney Pollard, *The Idea of Progress*, Harmondsworth, Penguin Books, 1971.

10. Frederick Perls, Ralph Hefferline and Paul Goodman, *Gestalt Therapy*, New York, Delta Books, 1951, p. 319.

11. This dynamic concept of human nature has received considerable support from evolutionary theory. See T. Dobzhansky, *The Biological Basis of Human Freedom*, New York, Columbia University Press, 1956.

12. See *Eschatology* edited by E. Schillebeeckx in *Concilium*, Vol. 1, No. 5, 1969 (special issue); H. Rondet, *Fins de l'homme et fin du monde*, Paris, Fayard, 1966; C. Dumont, 'De trois dimensions retrouvées en théologie: eschatologie-orthpraxie-hermeneutique', *Nouvelle Revue Théologique*, Vol. 92, No. 6, June–July 1970; Georges Didier, 'Eschatologie et engagement chrétien', *Nouvelle Revue Théologique*, Vol. 75, No. 1, January 1953; Mary-Ellen Muckenhirn (ed.), *The Future as the Presence of Shared Hope*, New York, Sheed and Ward, 1968; *In Search of a Theology of Development*, Geneva, Sodepax, 1970.

13. See Jürgen Moltmann, *Theology of Hope*, New York, Harper & Row, 1967. Moltmann's contribution, in spite of its political limitations, is undoubtedly one of the most important attempts to overcome the association between faith and fear of the future. For a more radical theological perspective see Ruben Alves, *Theology of Human Hope*, Washington, DC, Corpus Books, 1969.

14. See Ernst Bloch, *Man of His Own* (translated by E. B. Ashton), New York, Herder & Herder, 1970.

15. *Writings of the Young Marx on Philosophy and Society* edited and translated by Lloyd D. Easton and Kurt H. Guddat, Garden City, NY, Anchor Books, 1967, p. 402.

16. See Karl Marx and Frederick Engels, *Manifesto of the Communist Party*, in Karl Marx and Frederick Engels, *Selected Works*, New York, International Publishers, 1969.

17. For an analysis of the Marxist ethic of the truly human man, freed from alienation, see Eugene Kamenka, *Marxism and Ethics*, London, Macmillan & Co., Ltd, 1969. The same theme is developed by several writers (including Veliko Korác, Ivan Sviták, Mihailo Markoviè, Irving Fetscher, Eugene Kamenka, Maximilien Rubel) in *Socialist Humanism* edited by Erich Fromm, New York, Anchor Books, 1966.

18. For an interesting classification of human wants into 'self-preservation' needs (e.g. food, sex, shelter), 'community' needs (e.g. love, sense of belonging) and 'self-determination' needs (e.g. self-esteem) see Abraham Maslow, *Toward a Psychology of Being*, New York, Van Nostrand, 1962.

19. See Erich Fromm's discussion of the European Work Communities in *The Sane Society*, pp. 306–20; much of this material is drawn from *All Things Common* by Claire Huchet Bishop, New York, Harper and Brothers, 1950.

20. For a penetrating and thought-provoking analysis of the moral behaviour of children and their capacity for 'reciprocity', see Jean Piaget, *The Moral Judgment of the Child*, London, Kegan Paul, 1932.

21. For an illuminating analysis of the concept of 'caring, understood as helping the other to grow', see Milton Mayeroff, *On Caring*, New York, Harper & Row, 1971.

22. For a masterly analysis of the nature and significance of play in human culture, see Johan Huizinga, *Homo Ludens*, Boston, Beacon Press, 1955.

23. Herbert Marcuse, *Eros and Civilization*, New York, Vintage Books, 1955, p. 178.

24. Warren Wagar, *Building the City of Man*, p. 110.

25. Gurth Higgin, *Symptoms of Tomorrow*, London, The Plume Press, 1973.
26. For a penetrating exposition of the view that the scientific method is not quite as purely rational or objective as scientists would like to think, see Thomas Kuhn, *The Structure of Scientific Revolutions*, Chicago, University of Chicago Press, 1962. See also Michael Polanyi, *Personal Knowledge*, Chicago, University of Chicago Press, 1959, and Abraham Maslow, *The Psychology of Science*, New York, Harper & Row, 1966.
27. Theodore Roszak, *The Making of a Counter Culture*, p. 215.
28. Ivan D. Illich, *Tools for Conviviality*, pp. 14–15.
29. For a broad-ranging discussion of the relationship between human motivation and technological design see Charles A. Thrall and Jerold M. Starr (eds.), *Technology, Power and Social Change*, Lexington, Mass., Heath & Co., 1972.
30. Ivan D. Illich, *Energy and Equity*, London, Calder & Boyars, 1974, p. 17.
31. See Murray Bookchin, *Post-Scarcity Anarchism*, Berkeley, California, Ramparts Press, 1971; Robin Clarke, 'Technology for an Alternative Society', *New Scientist*, January 11, 1973; Colin Moorcraft, 'Design for Survival', *Architectural Design*, Vol. 42, July 1972.
32. Warren Wagar, *Building the City of Man*, p. 52.
33. *Ibid.*, p. 89
34. Pierre Teilhard de Chardin, *Human Energy* (translated by J. M. Cohen), London, Collins, 1969, p. 58.
35. *Ibid.*, p. 32.
36. Pierre Teilhard de Chardin, *Activation of Energy* (translated by Rene Hague), London, Collins, 1970, p. 90.
37. Pierre Teilhard de Chardin, *Human Energy*, pp. 152–3.
38. George Gaylord Simpson, 'Behaviour and Evolution' in Anne Roe and George Gaylord Simpson, *Behaviour and Evolution*, London, Yale University Press, 1958, p. 522.

Chapter 10. The politics of disorder

1. Relevant in this context is the notion developed by Leslie White, Marshall Sahlins and others that gradual cultural adaptation does not necessarily run parallel with general evolution and may actually lead society in the opposite direction. In this sense, the revolutionary overturn of the social system may be a precondition for the return to the path of true general evolution. See Marshall D. Sahlins and Elman R. Service (eds.), *Evolution and Culture*, Ann Arbor, University of Michigan Press, 1960. Similarly, James and Grace Lee Boggs have argued that revolution is a specific way in which human evolution may be advanced, 'a new plateau in which beings can continue to develop'. (*Revolution and Evolution in the Twentieth Century*, New York, Monthly Review Press, 1960).
2. For a most penetrating analysis of the dialectical relationship between revolutionary and counter-revolutionary change see W. F. Wertheim, *Evolution and Revolution: The Rising Waves of Emancipation*, Harmondsworth, Penguin Books, 1974.

3. Peter L. Berger, Brigitte Berger and Hansfried Kellner, *The Homeless Mind*, Harmondsworth, Penguin Books, 1974, p. 85.

4. For an incisive critique of the structural principle which underlies much of the work of such key sociological figures as Parsons, Weber and Marx and such contemporary writers as Marcuse, Dahrendorf and Rex, see Dick Atkinson, *Orthodox Consensus and Radical Alternative: A Study in Sociological Theory*, London, Heinemann Educational, 1972.

5. Among the more influential proponents of this conception of society one would include: E. F. Durkheim, *The Division of Labour in Society* (translated by George Simpson), New York, Free Press, 1964; Max Weber, *General Theory of Social and Economic Organization*, New York, Free Press, 1947; A. R. Radcliffe-Brown, *Method in Anthropology, Selected Essays*, edited by M. N. Srinivas, Chicago, University of Chicago Press, 1958; Talcott Parsons, *Politics and Social Structure*, New York, Free Press, 1969; Robert K. Merton, *Social Theory and Social Structure*, Glencoe, Illinois, Free Press, 1957.

6. Cf. Lewis F. Coser, *The Functions of Social Conflict*, Glencoe, Illinois, Free Press, 1956.

7. The deterministic implications of such categories as 'norms', 'roles' and 'structures', have become the subject of increasing concern in sociological theory. See, for example, Dennis H. Wrong, 'Oversocialized conception of man in Modern Sociology', *American Sociological Review*, Vol. 26, No. 2, April 1961; and George C. Homans, 'Bringing Men Back In', *American Sociological Review*, Vol. 29, No. 6, December 1964.

8. Here we are using the concepts of 'dependence' and 'periphery' which were introduced in chapter 5 to explain the phenomenon of under-development, but the terms are being applied to a much wider context to illuminate the global pattern of stratification within and across national boundaries.

9. For an incisive account of the institutional failure of the American pluralist system and of its counterproductive principles of delegation and manipulation, see Theodore J. Lowi, *The End of Liberalism: Ideology, Policy and the Crisis of Public Authority*, New York, W. W. Norton & Co., Inc., 1969. The author advances the argument by pointing to the value of disorder as a catalyst for desirable social and political change in *The Politics of Disorder*, New York, Basic Books Inc., 1971.

10. See Jürgen Habermas, 'What does a Crisis Mean Today? Legitimation Problems in Late Capitalism', *Social Research*, Vol. 41, No. 4, Winter 1973.

11. For a detailed survey of contemporary technological trends by the Stanford Research Institute see *Possible Non-Military Scientific Developments and their Potential Impact on Foreign Policy Problems of the United States*, a study prepared at the request of the Committee on Foreign Relations, US Senate, 86th Congress, 1st Session, Washington, DC, 1959.

12. *Der Spiegel*, No. 33, 1971.

13. For a penetrating analysis of this mechanism of self-deception see

Hannah Arendt, *Crises of the Republic*, Harmondsworth, Penguin Books, 1973.

14. See Abraham Brumberg (ed.), *In Quest of Justice: Protest and Dissent in the Soviet Union Today*, New York, Praeger, 1970; Abraham Rothberg, *The Heirs of Stalin: Dissidence and the Soviet Regime 1953–1970*, Ithaca, NY, Cornell University Press, 1972.

15. See Galia Golan *The Czechoslovak Reform Movement: Communism in Crisis 1962–1968*, Cambridge, Cambridge University Press, 1971.

16. W. F. Wertheim, *The Rising of Emancipation*, p. 112.

17. This mood of discontent underlies, for example, the ideology of a distinctive African socialism, which has received its most explicit formulation in the Arusha Declaration of 1967. For an elaboration of this point see Peter L. Burger *et al.*, *The Homeless Mind*, pp. 143–62.

18. Of particular interest is the J-Curve devised by James Davies according to which revolutionary conditions may be said to prevail when there has arisen an intolerable distance between the expected and actual satisfaction of needs. In this sense, psychological factors may be at least as important as economic factors in producing a particular 'state of mind', see James C. Davies, 'Toward a Theory of Revolution', *American Sociological Review*, Vol. 27, February 1962, pp. 1–19.

19. Cf. Peter L. Berger *et al.*, *The Homeless Mind*, pp. 163–79.

20. See Noam Chomsky, *For Reasons of State*, chapter 4.

21. For one of the clearest expositions of student aspirations see 'Students for a Democractic Society', *Port Huron Statement*, 1962.

22. The limitations of the revolutionary potential of student dissent are outlined in Peter Buckman, *The Limits of Protest*, London, Victor Gollancz, 1970.

23. For an analysis of the origins and direction of contemporary anarchist movement see David E. Apter and James Joll (eds.), *Anarchism Today*, London, Macmillan, 1970.

24. For a fuller discussion of the revolutionary implications of these various forms of protest see Ronald Segal, *The Struggle Against History*, Harmondsworth, Penguin Books, 1974.

25. In some cases hostility and discontent have given way to outright terrorism. See Paul Wilkinson, *Political Terrorism*, London, Macmillan, 1974.

26. The role of the peasantry in the revolutionary transformation of underdeveloped societies is discussed by Eric R. Wolf, 'On Peasant Rebellions', *International Social Science Journal*, Vol. 21, 1969; Eric R. Wolf, *Peasant Wars of the Twentieth Century*, London, Faber & Faber, 1971; Frantz Fanon, *The Wretched of the Earth* (translated by Constance Farrington), Harmondsworth, Penguin Books, 1967.

27. For an analysis of the Chinese Revolutionary model see J. L. S. Girling, *People's War: The Conditions and the Consequences in China and in Southeast Asia*, London, Allen & Unwin, 1969; Jerome Ch'en, *Mao and the Chinese Revolution*, London, Oxford University Press, 1965; Stuart R. Schram, *The Political Thought of Mao Tse-tung*, Harmondsworth, Penguin Books, 1969.

28. See F. Bergsten, 'Coming Investment Wars', *Foreign Affairs*, Vol. 53, No. 1, October 1974.

29. A brief but useful review of the role of the Catholic Church in the Latin American struggle for liberation is provided by John Gerassi in his introduction to *Camilo Torres, Revolutionary Priest*, Harmondsworth, Penguin Books, 1973. See also Alain Gheerbrant, *The Rebel Church in Latin America*, Harmondsworth, Penguin Books, 1974.

30. For a useful collection of some of the most important writings of Mao Tse-tung and Lin Piao on contemporary Chinese policy see *Mao Tse-tung and Lin Piao: Post-Revolutionary Writings* edited by K. Fan, New York, Anchor Books, 1972. For a graphic description of the moral and ideological impact of the Cultural Revolution on a Shensi Village see Jan Myrdal and Gun Kessle, *China: The Revolution Continued*, Harmondsworth, Penguin Books, 1973.

31. For an interpretation of the Cultural Revolution as a struggle between the Maoist line of 'politics in command' and the Liu Shao-chi line of 'technique in command', see William Hinton, *Turning Point in China: An Essay on the Cultural Revolution*, New York, Monthly Review Press, 1972.

32. See Stanely Hoffman, 'Nuclear Proliferation and World Politics' in, *A World of Nuclear Powers*, edited by Alastair Buchan, Englewood Cliffs, NJ, Prentice-Hall, 1966; Klaus Knorr, *On the Use of Military Power in the Nuclear Age*, Princeton, Princeton University Press, 1966; Kenneth Waltz, 'International Structure, National Force, and the Balance of World Power', *Journal of International Affairs*, Vol. 21, No. 2, 1967, pp, 215–31; Seyom Brown, *New Forces in World Politics*, Washington DC, The Brookings Institution, 1974, pp. 7–28, 109–22.

33. See Harold B. Malmgren, 'Coming Trade Wars? (Neo-Mercantilism and Foreign Policy)', *Foreign Policy*, No. 1 (Winter 1970–1), pp. 125–6; Richard N. Cooper, 'Economic Interdependence and Foreign Policy in the Seventies', *World Politics*, Vol. 24, No. 2, January 1972, pp. 159–81; Miriam Camps, 'Source of Strain in Transatlantic Relations', *International Affairs*, Vol. 48, No. 4, October 1972. The phenomenon of economic multipolarity is discussed at length by Douglas Evans *The Politics of Trade*, London, Macmillan, 1974.

34. See William E. Griffith, *The Sino-Soviet Rift*, Cambridge, Mass., MIT Press, 1964; Michel Tatu, *Le grand triangle: Washington–Moscou–Pekin*, Paris, Institut Atlantique, 1970; O. Edmund Clubb, *China & Russia*, New York, Columbia University Press, 1971; J. Camilleri and M. Teichmann, *Security and Survival: The New Era in International Relations*, Melbourne, Heinemann Educational 1973 (chapters 5–6).

35. Cf. Robert L. Heilbroner, 'The Multinational Corporation and the Nation-State' in *Continuing Issues in International Politics* edited by Yale H. Ferguson and Walker F. Weiker, Pacific Palisades, California, Goodyear Publishing Co., 1973.

36. Fred Bergsten, 'The Threat from the Third World', *Foreign Policy*, No.11, September 1973.

37. See, for example, Robert Cooley Angell, *Peace on the March: Transnational Participation*, New York, Van Nostrand Reinhold Co., 1969.

Chapter 11. The politics of survival

1.   The optimistic view that the problem of scarcity has been finally overcome is critically examined by Barrington Moore, Jr, *Reflections on the Causes of Human Misery*, Boston, Beacon Press, 1970 (especially pp. 40–9).

2.   Among the large and growing number of authors who are stressing the biophysical constraints on economic growth, particular mention may be made of Kenneth E. Boulding, 'The Economics of the Coming Spaceship Earth' in, *Environmental Quality in a Growing Economy* edited by Henry Jarrett and published for Resources for the Future Inc., Baltimore, Johns Hopkins Press, 1966; Garrett Hardin, 'The Tragedy of the Commons', *Science*, Vol. 162, December 13, 1968; C. Park, *Affluence in Jeopardy*, San Francisco, Freeman, Cooper & Co., 1968; P. R. Ehrlich and A. H. Ehrlich, *Population, Resources, Environment*, San Francisco, W. H. Freeman & Co., 1970.

3   The long-term inability of increased productivity to fulfil many of man's basic needs was, surprisingly enough, clearly understood by the most brilliant exponent of modern growth economics. See John Maynard Keynes, *Essays in Persuasion*, London, Macmillan, 1931, pp. 358–73.

4.   This is the underlying theme in E. F. Schumacher's *Small is Beautiful*, London, Abacus, 1974.

5.   See Fred L. Polak, *The Image of the Future*, 2 vols., translated by Elise Boulding, New York, Sythoff, Leyden and Oceana, 1961.

6.   C. S. Lewis, *The Abolition of Man*, New York, The Macmillan Company, 1947.

7.   John Stuart Mill, *Principles of Political Economy*, Books iv and v, edited with an introduction by Donald Winch, Harmondsworth, Penguin Books, 1970, pp. 111–17.

8.   K. E. Boulding, 'The Economics of the Coming Spaceship Earth', p. 9.

9.   E. F. Schumacher, 'Buddhist Economics', *Resurgence*, Vol. 1, No. 2, January–February 1968.

10. See Richard England and Barry Bluestone, 'Ecology and Social Conflict', in Herman E. Daly (ed.), *Toward a Steady-State Economy*.

11. Garret Hardin, *The Tragedy of the Commons*, p. 1247.

12. The quota concept is elaborated at some length by Herman E. Daly, 'The Steady-State Economy: Toward a Political Economy of Biophysical Equilibrium and Moral Growth' in, *Toward a Steady-State Economy*.

13. See Warren A. Johnson, 'The Guaranteed Income as an Environmental Measure' in, *Economic Growth vs the Environment* edited by Warren A. Johnson and John Hardesty, Belmont, California, Wadsworth Publishing Company Inc., 1971.

14. Edward L. Morse has argued persuasively that 'interdependence', especially in economic relations, has been a major source of friction and crisis. See 'Crisis Diplomacy, Interdependence and the Politics of International Economic Relations' in, *Theory and Policy and International Relations*.

15. See 'Final Statement: Humanism of Tomorrow and the Diversity of Cultures' in, *Interrelations of Cultures, Unity and Diversity of Cultures*, Paris, UNESCO, 1953, pp. 379–82.

16. Cf. David Mitrany, *A Working Peace System*, Chicago, Quadrangle, 1966, p. 27.

17. For a general discussion of the institutional requirements of a new world order see Richard A. Falk, *This Endangered Planet: Prospects and Proposals for Human Survival*, New York, Vintage Books, 1972, chapter 7.

18. The value of regional conceptions of world order is examined in the anthology, *International Political Communities*, Garden City, NY, Anchor Books, 1966. See also Joseph S. Nye, Jr, *Peace in Parts*, Boston, Little, Brown & Co, 1971.

19. A very succinct but critical outline of these world models will be found in Louis Rene Beres and Harry R. Targ, *Reordering the Planet: Constructing Alternative World Futures*, Boston, Allyn & Bacon Inc., 1974.

20. An increasingly dangerous trend is the inclination of several theorists to argue that a globalist perspective necessitates the creation of progressively more centralized decision-making structures. See Ernst B. Haas, *Beyond the Nation-State: Functionalism and International Organization*, Stanford, California, Stanford University Press, 1964.

21. See John Burton, *World Society*, Cambridge, Cambridge University Press, 1972.

22. For a stimulating analysis of the 'modern' concept and practice of mediation see John W. Burton, *Conflict and Communication*, London, Macmillan & Co., 1969. Refer also to Michael Bakun, 'Conflict Resolution Through Implicit Mediation', *Journal of Conflict Resolution*, Vol. 8, 1964; Oran Young, *The Intermediaries*, Princeton, NJ, Princeton University Press, 1967. There is now a vast literature on the subject of UN peacekeeping. Mention may be made of P. Lincoln Bloomfield (ed.), *International Military Forces: The Question of Peacekeeping in an Armed and Disarming World*, Boston, Little, Brown & Co., 1964; Arthur L. Burns and Nina Heathcote, *Peace-Keeping by U.N. Forces from Suez to the Congo*, New York, Frederick A. Praeger Inc., 1963; Arthur M. Cox, *Prospects for Peacekeeping*, Washington, DC, Brookings Institution, 1967.

23. For one of the most comprehensive discussions of the future role of transnational organizations see the collection of readings, *Transnational Relations and World Politics*, edited by Robert O. Keohane and Joseph S. Nye, Jr, Cambridge, Mass., Harvard University Press, 1972 (includes also a most useful bibliography).

24. For a discussion of the role of international personal and mass communications in promoting world community, see Jerome D. Frank, *Sanity & Survival: Psychological Aspects of War and Peace*, New York, Vintage Books, 1967, pp. 229–45.

Chapter 12. Transnational strategies and cultural change

1. A useful summary of such proposals may be found in Richard Falk, *This Endangered Planet*, (especially chapter 8). For a well documented

survey of some of the main techniques for the restraint of international violence, see D. W. Bowett (ed.), *The Search for Peace*, London, Routledge & Kegan Paul, 1971.

2. These responses are analysed with varying degrees of insight by a host of recent writings on the ecological crisis. For a critical analysis of many of the suggested remedies see Barry Commoner, *The Closing Circle: Nature, Man and Technology*, New York, Bantam Books, 1972.

3. For an analysis of the contemporary application of anarchist principles, see David Apter, 'The Old Anarchism and the Newsome Comments' in, *Anarchism Today*, edited by D. Apter and J. Joll; George Woodcock, 'Anarchism Revisited', *Commentary*, August 1968.

4. See Henri Lefebvre, *The Explosion: Marxism and the French Revolution*, New York, Monthly Review Press, 1969 (chapter 7).

5. The factors contributing to the failure of this revolutionary movement are discussed by E. J. Hobsbawm in *Revolutionaries*, New York, New American Library, 1973. See also Christian Charrière, *Le Printemps des Enragés*, Paris, Fayard, 1968; John Gretton, *Students and Workers: An Analytical Account of Dissent in France May–June 1968*, London, McDonald, 1969; Alain Touraine, *Le mouvement de mai ou le communisme utopique*, Paris, Editions du Seuil, 1968. For a first-hand statement of the movement's rationale by one of its leading instigators refer to Daniel and Gabriel Cohn-Bendit, *Obsolete Communism: the Leftwing Alternative*, translated by Arnold Pomerans, Harmondsworth, Penguin Books, 1969.

6. This argument is developed at some length by Paul Mattick in *Critique of Marcuse*, London, the Merlin Press, 1972.

7. It is this implicit threat which leads Erich Fromm to explore the possibilities of technological reform rather than political revolution in *The Revolution of Hope*, New York, Harper & Row, 1968.

8. This principle underlines the attempt of several modern writers to define possible strategies for revolutionary action in the western world. Apart from the important contributions by Ivan Illich and Erich Fromm, see Ronald Segal, *The Struggle Against History*, Harmondsworth, Penguin Books, 1974; George Lakey, *Strategy for a Living Revolution*, San Francisco, W. H. Freeman & Co., 1973. A more theoretical analysis of the rationale of cultural action and of the process of conscientization is provided by Paolo Freire, *Cultural Action for Freedom* and *Pedagogy of the Oppressed*. Harmondsworth, Penguin Books, 1972.

9. Peter L. Berger and Thomas Luckman, *The Social Construction of Reality*, Harmondsworth, Penguin Books, 1971, p. 177.

10. Cf. George Lakey, *Strategy for a Living Revolution*, pp. 102–22.

11. For a discussion of this question from the perspective of an American activist committed to a socialist revolution see Michael Lerner, *The New Socialist Revolution: An Introduction to its Theory and Strategy*, New York, Dell Publishing, 1973.

12. Erich Fromm, *The Revolution of Hope*, pp. 44–5.

13. Awareness of the dangers of excessive bureaucratization within the revolutionary party leads André Gorz, in spite of his strong commit-

ment to a proletarian revolution, to downgrade the importance of the Bolshevik concept of an organized vanguard and to emphasize the 'capacity for initiative, improvisation, and self-organization of the masses themselves' *Socialism and Revolution* (translated by Norman Denny), Garden City, NY, Anchor Books, 1973.

14. There is now a vast literature dealing with the concept and the practice of non-violence. Of particular interest are the following: Mohandas K. Gandhi, *Non-Violent Resistance*, New York, Schocken Books, 1964; Joan V. Bondurant, *Concept of Violence: The Gandhian Philosophy of Conflict*, Berkeley, University of California Press, 1969; H. J. N. Horsburgh, *Non-Violence and Aggression: A Study of Gandhi's Moral Equivalent of War*, London, Oxford University Press, 1968; Gene Sharp, *Exploring Non-Violent Alternatives*, Boston, Peter Sargeant, 1970, Barbara Duning, *Revolution and Equilibrium*, New York, Grossman, 1971; David Dellinger, *Revolution Nonviolence*, New York, Doubleday & Co., 1971; Jeffrie K. Murphy (ed.), *Civil Disobedience and Violence*, Belmont, California, Wadsworth Publishing Co., 1971.

15. The concept of civilian defence is the subject of a wide-ranging investigation in Adam Roberts (ed.), *Civilian Resistance as a National Defence*, Harrisburg, Pennsylvania, Stackpole Books, 1968. See also Gene Sharp, 'National Defence, Without Arms', *War/Peace Report*, Vol. 10, No. 4, April 1970.

INDEX